An End to the Upside Down Reset

Also by Mark Gober

AN END TO UPSIDE DOWN THINKING

Dispelling the Myth That the Brain Produces Consciousness,
and the Implications for Everyday Life

AN END TO UPSIDE DOWN LIVING

Reorienting Our Consciousness to Live Better and Save the
Human Species

AN END TO UPSIDE DOWN LIBERTY

Turning Traditional Political Thinking on Its Head to Break
Free from Enslavement

AN END TO UPSIDE DOWN CONTACT

UFOs, Aliens, and Spirits—and Why Their Ongoing Interaction
with Human Civilization Matters

Author's note: Throughout, some quoted material has been edited slightly for
spelling, punctuation, and clarity. Also, "emphasis added" is noted when I've
inserted bold or italics in a particular paragraph. If this is not noted, it means
that any bold or italics were in the original.

An End to the Upside Down Reset

The Leftist Vision for Society Under the "Great Reset"—and How It Can Fool Caring People into Supporting Harmful Causes

Mark Gober

Waterside Productions
Cardiff-by-the-Sea, California

First Printing, 2023
Printed in the United States of America

ISBN-13: 978-1-958848-55-5 (print edition)
ISBN-13: 978-1-958848-56-2 (ebook edition)
ISBN-13: 979-8-212434-17-1 (audiobook edition)

Waterside Productions
2055 Oxford Avenue
Cardiff-by-the-Sea, CA 92007
www.waterside.com

To those who value positive results more than the
appearance of positive intentions.

"It is the true believer's ability to 'shut his eyes and stop his ears' to facts that do not deserve to be either seen or heard which is the source of his unequaled fortitude and constancy. He cannot be frightened by danger nor heartened by obstacles nor baffled by contradictions because he denies their existence....And it is the certitude of his infallible doctrine that renders the true believer impervious to uncertainties, surprises and the unpleasant realities of the world around him....It is obvious...that in order to be effective a doctrine must not be understood, but has rather to be believed in....The devout are always urged to seek the absolute truth with their hearts and not their minds."[1]

—Philosopher Eric Hoffer in his book *The True Believer: Thoughts on the Nature of Mass Movements* (1951)

CONTENTS

THE GREAT RESET

"The Great Reset" initiative was announced in June 2020 by Klaus Schwab—the executive chairman and founder of the World Economic Forum (WEF)—alongside then–Prince Charles.[1] In Schwab's words, "The COVID-19 crisis has shown us that our old systems are not fit any more for the 21st century. In short, we need a great reset."[2] He elaborates: "The world must act jointly and swiftly to revamp all aspects of our societies and economies.... Every country, from the United States to China, must participate, and every industry, from oil and gas to tech, must be transformed."[3]

Former United States secretary of state John Kerry echoed these sentiments, stating: "This is a big moment. The World Economic Forum...is really going to have to play a front and center role in refining the Great Reset to deal with climate change and inequity."[4]

Schwab and his colleague Thierry Malleret also wrote a book titled *COVID-19: The Great Reset*. The authors state in the introduction: "At the time of writing (June 2020), the pandemic continues to worsen globally. **Many of us are pondering when things will return to normal. The short response is: never.**...The coronavirus pandemic marks a fundamental inflection point in our global trajectory....The world as we knew it in the early months of 2020 is no more….Radical changes of such consequence are coming that some pundits have referred to a 'before coronavirus' (BC) and 'after coronavirus' (AC) era."[5] Along these lines, Schwab states: "The pandemic…represents a rare but narrow window of opportunity to reflect, reimagine and reset our world."[6] [emphasis added]

The Great Reset is grand in its aims. It lays out a blueprint for the direction of society—globally. This book will examine the stated objectives of the Great Reset along with the deeper ideology that underpins it. Although some aspects of the Great Reset could be beneficial to society, others pose tremendous risks if citizens are not vigilant. **Ideas that have a veneer of compassion don't always translate into beneficial change.** And given that this initiative is coming from the WEF—one of the world's most powerful and influential organizations—a careful reflection on the Great Reset is not just necessary but essential for the future of our civilization.

What Is the World Economic Forum, and Who Is Involved?

Originally known as the European Management Forum upon its founding in 1971, the WEF is a nonprofit organization headquartered in Geneva, Switzerland.[7] It is well known for its annual meeting in Davos, Switzerland, where it hosts nearly 2,500 "business, government and civil society leaders…to consider the major global issues of the day and to brainstorm on solutions to address these challenges."[8]

The WEF considers itself "the International Organization for Public-Private Cooperation." **Furthermore, it "engages the foremost political, business, cultural and other leaders of society to shape global, regional and industry agendas."**[9] [emphasis added]

As of November 2022, the WEF's Board of Trustees includes a former vice president of the United States; heads of major investment companies; the president of a leading U.S. university; the president of the European Central Bank; high-level politicians in global governments; and senior executives who lead technology, energy, and consulting companies.[10]

The WEF also has a "Young Global Leaders" program that has included major influencers such as Emmanuel Macron, president of France; Justin Trudeau, prime minister of Canada; Vladimir Putin, president of Russia; H.R.H. Crown Prince Haakon of Norway; Sanna Marin, prime minister of Finland; Jacinda Ardern, prime minister of New Zealand; Carlos Alvarado Quesada, former president of Costa Rica; and others.[11]

In a conversation at the Harvard Kennedy School between Schwab and former United States presidential adviser David Gergen, Schwab commented on the reach of the Young Global Leaders program within governments: "We penetrate the cabinets. Yesterday I was at a reception for [Canadian] Prime Minister [Justin] Trudeau, and I know that...more [than] half of [his] cabinet are actually Young Global Leaders of the World Economic Forum."[12]

Additionally, the WEF has a long and impressive list of global companies who are "partners." A small sampling of the list, as of November 2022, is as follows: Abbott Laboratories, Amazon, Apple, the Bank of China, Bayer, BlackRock, Bloomberg, Boeing, The Coca-Cola Company, Credit Suisse, Deutsche Bank, Fujitsu, Goldman Sachs, Google, Huawei Technologies, Indian Oil, Johnson & Johnson, JPMorgan Chase & Co., Kaiser Permanente, KPMG, Lenovo, Lockheed Martin, Marriott International, Mastercard, McKinsey & Company, Microsoft, Morgan Stanley, Nasdaq, Nestlé, the *New York Times*, Nokia, Novartis, the NYSE, the Ontario Teachers' Pension Plan, PayPal, Pfizer, Procter & Gamble, Prudential, Qualcomm, Ralph Lauren, Schlumberger, State Street, TikTok, the Turkey Wealth Fund, Uber Technologies, UBS, Verizon Communications, Visa, Walmart, Williams-Sonoma, and many others.[13] (Note: The presentation of this exemplary list of partners does not imply that they are all in alignment with every WEF initiative or that they support the Great Reset. Rather, it is intended to show the WEF's access to important companies in many industries. The same caveat goes for individuals associated with the WEF—their association doesn't always imply philosophical alignment, though sometimes it can.)

What Are Some of the WEF's Ideas?

Outside the Great Reset, specifically, the WEF has presented perspectives on important global issues. A number of them have attracted criticism. For example, it released a 2016 video—now deleted from the WEF's website and YouTube[14]—laying out "8 predictions for the world in 2030." The first one is: "You'll own nothing and you'll be happy. Whatever you want you'll rent, and it'll be delivered by drone."[15] Similarly, the WEF posted an article in *Forbes* titled "Welcome To 2030: I Own Nothing, Have No Privacy and Life Has Never Been Better." The article begins with more rhetoric around the lack of private ownership, and then ventures into other areas in the future envisioned:

> I don't own anything. I don't own a car. I don't own a house. I don't own any appliances or any clothes. It might seem odd to you, but it makes perfect sense for us in this city. Everything you considered a product, has now become a service....

> In our city we don't pay any rent, because someone else is using our free space whenever we do not need it. My living room is used for business meetings when I am not there....

> When AI [artificial intelligence] and robots took over so much of our work, we suddenly had time to eat well, sleep well and spend time with other people....

> Once in a while I get annoyed about the fact that I have no real privacy. Nowhere [can I] go and not be registered. I know that, somewhere, everything I do, think and dream of is recorded. I just hope that nobody will use it against me."[16]

The WEF also aspires to tackle the "raging problem" of disinformation. A 2022 WEF article suggests the need for "far-reaching" government regulations.[17] This implies that the government gets to determine what information is acceptable for the public to hear. Propaganda could ensue without an ability for the public to challenge the narrative.

Overpopulation is another theme often mentioned in the WEF's circles. The idea is that there are too many people on the planet, and in order to save the environment, we need fewer of them. For instance, a 2018 WEF article is titled "Even as birth rates decline overpopulation remains a global challenge."[18] Similarly, in 2022, WEF adviser Yuval Noah Harari projected that in the future, technology will replace humans, so "we just don't need the vast majority of the population."[19] One wonders what measures would be used to reduce the population.

A cynic might look at this sampling and ask, "So, you're telling me that these people have a history of talking about reduced private ownership and limited privacy, wanting to regulate what we can say and the information we can see, and suggesting that there should be fewer of us on the planet? Why should we assume that their vision for society—the Great Reset—is for *our* benefit?"

What Does the Great Reset Plan to Achieve?

The term *Great Reset* is "new" in that it has only recently been used so regularly to describe the direction of a post–COVID-19 society. But the ideas themselves aren't new. As Schwab and Malleret put it: "The pandemic will accelerate systemic changes that were already apparent prior to the crisis."[20] Crisis thus provided an opportunity to enact the WEF's preexisting ideals.

The Great Reset includes aspirations that many citizens would likely agree with. For instance, Schwab and Malleret ask rhetorically, "Might the pandemic give birth to better selves and to a better world? Will it be followed by a shift of values? Will we become more willing to nurture our human bonds and more intentional about maintaining our social connections? Simply put, will we become more caring and compassionate?"[21] They continue: "Failing to act would equate to letting our world become meaner, more divided, more dangerous, [and] more selfish."[22] They even mention the importance of "well-being" and "lifestyle choices" such as "nature, diet, and physical exercise."[23]

Overall, the Great Reset has cultural, political, economic, environmental, technological, and metaphysical implications. What follows is an overview of those areas alongside potential concerns. The Great Reset literature is not explicitly organized in this manner, so the categories reflect my own synthesis of the most salient concepts:

- ○ Cultural Direction

  - ■ Description: Schwab and Malleret highlight "issues of inequality, the ineffectiveness of most redistribution policies, a sense of exclusion and marginalization, and a general sentiment of unfairness."[24] They think we need to move toward a world that is "more equitable and fairer" while avoiding "injustice."[25] Their book mentions inequality as one of the world's "existential problems,"[26] and the authors even call it a possible "disaster."[27]

  - ■ Concerns: Terms like *equality*, *equity*, *fairness*, and *justice* are vague and can mean whatever people want them to mean. Thus, they can be weaponized to control people and create a divided society.

- ○ Political Direction

  - ■ Description: The authors argue for "the return of 'big' government"[28] and add that "taxation will increase."[29] They also believe that a centralized global authority is needed through what they call "improved global governance."[30] They lament: "We live in a world in which nobody is really in charge."[31] Moreover, they feel that "societies around the world [will] reconsider and redefine the terms of their social contract"[32] between "individuals and institutions."[33] (Note: The authors also opine on geopolitical matters, such as the power dynamics between the United States and China.[34] This book will not evaluate these issues but rather will examine the higher-level view of government within the Great Reset.)

- Concerns: Governments throughout history have been responsible for countless horrors, including mass murder. Human beings can become monsters when placed in positions of power. Centralizing authority creates the potential for great evil to emerge.

○ Economic Direction

  - Description: Schwab and Malleret state: "In general, there will be more regulation."[35] Schwab also declares that "we need a 'Great Reset' of capitalism."[36] In lieu of traditional shareholder capitalism, which he says is "driven by selfish values,"[37] he argues for "stakeholder capitalism." In other words, companies shouldn't just be responsible to their financial shareholders, but to all other "stakeholders," such as customers, employees, suppliers, lenders, the economy, the state, and society.[38]

  - Concerns: Government influence over the economy, as opposed to a free-market system, can create fertile ground for manipulation. Enforcement of "stakeholder" capitalism could similarly be used to exert control over the market.

○ Environmental Direction

  - Description: Schwab and Malleret's book mentions climate change as an "existential" problem,[39] which, like inequality, the authors consider to be a potential "disaster."[40] They remind readers that, in their view, "acute crises contribute to boosting the power of the state."[41] They also suggest that "excessive consumption of any kind is neither good for us nor for our planet."[42] Al Gore even stated in 2020: "I think this is a time for a 'Great Reset.'" And "the climate crisis" represents "an opportunity."[43]

  - Concerns: Crises can be weaponized to take away citizens' freedoms, reduce their quality of life, control what they consume and how they use transportation, and give more power to governments. COVID-19 demonstrated this, and environmental issues—in particular, climate change—could be used in a similar manner.

○ Technological Direction

  ▪ Description: The authors suggest that the pandemic will "accelerate innovation."[44] This sentiment aligns with Schwab's notion of a "fourth industrial revolution" that will include "breakthroughs in areas ranging from gene sequencing to nanotechnology, from renewables to quantum computing. It is the fusion of these technologies and their interaction across the physical, digital, and biological domains that make the fourth industrial revolution fundamentally different from previous revolutions."[45]

  ▪ Concerns: Technological improvements could enable sophisticated surveillance systems that take away freedom. Additionally, altering biology and merging humans with artificial intelligence (transhumanism), could further enslave people.

○ Metaphysical Direction

  ▪ Description: The Great Reset does not include an explicit discussion about the nature of reality. Implicit in the vision is a metaphysics devoid of God or any transcendent, spiritual dimension.

  ▪ Concerns: Without a spiritual compass, the self-appointed leaders of the world could "play God" and feel that there are no metaphysical consequences to their actions. They might also be more likely to develop their own "religions" around social and environmental causes, resulting in zealous dogmatism. However, quietly, there exists a substantial body of credible science suggesting that we are inherently spiritual beings.[46] To ignore this misses a fundamental aspect of our existence and creates additional danger for the society envisioned under the Great Reset.

What Do the Critics Say?

The Great Reset's aims are broad and sweeping. And they come from an immensely prominent—but unelected and unappointed—group of people who seek to impose their vision upon the rest of the world. This has brought about harsh condemnation. What follows are examples:

○ Former congressman Ron Paul, MD, warns: "This Great Reset is about expanding government power and suppressing liberty worldwide. Schwab envisions an authoritarian system where big business acts as a partner with government."[47]

○ Political writer Michael Anton says about the Great Reset: "Its mission is to persuade people, at least in the developed West, to accept lower standards of living in order to create a more just and 'equitable' world."[48]

○ Author Glenn Beck gives an extended opinion in his book *The Great Reset* (2022), describing the initiative as "something like 'modern corporate cronyist techno socialistic international fascism.'"[49] He adds: "The Great Reset is a proposal that is breathtaking in its scope. Its backers support altering nearly every part of society, from the cars we drive to the food we eat to the news reports we watch on television. Its core foundation was shaped almost entirely by a small, extremely wealthy and well-connected group of people, one that includes highly influential business leaders, environmentalists, government officials, and bankers. The goal of the Great Reset is both shocking and wildly ambitious: to transform the global economy, eliminate free markets, impose a new, more easily controllable and malleable economic system, and change the way people think about private property and corporations."[50] Furthermore, he writes:

"Its confusing terminology and vague language are what make the Great Reset so dangerous—and frankly, brilliant,"[51] and likewise, he warns about "the smiley face stuff they put in the brochures."[52] Beck feels that "the Great Reset is not really about helping the poor or saving the planet. It is about making the rich richer and expanding the power of the ruling class—goals that many elites have shared across cultures, historical eras, and geographies."[53] He calls the Great Reset "the single most important topic I have covered in my career, and **the movement that could finally snuff out the flame of liberty in America**."[54] [emphasis added]

○ Author Marc Morano also wrote a book called *The Great Reset* (2022), in which he voices similar concerns: "The merging of government and corporate power has proven to be the greatest threat to individual liberty. It is driven in part by the ideology that holds that citizens can't be left to their own devices or they will ruin the Earth, create inequity, become white supremacists, not know how to raise their kids, destroy the climate, and generally make poor decisions. The adherents of the bureaucratic state believe that people must have their lives essentially planned and boxed: the masses need credentialed experts to lay out their lives."[55]

○ Author Victor Davis Hanson wrote a chapter titled "The Great Regression" in Michael Walsh's book *Against the Great Reset* (2022). He views the Great Reset as a plan made by people "who have done well for themselves [and] could do even better for the rest of us—*if* these anointed could just be unbound and given enough power and authority to craft rules for nearly eight billion of the planet's ignorant."

He also writes: "A word of caution is needed about the pretentious and supposedly benign signature title of the Great Reset project. Assume the worst when the adjective 'great' appears in connection with envisioned fundamental, government-driven, or global political changes. What was similar between Lyndon Johnson's massively expensive but failed 'Great Society' and Mao's genocidal 'Great Leap Forward' [in China] was the idea of a top-down, centrally planned schema, cooked up by elites without any firsthand knowledge, or even worry, how it would affect the middle classes and the poor. So often, the adjective 'great' is a code word of supposed enlightened planners for radical attempts at reconstruction of a society that must be either misled or forced to accept a complete overhaul."[56]

What Is the Real Intention behind the Great Reset?

Without being inside the mind of each person who endorses the Great Reset, it's difficult to know with certainty *why* each of them expresses support. There are three basic possibilities: (1) They honestly believe they are doing the right thing, and their *intent* is to make the planet a better place. (2) They are genuinely psychopathic individuals—who don't think the same way most normal, decent people do—and they want to enslave and depopulate the masses. Psychopaths can sometimes appear to be magnanimous on the surface, but in reality they lack empathy, love power, and crave control—that is, they can be "wolves in sheep's clothing."[57] (3) Their behavior is being manipulated by a third party who is leveraging blackmail, bribery, threats, and/or mind-control tactics.[58]

At the very least—regardless of the intentions of each actor—**the Great Reset is based on an elitist mindset.** It is the belief that a small number of individuals know what is best for billions of people. They believe they have superior knowledge and a right to use that knowledge to impose their views on others. Among individuals claiming to have benevolent intentions, the rationale is that their impositions are "for people's own good." But "meaning well" doesn't always result in "doing well." As the saying goes: "The road to Hell is paved with good intentions."[59]

Author Naomi Wolf, a former adviser to the presidential campaigns of Bill Clinton and Al Gore, gives revealing insights into the elitist mentality in her book *The Bodies of Others* (2022). She recalls being at a New York City dinner party hosted by a hedge-fund manager. Her "host" at the party was an Ivy League–trained "lovely guy" who introduced her to his protégé—a young Ivy League–educated woman. Wolf—herself an Ivy League graduate—and the young woman were discussing events in Greece, and Wolf asked her whether the Greek people "should have a say in outcomes about their economic futures." The young woman "calmly responded with all the confidence and certainty of a now-privileged twentysomething," stating, "No, the ordinary people of any given country don't have the skills to make the right economic decisions for themselves or their nations. We should be deciding for them." Wolf's host "confirmed proudly," stating, "That's right."[60]

Additionally, the Great Reset is antihuman: it implicitly views humans as parasites on the planet who negatively impact nature and need to be tightly controlled and micromanaged. Human flourishing doesn't appear to be a primary objective—at least as it relates to the flourishing of the masses.[61]

These themes—the elitist mentality and an antihuman worldview—will be recurring throughout the forthcoming examinations of the Great Reset's aims.

What Is the Structure of This Book?

Part I examines the ideology that underlies much of the Great Reset. Its characteristics are explored in chapter 1, while chapter 2 provides examples of its dominance in our culture. Chapter 3 explores often-unconscious psychological biases that make it "stick" so well. The prevalence of this ideology renders the Great Reset particularly hazardous because it risks going unnoticed—and not being resisted—by those under the ideology's effective spell.

Part II of the book examines the six categories of the Great Reset that were previously mentioned: culture (chapter 4), politics (chapter 5), economics (chapter 6), environment (chapter 7), tech-nology (chapter 8), and metaphysics (chapter 9). Each chapter discusses the Great Reset's stated objectives, followed by an anal-ysis of the potential dangers in light of ongoing trends. Some of the examples are focused on America (and the West in general). A Western focus is important because if the freest countries in the world fall to dictatorial tendencies, the impact would likely be disproportionately negative for the world at large.

The book concludes with ideas about positively advancing society. Frameworks for our collective evolution are discussed—with the intent of transcending the Great Reset.

PART I
WHAT IS THE IDEOLOGY UNDERLYING THE GREAT RESET?

CHAPTER 1

THE PSYCHOLOGICAL FOUNDATIONS OF LEFTISM

Precisely how the Great Reset will play out is still unknown. However, projections can be made by examining a popular societal ideology that parallels many sentiments expressed under the Great Reset's vision. It is an ideology that has a tremendous impact on the hearts and minds of citizens through its dominance in the realms of education, media, technology, and entertainment (as we'll discuss in the next chapter). **The ideology is known as** *leftism*.

While it might not have 100 percent alignment with every aspect of what's been disclosed publicly about the Great Reset, it has similarities. **The Great Reset can thus be interpreted as a largely leftist movement.** Therefore, by studying leftism, we can better understand the Great Reset and its potential dangers. And we can deconstruct the manner in which leftists might be blindsided, causing them to support initiatives that they might otherwise resist.

What Is Leftism?

The term *Left*, in a political context, comes from the French Revolution. In the summer of 1789 during the French National

Assembly, those who opposed the monarchy sat to the left of the presiding officer.[1] Today, *Left* often denotes opposition to conservatism, Republicans, and the political Right. **The Left is also associated with *progressives*, *liberals*, and *Democrats*.**

These Left-related terms are typically used interchangeably. But some argue that leftism has distinct features. For example, conservative political commentator Dennis Prager—a vocal opponent of the Left—believes that leftism and liberalism differ substantially. He says that they have divergent takes on race, free speech, capitalism, nationalism, America, Western civilization, and Judaism and Christianity. What follows is a summary of Prager's perspective:[2]

- ○ *Race:* Liberals consider the color of one's skin insignificant, whereas the Left judges based on skin color (paradoxically, in the name of "antiracism"). To the Left, all black dormitories and separate black graduations are good things, whereas liberals favor racial integration. For instance, students at one college claim that such segregation would make the school a "more welcoming, supportive and safe community for minoritized students."[3] Furthermore, Prager comments: "To the Left, the notion that race is insignificant is itself racist. Thus, the University of California officially regards the statement 'There is only one race, the human race' as racist." According to leftists, this statement is offensive because it denies "the significance of a person of color's racial/ethnic experience and history."[4]

- ○ *Capitalism:* Liberals appreciate the way in which capitalism has helped to alleviate poverty by bringing about economic growth. Liberals might want the government to play a greater role in the economy than conservatives do, but they still see its value. The Left opposes capitalism and sometimes outright supports socialism or communism.

- ○ *Free Speech:* Liberals support the phrase "I disapprove of what you say, but I will defend to the death your right to say it." On the other hand, leftists support the suppression of speech that they—subjectively—deem to be objectionable or "hateful."

○ *Nationalism:* In Prager's words: "Liberals deeply believed in the nation-state, whether their nation was the United States, Great Britain or France. The Left has always opposed nationalism because leftism is rooted in class solidarity, not national solidarity. The Left has contempt for nationalism, seeing in it intellectual and moral primitivism at best, and the road to fascism at worst. Liberals always wanted to protect American sovereignty and borders."

○ *America:* Liberals "venerate" America, whereas the Left views America as "essentially a racist, sexist, violent, homophobic, xenophobic and Islamophobic country."

○ *Western Civilization:* Liberals have a "deep love" for Western civilization, whereas leftists are inclined to believe "not only that Western civilization is not superior to any other civilization but also that it is no more than a euphemism for white supremacy."

○ *Judaism and Christianity:* Liberals appreciate the Judeo-Christian religious roots of America, whereas leftists have "contempt" for them.

Within the Great Reset discourse, these leftist undertones appear: there is a focus on race-related issues like "equity," "fairness," and "injustice"; there is a concern about allowing freedom of speech; there is a desire to change capitalism with government intervention; there is a globalist—rather than a nationalist—outlook arguably lacking veneration for the successes of Western civilization; and there is a dearth of overtly religious or spiritual values. In essence, Prager's brief summary suggests that leftism spans metaphysics, politics, and many other aspects of society. **We could call it a metaphysical-sociopolitical ideology—a comprehensive way of looking at the world.**

Additionally, leftism tends to view many aspects of society as problematic and not worth preserving. So the notion of a "reset" is in alignment with its basic worldview. The late conservative commentator Roger Scruton commented on this psychology:

> It's...what [Georg Wilhelm Friedrich] Hegel calls the "labor of the negative."...The initial instinct on the Left is that negative instinct: things are wrong and [they] must be rectified. They can only be rectified, however, by the seizure of power. And so, [leftists say], "We're going to seize power in order to rectify [the things that are wrong]." But once [they've] got the power, the negative is still there in [their] heart because it's driven [them] all along. That's the thing that has inspired [them], so [they] set about destroying things and punishing people. [They] find classes who are to blame....And [they] don't get out of that negative structure."[5]

This is not to imply that the extreme Right isn't problematic too. But clinical psychologist Jordan Peterson explains why leftist extremism is uniquely dangerous:

> On the Right, I think we've identified markers for people who have gone too far in their ideological presuppositions. And it looks to me like the marker we've identified is racial superiority. I think we've known that probably since the end of World War II....So what's interesting is that on the conservative side of the spectrum we've figured out how to box in the radicals and say, "No, you're outside the domain of acceptable opinion." Now here's the issue: We know that things can go too far on the Right, and we know that things can go too far on the Left. But we don't know what the markers are for going too far on the Left. And I would say that it's ethically incumbent on those who are liberal or Left-leaning to identify the markers of pathological extremism on the Left and to distinguish themselves from the people who hold those pathological viewpoints. And I don't see that that's being done. And I

think that's a colossal ethical failure, and it may doom the liberal-Left project....It is definitely the case that you can go too far on the Left, and it's definitely the case that we don't know where to draw the line. And that's a big problem.[6]

Michael Rectenwald, a formerly far-Left Marxist and professor of liberal studies at New York University, voices similar concerns. He laments "the absence of critiques of leftist ideology by academics."[7] He further observes:

Rightist ideology is studied because it is "problematic."...Leftist ideology is not examined because leftism purportedly poses no danger; it is not pernicious and is nothing to be concerned about. By default, the standard leftist regards leftist ideology as benign but also as obviously beneficial....Leftist ideology is "on the right side of history." The implication is clear. Leftists do not believe that leftist ideology is ideological at all....

Intrinsic to leftist ideology is precisely the notion that no symmetry between right and left can be permitted—on the basis of...its obvious and indisputable political and moral superiority to rightist ideology....That is, *le point de capiton* of leftist ideology is the belief in its own, unique moral superiority and ultimate innocence.

How is this belief manifest? For one, leftist ideology presents itself—to itself and to others—as the default no-fault political belief system. While the crimes of right-wing political villainy are kept in circulation and replayed regularly—in classrooms, the media, casual conversations, and so on and so forth—the left's political crimes are swept under the carpet, ignored, or justified. Yes, in passing, once in a blue moon, someone...will acknowledge the [estimated] 94 million [people] murdered by communist regimes.[8]

One might then wonder: If leftism is generally aligned with the Great Reset initiative, does it run the risk of "going too far" before a critical mass of people notices its problems?

What Do Leftists Tend to Value?

Moral psychology, and related studies, reveal that individuals on the Left have distinct areas of focus. The insights here are important because they give clues about the manner in which leftists might be swayed by rhetoric about the Great Reset.

For example, in Arnold Kling's book *The Three Languages of Politics*, he lays out a basic, but helpful, generalization. In his three-axis model of political communication, he asserts:[9]

○ Progressives (that is, those who lean Left) communicate along the oppressor-oppressed axis.

○ Conservatives communicate along the civilization-barbarism axis.

○ Libertarians communicate along the liberty-coercion axis.

In other words, those on the Left might resonate strongly with causes where they see oppression, and they might care relatively less about being "civilized" or about liberty. That is, they will look to frame world issues from the lens of who is the oppressor and who is being oppressed.

In his book *The Psychopathology of Political Ideologies* (2022), University of California, Santa Barbara lecturer Robert Samuels elaborates on the leftist mentality. He attempts to pathologize political ideologies (not limited to the Left), so he uses strong language:

> Left-wing ideology…is centered on a hysterical identification with suffering and the use of a victim-based fantasy structure to influence others on an emotional level. Part of this ideology is determined by a desire to reverse the social hierarchies shaping premodern culture. For instance, instead of men dominating women, women seek to gain more social power. The postmodern period is then shaped by minority-based social movements seeking to expand the modern system of democratic justice, but…these movements often

become fixated on a particular group identity. Since in order to promote in-group solidarity, it is necessary to draw a clear distinction between the good "us" and the evil "other," this type of political polarization tends to create an ideology centered on conflict between the pure and innocent victim and the evil perpetrator. **Moreover, in this structure, the victim's vengeance is always justified, and the victim cannot be criticized or questioned**, and so this group psychopathology makes it difficult to resolve conflicts and embrace the modern ideals of neutrality, objectivity, and universality.[10] [emphasis added]

This concept aligns with the work of cognitive linguist and philosopher George Lakoff in his book *Moral Politics: How Liberals and Conservatives Think* (1996). He suggests that the liberal worldview (which we can use as a proxy for the leftist worldview) is based upon the ideal of a "Nurturant Parent." On the other hand, the conservative ideal is that of a "Strict Father." For the Nurturant Parent, according to Lakoff, "love, empathy, and nurturance are primary,"[11] whereas the Strict Father morality "assigns highest priorities to such things as moral strength…, respect for and obedience to authority, the setting and following of strict guidelines and behavioral norms, and so on."[12]

Social psychologist Jonathan Haidt digs deeper into these matters in his book *The Righteous Mind: Why Good People Are Divided by Politics and Religion* (2012). He describes six different foundations of morality and finds that liberals and conservatives differ in terms of what they value. Of the six moral categories, liberals tend to focus on only three of them, whereas conservatives focus on all six. For instance, *both* liberals and conservatives view care, fairness, and liberty as moral foundations, but only conservatives tend to view loyalty, authority, and sanctity as moral foundations.[13] Haidt also notes that "liberals [often] turn out to be more disturbed by signs of violence and suffering, compared to conservatives."[14]

When applied to the rhetoric of the Great Reset, the implications are profound: the Left might thus be more persuaded by initiatives claiming to come from a place of compassion and tolerance. "Care" makes up a higher percentage of their overall moral foundation matrix and might be weighted more heavily in their evaluations of societal issues.

Leftists' ability to empathize with others is in many ways an admirable and beneficial quality. But it might also be a weak spot whereby they can be more easily fooled. They might automatically gravitate toward ideas that on the surface are presented as compassionate, when the deeper meaning is less wholesome.

For instance, consider Klaus Schwab and Thierry Malleret's explicit statement that the Great Reset will involve "an augmented search for the common good as a policy objective."[15] Focusing on the "common good" can be a negative if it comes at the expense of individuals within society. In fact, governments have historically weaponized this idea. In the most extreme cases, communistic and fascistic governments have used "the greater good" as a justification to do horrible things to individuals. This way of thinking—known as *collectivism*—ignores the reality that "the collective" is, by definition, made of individuals.[16] Perhaps the leftist mentality is more prone to this dangerous fallacy because collectivistic branding sounds caring on the surface.

Additionally, because compassion is so highly regarded among leftists, they likely have a greater psychological incentive to ignore instances in which they, themselves, violate this core value—because acknowledging it would be too painful. So instead of pinpointing where they're not being compassionate, they might instead (unconsciously) choose to ignore it.[17] The result is hypocrisy.

For example, imagine a scenario in which leftists express outrage over violent protests that they see on television involving people on the Right. Then riots emerge in favor of a leftist cause, and they choose to ignore the destructive aspects of the event while praising the rioters for their willingness to bravely stand up for their values. Or imagine a company that wants to be more "inclusive," so its new hiring process involves hiring people from ethnic group A …but in so doing, it actively chooses *not* to hire people from ethnic group B. Yet it keeps the hiring practice intact and boasts publicly about how inclusive it is. Larry Elder's 2017 book, *Double Standards: The Selective Outrage of the Left*, is aptly named.

Furthermore, narcissism can arise from ostensibly compassionate leftists. Psychologist Sam Vaknin comments: "Altruistic, charitable behaviors can easily become 'narcissized'….It's like ostentatious altruism….[It's] the kind of social activism that is intended to promote attention rather than to accomplish goals."[18] This is visible in the promotion of leftist social causes, environmental activism, and so forth.

Finally, Lakoff points to another significant challenge that leftists face, which could drastically impact their ability to evaluate the Great Reset: leftists seem to be relatively unaware of their own biases. Lakoff is Left-leaning himself, but writes: "What I have found is that conservatives have a deeper insight into their worldview than liberals have into theirs….Liberals are less aware of the implicit view of morality…that organizes their own political beliefs."[19] Without having analyzed their beliefs as deeply, leftists might be less inclined to overcome their biases than others.

THE DOMINANCE OF LEFTISM

Now that we've examined the basic psychology underlying leftism, we'll briefly explore its increasing dominance in Western thinking. In the next chapter, we'll examine why that thinking will be difficult to overcome, which will then lead to a deeper exploration of the vision for society under the Great Reset. Ultimately, the overrepresentation of leftism in our world might mean that negative aspects of the Great Reset—including its elitist and antihuman tendencies—will be overlooked by vast segments of the population.

Leftist Bias in Education

College campuses in America increasingly lean Left. Greg Lukianoff and Jonathan Haidt show in their 2018 book *The Coddling of the American Mind* that the Left-to-Right ratio among college professors was roughly 5 to 1 in 2011. In 1996, it was 2 to 1.[1]

Gad Saad, a professor of marketing at Concordia University in Quebec, likewise mentions research revealing a similar bias. He cites a study on political donations across industries, which showed a "90 to 10 Democrat-to-Republican ratio" in academia.[2] He references additional data that makes this point:

In a 2016 study of professors' voting registration at forty leading American universities across five disciplines, the Democrat-to-Republican ratios were 4.5 (economics), 33.5 (history), 20.0 (journalism), 8.6 (law), and 17.4 (psychology). The total across the five disciplines was an 11.5 to 1 ratio favoring Democratic professors. A detailed examination of law professors at American universities found that only 15% were classified as conservative (based on data from political donations)….A recent study of professors' political registrations at fifty-one out of the sixty top liberal arts colleges in the United States uncovered a 10.4 to 1 Democrat to Republican ratio….Incredibly, twenty institutions had a proportion of Republican professors that, statistically speaking, was zero. Of note, the more prestigious a school is, the more lopsided the Democrat ratio.[3]

As economist Thomas Sowell puts it: "The next time some academics tell you how important 'diversity' is, ask how many Republicans there are in their sociology department."[4] [emphasis added]

Saad also references a 2018 *New York Times* opinion piece by Samuel J. Abrams—a professor of politics at Sarah Lawrence College—which reported data from a survey of 900 administrators who managed student life on college campuses. The result was a liberals-to-conservatives ratio of 12 to 1. He wrote: "This warped ideological distribution among college administrators should give our students and their families pause. To students who are in their first semester at school, I urge you not to accept unthinkingly what your campus administrators are telling you. **Their ideological imbalance…threatens the free and open exchange of ideas, which is precisely what we need to protect in higher education in these politically polarized times."**[5] [emphasis added]

The tale of Michael Rectenwald, a former New York University (NYU) professor, is telling. Previously a Marxist, he decided to break ranks with the prevailing orthodoxy. He explains what happened after he went "on the record" with his views about social trends during a 2016 interview. (For reference, he uses the term *bias reporting hotline*, which refers to a 24/7 phone number that can be called to report "bias incidents" by members of a university community; *safe spaces*, which refers to "places reserved for marginalized individuals to come together and discuss their experiences"; and *trigger warnings*, which give notice of potentially disturbing material that will follow the warning.[6]):

> I criticized the adoption of the new "social justice" creed by NYU and most other North American colleges and universities, including the establishment of "bias reporting hotlines" at NYU and at over 230 other institutions, the use of safe spaces, the adoption of trigger warnings, and the now-routine no-platforming of speakers, which made it impossible for alternative perspectives to be heard on most campuses....
>
> I was universally shunned by over 100 fellow faculty members, some of whom wouldn't let me on an elevator with them....A group of colleagues issued a series of blistering emails, attacking me for announcing on Twitter the forthcoming publication of my new book. I was called "alt-right," "Nazi," "short-pants White Devil," "fragile white male," and "Satan."[7]

Rectenwald later sued the university and several colleagues for defamation and negotiated a retirement settlement. He writes: "Most people who hear my story do not wonder why I broke with the left when I did. They wonder why it took so long....Consider this: I was subjected to this very indoctrination for over twenty-five years. My escape was a minor miracle."[8]

Similarly, there has been a rise in "disinvitations" of guest speakers on college campuses. In the year 2000, there was just a handful of disinvitations, and they came equally from the Left and the Right. By 2017, the number of disinvitations increased to thirty from the Left, whereas there were only five disinvitations from the Right. According to Lukianoff and Haidt, around 2013 there was a shift: students began adopting the predominantly leftist concern about being exposed to "offensive" ideas. They add: "In 2017, 58 percent of college students said it is 'important to be part of a campus community where I am not exposed to intolerant and offensive ideas.'" While some conservative students supported this idea (45 percent), relatively more Left-leaning students supported it (63 percent).[9]

As an example, in 2015, a black student at Williams University invited "a conservative critic of feminism and an advocate of traditional gender roles" to speak. Students were so enraged that the event had to be canceled. One student commented, "When you bring a misogynistic, white supremacist men's rights activist to campus in the name of 'dialogue' and 'the other side,' you are not only causing mental, social, psychological, and physical harm to students, but you are also—paying—for the continued dispersal of violent ideologies that kill our black and brown (trans) femme sisters….Know, you are dipping your hands in their blood."[10]

Pre-college American schools are also accused of biasing children with leftism. Documents uncovered in 2022 from a law-suit reveal teacher trainings geared toward a "School Transformation Action Plan" based on "equity/anti-racism," "examining presence and role whiteness," and "critical race theory." The training materials also include a document titled "What Is Whiteness?" and talks about "white privilege," "white racial bonding," and "white racial identity development."[11]

Leftist Bias in the Technology Industry

Many technology platforms reflect a leftist bias as well. Larry Sanger, a cofounder of Wikipedia who is no longer with the company, stated in a 2021 interview: "You can't cite the *Daily Mail* at all. You can't cite Fox News on sociopolitical issues either….It's banned. So what does that mean? It means that if a controversy does not appear in the mainstream center-Left media, then it's not going to appear on Wikipedia." He added that Wikipedia articles "are simply mouthing the view of the…World Economic Forum, and the World Health Organization, the CDC and various other establishment mouthpieces....There's a global enforcement of a certain point of view...which is amazing to me."[12]

Social media platforms like Facebook, Instagram, and Twitter have similarly demonstrated a preference for leftist perspectives. After being accused of "bias and political censorship," Facebook's founder, Mark Zuckerberg, stated in a 2018 congressional hearing: "I understand where that concern is coming from because Facebook and the tech industry are located in Silicon Valley, which is an extremely Left-leaning place."[13]

Facebook, along with Twitter, were also involved in censoring the incriminating story about then–presidential candidate Joe Biden's son's laptop. Zuckerberg claims he censored the story because the FBI had warned Facebook about the potential for misinformation leading up to the 2020 presidential election,[14] and Twitter's then-CEO Jack Dorsey later admitted it was "wrong" to censor the information.[15] One survey revealed that roughly 80 percent of Americans believe that if the story hadn't been censored, Democrat Joe Biden would not have won the presidency.[16]

Google's actions might have swayed public opinion about that election as well. Author Vivek Ramaswamy summarizes what happened:

> In the summer of 2020, ahead of the election, a curious trend emerged. In the first half of the year, individual clicks and impressions of the conservative news website Breitbart News resulting from Google searches for "Joe Biden" were steadily high. But suddenly, starting in the middle of the year, activity on Breitbart from the same search took a nosedive. Why did this happen? As it turns out, Google had allegedly kept a "blacklist" of "right-wing" conservative websites and news outlets to be suppressed from its search results. Breitbart was on the list.
>
> Dr. Robert Epstein, a renowned psychologist and researcher and a Democrat, is a longtime expert on deceptive business practices by Big Tech companies....

In 2019, Dr. Epstein testified before the Senate Judiciary Committee and claimed that Google could manipulate "upwards of 15 million votes" in the upcoming 2020 election without anyone knowing they were manipulated and without leaving a trace. Ahead of the election, Dr. Epstein's team of 733 field agents were deployed in three key swing states. They preserved approximately 500,000 ephemeral online experiences and found that Google search results were strongly biased in favor of liberals. While bias was shown to every group in Google searches, conservatives were shown slightly *greater* liberal bias in their search results.[17]

These actions aren't surprising when considering the biased nature of political donations in the technology industry. Saad references a study in which "the percentage of contributions that went to Democratic candidates from Netflix was 99.6 percent; from Twitter, 98.7 percent; from Apple, 97.5 percent; from Google/Alphabet, 96 percent; from Facebook, 94.5 percent; from PayPal, 92.2 percent; and from Microsoft, 91.7 percent."[18]

Furthermore, technology platforms use algorithms that keep people in an "echo chamber" and prevent them from hearing alternative perspectives. Lukianoff and Haidt write: "The 'filter bubble,' in which search engines and YouTube algorithms are designed to give you more of what you seem to be interested in…[leads] conservatives and progressives into disconnected moral matrices backed up by mutually contradictory informational worlds. Both the physical and electronic isolation from people we disagree with allow the forces of confirmation bias, groupthink, and tribalism to push us still further apart."[19]

Leftist Bias in Entertainment

The entertainment world has similarly developed a reputation for its leftist leanings. Actress Alyssa Milano commented in a 2017 interview with AOL: "[Hollywood] is left-leaning for sure, for better or for worse….There's a certain tunnel vision to these ideologies. I think artists…are always going to be left-leaning because

CHAPTER 2 | THE DOMINANCE OF LEFTISM   19

it's just more inclusive. More tolerant."[20] The *New York Times* also explored this concept in a 2018 article titled "Why Is Hollywood So Liberal?"[21]

In fact, Saad cites a study on political donations revealing that "the film and stage production industry has a 93 to 7 Democrat-to-Republican ratio." The bias extends into the book and magazine publishing industry (which has a 92 to 8 Democrat-to-Republican ratio).[22]

The world of professional sports seems to have a leftist bias as well. According to a 2017 survey, 30 percent of 1,423 adults said they detected a bias on the popular sports network ESPN. Of that 30 percent, 63 percent noticed a leftist political bias, while 30 percent thought the network leaned Right.[23] Broadcaster Tim Donner comments: "The sports media has become just as leftist as their brethren in the 'news' business."[24]

Leftist Bias in the Media and Journalism

The media is known for being largely Left-leaning. Ari Fleischer tells a revealing story in his 2022 book *Suppression, Deception, Snobbery, and Bias: Why the Press Gets So Much Wrong—And Just Doesn't Care*. He writes:

> Jane Coaston is the host and editor of the *New York Times*'s opinion podcast *The Argument*. She was previously [a] senior politics reporter at Vox. In May 2021, Coaston appeared on Hugh Hewitt's radio show, where she was asked a series of questions about the makeup of her fellow mainstream journalists. Her answer blew the cover off the press as she revealed how lopsided her colleagues are.
>
> Hewitt stipulated there are some 5,000 elite people who make up the mainstream media, consisting of reporters and producers at the *New York Times*, the *Washington Post;* the *Wall Street Journal;* the Associated Press; Reuters, Bloomberg; networks ABC, NBC, CBS, PBS, CNN, [and] MSNBC; the *Atlantic;* the *New Republic;*

and *Time* magazine, along with the Sunday shows and most columnists.

How many of these 5,000, Hewitt asked Coaston, voted for Trump in 2020? Her reply was 2 percent. How many for Trump in 2016? he asked. About 4 percent, she said. What about Romney in 2012? Maybe 7 or 8 percent, she replied. McCain in 2008? Coaston estimated 4 percent for McCain. Bush in 2004, she said, came in at about 7–9 percent. Hewitt continued: "I love that you're doing this with me. Thank you. A lot of media refuse to play this exercise, but it's very useful for the audience."[25]

The existence of a leftist media bias is reiterated by George Mason University economics professor Tim Groseclose in his 2011 book *Left Turn: How Liberal Media Bias Distorts the American Mind*. To him, "the most important fact about media bias…[is]: in a typical presidential election, only about 7 percent of Washington correspondents vote for the Republican."[26] Along these lines, Saad cites a 2013 study from Indiana University's School of Journalism, which "revealed that American journalists were nearly four times more likely to be Democrats than Republicans."[27]

This is now true in financial journalism as well. A 2018 study conducted by researchers from Arizona State University and Texas A&M University demonstrated that nearly 60 percent of 462 financial journalists surveyed were Left-leaning, and almost all the rest identified as moderate. Fewer than 5 percent of financial journalists were "very" conservative or "somewhat" conservative. *Investor's Business Daily* comments: "It's now pretty much a fact that journalism is one of the most left-wing of all professions. But until recently, that wasn't thought to be true of financial journalists—who have a reputation for being the most right-leaning and free-market-oriented among mainstream journalists."[28]

Groseclose also brings to light what he calls a "second-order problem" with the leftist bias in the media. He comments that because "U.S. newsrooms are extremely one-sided…any reporter, even if she is a conservative, will be surrounded at her work environment almost entirely by liberals."[29] Consider an instance in which a conservative journalist, who is a minority in the newsroom, wants to present a factually accurate story that contradicts the leftist narrative. As Groseclose writes: "Although her story may be true, if all her colleagues tell her that it is not—or, perhaps instead, they chide her that it is irresponsible or hurtful or racist to report it—then she will need a strong dose of courage and persistence to continue to pursue it."[30]

Political commentator Chris Rossini summarizes the situation well when he rhetorically asks: "Does the media ever print the words 'far Left'? If so, I rarely see it."[31] On the other hand, it doesn't take much detective work to find media reports about the "far Right." The mainstream media has gone so far to the Left that relative to where it sits, nothing is "far Left," but a significant amount of material is *relatively* "far Right."

As political commentator Larry Elder puts it: "The [conservative] position [is one] you won't hear unless you watch Fox News or listen to talk radio, and a lot of people [on the Left] won't do it if you…pay them."[32] (Note: I would add "alternative" media to Elder's comment, which often offers opinions that mainstream conservative outlets don't talk about either.)

These examples of leftist bias represent only a small sampling, but the basic point is clear: leftism has a dominant influence in the Western world. Those who get a mainstream education, use social media, and listen to traditional sources for media and entertainment run the risk of developing a leftist bias simply because that's what they're familiar with. And, unfortunately, that can lead to one-sided thinking, with blind spots regarding the direction of society—including the Great Reset.

Groseclose summarizes the situation well:

> What happens when our view of the world is filtered through the eyes, ears, and minds of such a liberal group?...The filtering prevents us from seeing the world as it actually is. Instead, we only see a distorted version of it. It is as if we see the world through a glass—a glass that magnifies the facts that liberals want us to see

and shrinks the facts that conservatives want us to see. The metaphoric glass affects not just what we see, but how we think....Perhaps worst of all, [the] bias feeds on itself. That is, [it] makes us more liberal, which makes us less able to detect the bias, which allows the media to get away with more bias, which makes us even more liberal, and so on.[33]

CHAPTER 3
THE STICKINESS OF LEFTISM

Imagine a leftist who went to college, keeps up with world events by watching CNN and reading the *New York Times*, enjoys Hollywood entertainment and sports, and avoids conservative or alternative media sources. A person with that profile will naturally have a skewed perspective on the world, simply because of the information he or she consumes.

But on top of that, psychological phenomena that often occur outside of conscious awareness can make a worldview shift even *more* difficult. That is, characteristics of the human mind make people naturally susceptible to manipulation.

A "stickiness" of leftist beliefs might then persist, unchallenged. And that can cause people to overlook the dangers of the Great Reset.

Being aware of the invisible forces that govern human judgment and decision making can help individuals overcome blind spots, however. In this chapter, the following psychological phenomena will be examined as they relate to biased thinking, and a discussion of escaping the Left will follow:

⭘ The Fundamental Attribution Error

- ○ "What You See Is All There Is"
- ○ The Dunning-Kruger Effect
- ○ Framing Effects
- ○ The Halo Effect
- ○ The Anchoring Effect
- ○ The Mere Exposure Effect
- ○ The Availability Heuristic
- ○ Motivated Reasoning
- ○ Tribal Biases

Before beginning, it's important to keep in mind the fact that these psychological biases are problematic for all people— including non-leftists. But because the focus of this book is on the dangers of leftist ideology, and the associated dangers of the Great Reset, that's what will be emphasized here.

The Fundamental Attribution Error

Human beings can act differently depending on the situation in which they find themselves. Consider the following hypothetical example: Joe is typically introverted and antisocial. On one rare occasion, he attends a party hosted by his close friends, and because he is in a comfortable situation, he acts in a much more extroverted manner than usual. Several of the party's attendees who had never met Joe, and knew nothing about him previously, observed his behavior and left the party thinking that he is a gregarious extrovert. But their assessment was inaccurate. They failed to take into account the power of the situation; and falsely attributed Joe's behavior to innate, more typical personality traits.

This is the fundamental attribution error: "overestimating the role of traits and underestimating the importance of situations," in the words of University of Michigan psychologist Richard Nisbett.[1]

This bias often relates to opinions of people we don't know very well. Public opinion can thus be manipulated by the media accordingly: it can selectively share clips and quotes of a public figure that aren't representative of his or her typical traits. Examples can be selected to show the person acting out of normal character due to the situation. If media consumers aren't savvy, they might develop an incorrect opinion about that person.

In a Left-biased world, one might wonder: What incorrect opinions—whether positive or negative—do leftists hold because they've been selectively presented with information that misrepresents a person's true character? How might this apply to leftists' trust in those who support the Great Reset? Do they view them in a more positive manner than is warranted? And do they view opponents of leftist, Great Reset ideologies in an unnecessarily negative light, based on what the media has shown them?

"What You See Is All There Is"

Nobel Prize–winning psychologist Daniel Kahneman observes a phenomenon that's even broader than the fundamental attribution error. In his words: "Information that is not retrieved (even unconsciously) from memory might as well not exist."[2] In other words: "What you see is all there is." Kahneman defines this common phenomenon as "jumping to conclusions on the basis of limited evidence."[3]

Often, this cognitive shortcut can be helpful. Kahneman writes: "Much of the time, the coherent story we put together is close enough to reality."[4] But it can lead us astray. **We might underestimate the amount of information about which we are simply unaware.** For example, people who use the *New York Times* as their primary news source might be oblivious to alternative perspectives because they only see what the *New York Times* shows them. Using Kahneman's terminology, "what they see" in their news source "is all there is."

The Dunning-Kruger Effect

A related phenomenon is the Dunning-Kruger Effect. This cognitive bias suggests that people believe they know more than they do. An article in *Psychology Today* summarizes the work of Cornell University psychologists David Dunning and Justin Kruger:

> The pair [of psychologists] tested participants on their logic, grammar, and sense of humor, and found that those who performed in the bottom quartile rated their skills far above average. For example, those in the 12th percentile self-rated their expertise to be, on average, in the 62nd percentile.
>
> The researchers attributed the trend to a problem of metacognition—the ability to analyze one's own thoughts or performance. "Those with limited knowledge in a domain suffer a dual burden: Not only do they reach mistaken conclusions and make regrettable errors, but their incompetence robs them of the ability to realize it," they wrote.[5]

This effect also applies to people who are very intelligent. As stated in *Psychology Today*: "Individuals rating as high as the 80th percentile for a skill have still been found to overestimate their ability to some degree. **This tendency may occur because gaining a small amount of knowledge in an area about which one was previously ignorant can make people feel as though they're suddenly virtual experts.** Only after continuing to explore a topic do they realize how extensive it is and how much they still have to master."[6] [emphasis added]

Dunning suggests that this bias of overconfidence can be tamed by playing "devil's advocate." Challenging one's own beliefs is therefore critical. He's advocating for intellectual humility.[7]

A danger of the Dunning-Kruger effect, when applied to leftism and the Great Reset, is that people might overlook their blind spots. **They might incorrectly believe that they know enough**

already, leading them to underestimate what they're unaware of and potentially falling prey to harmful movements.

Framing Effects

The way in which identical information is presented can influence opinions about that information. In other words, the "framing" of information matters. Kahneman gives an example: "The statement that 'the odds of survival one month after surgery are 90%' is more reassuring than the equivalent statement that 'mortality within one month of surgery is 10%.' Similarly, cold cuts described as '90% fat-free' are more attractive than when they are described as '10% fat.' The equivalence of the alternative formulations is transparent, but an individual normally sees only one formulation, and what she sees is all there is."[8]

How, then, might opinions of world issues be influenced by the way in which they are framed? Given the current leftist bias, is it possible that issues are framed in specific ways that skew perception?

The Halo Effect

Kahneman describes the halo effect—also known as exaggerated emotional coherence—as follows: "The tendency to like (or dislike) everything about a person—including things you have not observed."[9] He gives a hypothetical example:

> You meet a woman named Joan at a party and find her personable and easy to talk to. Now her name comes up as someone who could be asked to contribute to a charity. What do you know about Joan's generosity? The correct answer is that you know virtually nothing, because there is little reason to believe that people who are agreeable in social situations are also generous contributors to charities. But you like Joan, and you will retrieve the feeling of liking her when you think of her. You also like generosity and generous people. By association, you are now predisposed to believe that Joan is generous. And

now that you believe she is generous, you probably like Joan even better than you did earlier, because you have added generosity to her pleasant attributes.

Real evidence of generosity is missing in the story of Joan, and the gap is filled by a guess that fits one's emotional response to her. In other situations, evidence accumulates gradually, and the interpretation is shaped by the emotion attached to the first impression.[10]

How might opinions be shaped—in an inappropriately positive or negative direction—based upon what leftist programming has taught the public? Tightly held opinions about public figures, for instance, might be silently divorced from reality.

The Anchoring Effect

Kahneman calls anchoring "one of the most reliable and robust results of experimental psychology." He gives some examples to illustrate what it is: "If you are asked whether Gandhi was more than 114 years old when he died, you will end up with a much higher estimate of his age at death than you would if the…question referred to death at 35." In other words, people's guesses differ depending on the number given within the question.

Kahneman provides another example: "If you consider how much you should pay for a house, you will be influenced by the asking price. The same house will appear more valuable if its listing price is high than if it is low, even if you are determined to resist the influence of this number….The list of anchoring effects is endless."[11] One of the key insights is that anchoring occurs even when the number presented is "uninformative." Kahneman summarizes the implication: "The psychological mechanisms that produce anchoring make us far more suggestible than most of us would want to be."[12]

We might then wonder: How is leftist bias impacting—or inappropriately anchoring—people's views of society?

The Mere Exposure Effect

Repeated exposure to something can often induce liking of that thing. One of the key studies in this area, referenced by Kahneman, was conducted at the University of Michigan and Michigan State University: for several weeks an advertisement appeared on the front page of the student newspaper and contained Turkish or Turkish-sounding words. Kahneman explains:

> One of the words was shown only once, [whereas] others appeared on two, five, ten, or twenty-five separate occasions....When the mysterious ads ended, the investigators sent questionnaires to the university communities, asking for impressions of whether each of the words "means something 'good' or something 'bad.'" The results were spectacular: the words that were presented more frequently were rated much more favorably than the words that had been shown only once. This finding has been confirmed in many experiments....
>
> The mere exposure effect does not depend on conscious experience of familiarity. In fact…it occurs even when the repeated words or pictures are shown so quickly that observers never become aware of having seen them. **They still end up liking the words or pictures that were presented more frequently.**[13] [emphasis added]

Political campaigns can use this to their advantage by generating as much exposure to their material as possible.

Furthermore, psychologist Robert Zajonc, a leading investigator in this field, argued that this effect is part of our biology and even applies to animals. As Kahneman summarizes the argument: "Survival prospects are poor for an animal that is not suspicious of novelty. However, it is also adaptive for the initial caution to fade if the stimulus is actually safe. The mere exposure effect occurs, Zajonc claimed, because the repeated exposure of a stimulus is followed by nothing bad. Such a stimulus will eventually become a safety signal, and safety is good."[14]

This begs the question: How might repetitive exposure to certain ideas in the media contribute to what leftists think is "good"?

The Availability Heuristic

Kahneman defines this cognitive heuristic (that is, a mental short-cut) as "the process of judging frequency by 'the ease with which instances come to mind.'"[15] For example, in one study spouses were asked, "How large was your personal contribution to keeping the place tidy, in percentages?" The results should have added up to 100 percent, but they added up to more than 100 percent. Kahneman explains the results: "Both spouses remember their own individual efforts and contributions much more clearly than those of the other, and the difference in availability leads to a difference in judged frequency."[16]

Psychologist Fritz Strack provides another example: "An employer wishing to gauge the rate of unemployment in their community may go to the trouble of obtaining the relevant information from official sources. But if they are not motivated or able to do that, they can try to think of unemployed friends or acquaintances. The more easily they are able to do so, the higher will be their estimate of the rate of unemployment."[17]

Similarly, the information provided by Left-leaning media sources can skew perception. It can result in the belief that certain ideas are common when in fact they aren't. The reverse might be true as well: ideas that aren't presented by the leftist outlets might be regarded as more "fringe" than they truly are.

Motivated Reasoning

Humans have a natural tendency to gravitate toward information that confirms their existing beliefs (sometimes called *confirmation bias*). Social psychologist Jonathan Haidt explains that people are "really good at…finding evidence to support the position [they] already [hold], usually for intuitive reasons."[18] In other words, they pay "selective attention" to certain information, which can lead to the "perseverance of beliefs" that they might otherwise drop or modify.[19]

Similarly, people tend to resist information that challenges their worldview. For instance, Haidt explains: "If you ask people to believe something that violates their intuitions, they will devote their efforts to finding an escape hatch—a reason to doubt your argument or conclusion. They will almost always succeed."[20] Encountering information that challenges existing beliefs can cause psychological discomfort known as *cognitive dissonance*.

Haidt elaborates on these dynamics:

> The social psychologist Tom Gilovich studies the cognitive mechanisms of strange beliefs. His simple formulation is that when we *want* to believe something, we ask ourselves, "*Can* I believe it?" Then...we search for supporting evidence, and if we find even a single piece of pseudo-evidence, we can stop thinking. We now have permission to believe. We have a justification, in case anyone asks.
>
> In contrast, when we *don't* want to believe something, we ask ourselves, "*Must* I believe it?" Then we search for contrary evidence, and if we find a single reason to doubt the claim, we can dismiss it. You only need one key to unlock the handcuffs of *must*.
>
> Psychologists now have file cabinets full of findings on "motivated reasoning," showing the many tricks people use to reach the conclusions they want to reach. When subjects are told that an intelligence test gave them a low score, they choose to read articles criticizing (rather than supporting) the validity of IQ tests. When people read a (fictitious) scientific study that reports a link between caffeine consumption and breast cancer, women who are heavy coffee drinkers find more flaws in the study than do men and less caffeinated women. Pete Ditto, at the University of California at Irvine, asked subjects to lick a strip of paper to determine whether

they have a serious enzyme deficiency. He found that people wait longer for the paper to change color (which it never does) when a color change is desirable than when it indicates a deficiency, and those who get the undesirable prognosis find more reasons why the test might not be accurate (for example, "My mouth was unusually dry today").[21]

Along these lines, Haidt describes research showing that when participants observed their preferred political candidate exhibiting hypocrisy, it "immediately activated a network of emotion-related brain areas—areas associated with negative emotion and responses to punishment."[22] In other words, it's painful to see that someone you support is a hypocrite, and there is a neurochemical incentive to prevent that pain by avoiding instances that could reveal hypocrisy.

Researchers were able to alleviate the pain by then presenting evidence that reconciled the politician's previous hypocrisy. Then their brain gave them positive signals—in Haidt's words "a little hit of that dopamine" (which is the same neurochemical triggered by addictive drugs like heroin and cocaine). So there is a neurochemical bias toward finding evidence that supports one's previously held beliefs about a politician.

In summary, Haidt theorizes: "[This] would explain why [strong supporters of a political cause] are so stubborn, closed-minded, and committed to beliefs....[They've] been [neurochemically] reinforced so many times for performing mental contortions that free it from unwanted beliefs. Extreme partisanship may be literally addictive."[23]

Put together, the accumulated research suggests that people will tend to gravitate toward ideas that support their existing beliefs and avoid ideas that challenge their existing beliefs. If their worldview is largely informed by pervasive leftist biases, might they be more inclined to believe those ideas and reject anything that contradicts them? These dynamics can cause leftist beliefs to become entrenched.

Tribal Biases

The feeling of belonging to a particular group also has a great impact on one's psychology. As Haidt says: "Our politics are groupish, not selfish."[24] Political scientist Don Kinder explains that people care about their groups sometimes more than they care about themselves: **"In matters of public opinion, citizens seem to be asking themselves not 'What's in it for me?' but rather 'What's in it for my group?'"**[25] So political opinions end up being like "badges of social membership."[26] People can be drawn toward certain ideas and away from others, simply because of tribal dynamics. [emphasis added]

In fact, neuroscience backs up this notion. As summarized by Greg Lukianoff and Haidt:

> Neuroscientist David Eagleman used functional magnetic resonance imaging (fMRI) to examine the brains of people who were watching videos of other people's hands getting pricked by a needle or touched by a Q-tip. When the hand being pricked by a needle was labeled with the participant's own religion, the area of that participant's brain that handles pain showed a larger spike of activity than when the hand was labeled with a different religion. When arbitrary groups were created (such as by flipping a coin) immediately before the subject entered the MRI machine, and the hand being pricked was labeled as belonging to the same *arbitrary* group as the participant, even though the group hadn't even existed just moments earlier, the participant's brain still showed a larger spike. **We just don't feel as much empathy for those we see as "other."**[27] [bold added, italics in original]

These biases might leave leftists with a warped view of themselves and others.

Escaping Leftist Biases

Let's review the situation: Leftism is the predominant ideology in education and all forms of media. The slanted information leftists see likely "sticks" even more because of the many psychological biases just discussed.

Leftist beliefs, therefore, can be difficult to get out of—but they *can* be overcome. One place to start is simply being aware of the plethora of invisible psychological biases we all face. Kahneman comments on this idea: "Maintaining one's vigilance against biases is a chore—but the chance to avoid a costly mistake is sometimes worth the effort."[28]

Another way to potentially break free is to do what's uncomfortable and seek out new information and alternative opinions. Consider the example of Thomas Sowell, a renowned conservative/libertarian economist, who used to be on the far Left. He even identified as a Marxist. But his worldview changed dramatically. When asked what led to his shift, he replied with one word: "Facts."[29] Stated another way, Sowell became aware of new information, and he then underwent a remarkable transformation. He's since been a highly influential author, thinker, and critic of the leftist ideology.

Dave Rubin, a former leftist, and host of *The Rubin Report* political show, had a dramatic shift as well. It began in an entirely public manner when he was interviewing the prolific conservative/libertarian thinker Larry Elder. During the January 2016 interview, they discussed many issues, but Elder—who is black—challenged Rubin's then-leftist views. Rubin—who is a white, Jewish, gay man—reflects on what happened in his book titled *Don't Burn This Book* (2020): "Leftism…was still strongly running through my veins, so I was blind to my own ignorance. It all became painfully obvious when I asked [Elder] about 'systemic racism' in America—a social theory I presented as fact."[30] (Note: To be clear, the discussion is about whether racism is truly *systemic* in America and does not deny the fact that racism exists today and has existed for a very long time.)

What follows is an excerpt from the part of the conversation that discusses systemic racism:

> **Elder:** The goal is to tell black people that we're victims, that discrimination and racism remain major problems in America, when in fact they don't. And they want black people to vote for the Democratic Party. The Democratic Party gets 95 percent of the black vote, and the reason they get it is because blacks are convinced that the number-one issue facing the country right now is social justice, racist white cops, discrimination, systemic racism, microaggression—whatever new word they come up with. And it's a bunch of nonsense. The number-one problem domestically faced in this country is a breakdown of the family, and President Obama said it. I didn't....A kid—not just a black kid, [any] kid—raised without a dad is five times more likely to be poor and commit crimes, nine times more likely to drop out of school, and twenty times more likely to end up in jail. So you're far more likely to end up in jail without having a dad than you are because of a white racist cop.

> **Rubin:** Right, but you wouldn't *not* acknowledge that there are some systemic issues?

> **Elder:** Give me an example. Tell me what you think the most systemic, racist issue is. What is it?

> **Rubin:** Well, I would say that because black people in most cases, in many cases, were descendants of slaves, that racism as an institution...that a certain amount of it just exists.

> **Elder:** Give me the most blatant racist example you can come up with right now.

> **Rubin:** I think you could probably find evidence that, in general, that cops are...more willing to shoot if the perpetrator is black.

> **Elder:** What's your data? What's your basis for saying that?

Rubin: Well, look, I know a lot of people would say, "Look at what's going on in Chicago."

Elder: I know what they would say. I'm talking about what the facts are: 965 people were shot by cops last year [in 2015]….4 percent of them were white cops shooting unarmed blacks. In Chicago in 2011, 21 [black] people were shot and killed by cops. In 2015, there were 7. [Chicago's population] is a third black, a third white, and a third Hispanic. 70 percent of the homicides are black-on-black….The idea that a racist white cop shooting unarmed black people is a peril to black people is BS.[31]

The conversation then migrated to a discussion about Freddy Gray, a black man who died in the back of a police van in 2015. This had been regarded by the mainstream, leftist media as an example of systemic racism. Elder commented: "[Baltimore] is a city that's 45 percent black….The city council is 100 percent Democrat. The majority of the city council is black. The top cop at the time was black. The number-two cop was black. The majority of the command staff was black. The mayor is black. The attorney general is black. And yet here we are talking about racism? It's absurd."

Looking back on this part of the conversation, Rubin comments:

I remember feeling physically uncomfortable in my chair as [Elder] laid out the incontrovertible truth. I'd lost control of the interview and had to grab it back…. In order to do this, I shamefully played the "liberal hero" card, [responding to Elder]: "It's funny, I find myself caught in the middle….As a liberal, I always want to try and defend others—in this case, blacks. I'm always sympathetic to that." Even though I didn't realize it, this was a cop-out lefties almost always use when confronted with reality. Sure, he had just laid out a ton of stats that disproved my original position, but hey, I'm still a liberal, a good guy, so cut me some slack.[32]

But Elder didn't let up. He said to Rubin, "I asked you to name the most important example of racism. You gave me white cops going after black people, and I gave you the facts on that....You must have something else....I need some specifics....You're the one who made the assertion....You didn't hold it up very well. What's the other argument you have?...I'm not mad, I just want know what it is you're talking about." Elder later added, "I give facts...and [according to the Left] the facts are racist."[33] (Note: The *Los Angeles Times* even called Elder the "black face of white supremacy."[34])

Rubin recalls that after the interview, he was "too embarrassed to even look at the camera operators in the eye because they'd witnessed my intellectual execution firsthand."[35] The conversation with Elder was like the first domino that led to a revision of Rubin's old worldview. To Rubin's credit, he was willing to consider new ideas and challenge his deeply held assumptions: he had the humility to acknowledge where he lacked data, and he changed his perspectives accordingly. And that allowed him to break through the many psychological biases that otherwise would have made this transition nearly impossible.

Rubin provides additional color on the situation during a 2022 interview with *Sky News Australia*:

> Elder just basically beat me senseless with facts.... From there [that is, the Elder interview], I started talking to other [conservatives]....And I started to find that although I had some disagreements with...some of these people on the Right—and I still do, by the way—they were very open to discussing....They knew what they thought and why they thought it. And... this was the most shocking part—I found them nicer. That really was the...shocking part, because you know there's this meme...on the Left, the Left must love... tolerance. **So the implication is that the people on the Right are bigots and angry. And it just simply is not true.** Since I have gone through this metamorphosis, transition, whatever you want to call it, and now I hang out with all these scary right-wingers—they are happier, they are more generous of spirit, they smile more,

they laugh more, and most importantly, they're willing to agree to disagree. So you can sit at a table, and I've done it with the great thinkers, and they don't agree on everything of course, and we can argue it out….We can disagree on a million things…and then we're still good to go at the end of the day. And that's very different, unfortunately, than what has happened on the Left.[36] [emphasis added]

Now, Rubin is a popular conservative commentator and an avid critic of the Left—as someone who knows deeply about their psychology, from his own personal experience. In his book, he further remarks on the journey away from leftism:

Getting to this point isn't easy. In fact, it usually takes years of hard labor because our factory settings— everything the system teaches us to believe—are programmed into us from a young age. These include a range of 2D arguments that simplify life and position our starting point on the left, such as Democrats = good, Republicans = bad, progressives = humane, conservative = merciless, socialists = generous, capitalists = greedy, etc. These presumptions are obviously fallacies, but they aren't easily swallowed by the idealistic and impressionable youth. The message is even more appealing when it's constantly reinforced through academia, the media, and celebrity, which make it look cool and credible.[37]

But not everyone on the Left is as receptive to new ideas as Rubin proved to be. Elder presented data about police violence in an interview on *TMZ Live*. He even cited evidence from a black Harvard professor's study. One of the hosts of *TMZ Live*—a leftist white man—became visibly upset with Elder's pushback against the leftist narrative on systemic racism. Elder replied, "The facts are on my side. The facts are not on your side." The host's response was: **"You are relying on statistics, and you are not looking at humanity."**[38] [emphasis added]

The host's psychological biases were on full display. He wasn't able to process information that challenged his beliefs, so he got angry. But also, his Left-specific bias shined brightly: he wanted to look at "humanity" rather than facts. "Humanity" sounds much more compassionate than cold, hard data. **As conservative Dennis Prager often says, the Left cares about what *feels* good rather than what *does* good.**[39] **The desire to preserve a feeling can thus get in the way of the truth.**

This concept will be important to keep in mind in the forthcoming chapters. We'll be moving on to an analysis of the Great Reset's initiatives. Many of the ideas might *sound* good on the surface, and they might make someone *feel* good by supporting them. But when they're investigated beyond their superficial appearances, many dangers become apparent. That is, the ideas won't always *do* good.

PART II
WHAT ARE THE MAIN AREAS OF THE GREAT RESET, AND WHY ARE THEY CONCERNING?

CHAPTER 4

CULTURE

So far, two primary areas have been covered in this book:

1. An overview of what the Great Reset is and aims to achieve
2. The leftist ideology that parallels much of the Great Reset's rhetoric, along with the dominance and psychological stickiness of that worldview

We will now engage in an analysis of the six primary societal categories related to the Great Reset (each is its own chapter):

1. Culture
2. Politics
3. Economics
4. Environment
5. Technology
6. Metaphysics

Within each category, the vision under the Great Reset poses dangers to our future. However, because the content of each category relates to deeply entrenched leftist beliefs, large segments of the population might be overlooking the downsides. That's why deconstructing them is so essential—and might even help some individuals break through their blinders.

This chapter focuses on the cultural aspects of the Great Reset. Recall from the introduction that Klaus Schwab and Thierry Malleret's book *COVID-19: The Great Reset* advocates for a world that is "more equitable and fairer" and avoids "injustice."[1]

This rhetoric can be viewed in a positive light. Human history is littered with the horrors of racism and bigotry. Although humanity has made great strides in these areas, there is certainly room for continued improvement. And understandably, there are calls by activists to accelerate progress.

Unfortunately, however, there's a darker side to this.

Equality and Equity

Consider the notion of *equality*, which certainly sounds like a nice thing to support. But what does it really mean? It seems to have different definitions depending on who uses the term. It has often been used to address rights under government law: in a society that supports equality, superficial issues like gender, race, ethnicity, and sexual orientation would have no bearing on an individual's basic rights. Most people would probably agree that this form of equality is a good thing.

But increasingly the term has come to mean that differences are bad, so they need to be forcefully corrected. That notion ignores the fact that human beings are inherently unique. Each of us is different—unequal—in certain ways, whether it's our genetic makeup, the way we look, the way we think, and so on.

Our diversity is part of what makes society special and interesting.

Murray Rothbard, a political economist, summarized this issue in his 1970 essay titled "Egalitarianism as a Revolt Against Nature":

> What, in fact, is "equality"? The term has been much invoked but little analyzed. A and B are "equal" if they are identical to each other with respect to a given

attribute. Thus, if Smith and Jones are both exactly six feet in height, then they may be said to be "equal" in height. If two sticks are identical in length, then their lengths are "equal," etc. There is one and only one way, then, in which any two people can really be "equal" in the fullest sense: they must be identical in all of their attributes. This means, of course, that equality of all men—the egalitarian ideal—can only be achieved if all men are precisely uniform, precisely identical with respect to all of their attributes. The egalitarian world would necessarily be a world of horror fiction—a world of faceless and identical creatures, devoid of all individuality, variety, or special creativity.

Indeed, it is precisely in horror fiction where the logical implications of an egalitarian world have been fully drawn....The depiction of such a world [is shown] in the British anti-Utopian novel *Facial Justice*, by L. P. Hartley, in which envy is institutionalized by the State's making sure that all girls' faces are equally pretty, with medical operations being performed on both beautiful and ugly girls to bring all of their faces up or down to the general common denominator. A short story by Kurt Vonnegut provides an even more comprehensive description of a fully egalitarian society. Thus, Vonnegut begins his story, "Harrison Bergeron":

"The year was 2081, and everybody was finally equal. They weren't only equal before God and the law. They were equal every which way. Nobody was smarter than anybody else. Nobody was better looking than anybody else. Nobody was stronger or quicker than anybody else. All this equality was due to the 211th, 212th, and 213th Amendments to the Constitution, and to the unceasing vigilance of agents of the United States Handicapper General."

The "handicapping" worked partly as follows:

"Hazel had a perfectly average intelligence, which meant she couldn't think about anything except in short bursts. And

George, while his intelligence was way above normal, had a little mental handicap radio in his ear. He was required by law to wear it at all times. It was tuned to a government transmitter. Every twenty seconds or so, the transmitter would send out some sharp noise to keep people like George from taking unfair advantage of their brains."

The horror we all instinctively feel at these stories is the intuitive recognition that men are *not* uniform, that the species, mankind, is uniquely characterized by a high degree of variety, diversity, differentiation; in short, inequality.[2]

Nobel Prize–winning economist Friedrich Hayek further critiqued the notion of equality as it is often presented. Ironically, achieving equality necessarily entails the introduction of inequality: "The classical demand is that the state ought to treat all people equally in spite of the fact that they are very unequal. You can deduce from this that because people are unequal, you ought to treat them unequally in order to make them equal. And that's what social justice amounts to. It's a demand that the state should treat different people differently in order to place them in the same position....Making people equal, [as] a goal of governmental policy, would force government to treat people very unequally indeed."[3]

A related—and increasingly popular—buzzword is that of *equity*. It means "equal outcomes." Larry Elder pokes fun at the implications: "Isn't the fact that [female] supermodels make a lot more money than male supermodels a lack of equity? What about plumbers? Have you noticed most plumbers tend to be men? Isn't that a lack of equity?...And what about people who are behind bars? Have you ever noticed 90 percent of prisoners are men? Isn't that a decided, dramatic, scandalous lack of equity?"[4]

At first glance, equity might sound like a compassionate notion—which is perhaps why the Left is so drawn to it and why it's part of the movement to enact "diversity, equity, and inclusion" initiatives within organizations. But it is only *selectively* compassionate because it gives some people a boost and not others. It can even involve taking something away from one person (not so compassionate) and giving to another person (allegedly compassionate)—in order to make them equal.

In summary, these "feel good" utopian concepts that are so important in modern leftist discourse, and emphasized in the Great Reset, are in fact highly dystopic. Rothbard summarizes the implications of creating a world with equal outcomes: "An egalitarian society can only hope to achieve its goals by totalitarian methods of coercion....When the implications of such a world are fully spelled out, we recognize that such a world and such attempts are profoundly antihuman; being antihuman in the deepest sense, the egalitarian goal is, therefore, evil."[5]

Is this what the Great Reset's advocates aim to achieve?

Fairness

The Great Reset also incorporates the related notion of "fairer outcomes." Klaus Schwab uses it almost interchangeably with the notion of "more equitable outcomes."[6]

In his book *Dismantling America* (2010), Thomas Sowell devotes several chapters to an analysis of fairness, writing: "If there is ever a contest to pick which word has done the most damage to people's thinking, and to actions to carry out that thinking, my nomination would be the word 'fair.'…[Its] mushy vagueness may be a big handicap in logic but it is a big advantage in politics. All sorts of people, with very different notions about what is or is not fair, can be mobilized behind this nice-sounding word, in utter disregard of the fact that they mean very different things when they use that word."[7]

Sowell elaborates:

> Some years ago…there was a big outcry that various mental tests used for college admissions or for employment were biased and "unfair" to many individuals and groups. Fortunately there was one voice of sanity…who

said: "The tests are not unfair. *Life* is unfair and the tests measure the results."

If by "fair" you mean everyone having the same odds for achieving success, then life has never been anywhere close to being fair, anywhere or at any time. If you stop and think about it…it is hard even to conceive of how life could possibly be fair in that sense.

Even within the same family, among children born to the same parents and raised under the same roof, the first-borns on average have higher IQs than their brothers and sisters, and usually achieve more in life.

Unfairness is often blamed on somebody, even if only on "society." But whose fault is it if you were not the first born? Since some groups have more children than others, a higher percentage of the next generation will be first-borns in groups that have smaller families, so such groups have an advantage over other groups.

Despite all the sound and fury generated in controversies over whether different groups have different genetic potential, even if they all have identical genetic potential, the outcomes can still differ if they have different birth rates....

Many people fail to see the fundamental difference between saying that a particular thing—whether a mental test or an institution—is conveying a difference that already exists or is creating a difference that would not exist otherwise.

Creating a difference that would not exist otherwise is discrimination, and something can be done about that. But, in recent times, virtually any disparity in outcomes is almost automatically blamed on discrimination, despite the incredible range of other reasons for disparities between individuals and groups.

Nature's discrimination completely dwarfs man's discrimination.[8] [emphasis added]

Sowell notes that the quest for "fairness" often results in "equalizing downward, by lowering those at the top."[9] Again, it's being compassionate toward some people but not compassionate toward others.

The reluctance to accept these notions, it seems, reflects a reluctance to accept reality.

Antiracism

The desire for a more equal, equitable, and fair society is often associated with the desire for a society devoid of racism. Dr. Martin Luther King famously summarized the basic idea in 1963: "I have a dream that my four little children will one day live in a nation where they will not be judged by the color of their skin but by the content of their character."[10]

But that ideal has been warped into something else. As stated by author and organizational psychologist Dr. Karlyn Borysekno, the opposite of King's vision has emerged in certain leftist circles: "The color of one's skin is the only thing that matters, with no regard to the content of their character."[11]

This way of thinking often arises in *critical race theory*, a formerly fringe academic concept derived from the Marxist "Frankfurt School" that is now prevalent in parts of Western society, including the American education system (see Helen Pluckrose and James Lindsay's book *Cynical Theories* [2020] for more on this subject). Borysenko summarizes the basic assertion: "Racism exists everywhere—in every person, every interaction, every organization, and every institution—and the goal of the critical theorist is to explore how (not if) racism occurred in each instance. Racism is always assumed to have occurred, and white people (the ones who built the system) are assumed to be racist from birth."[12] Caucasian author Robin DiAngelo writes in her 2018 book *White Fragility*: "Indeed, the forces of racism were shaping me even before I took my first breath."[13]

As noted by author Vivek Ramaswamy, "Coca-Cola made the news recently when some images leaked of a DiAngelo diversity training course it had its employees take on LinkedIn—she instructed them 'to be less white' and said that amounts to being less oppressive, arrogant, defensive, ignorant, and so on. I took a look at the training course and noticed that DiAngelo added that Asians are guilty of these sins too because they're 'white-adjacent.'"[14]

These ideas train people to feel that their skin color relates to their innate character. The ideology creates division rather than unity and promotes a hierarchy based upon superficial qualities.

Along these lines, Ibram X. Kendi writes in his 2019 book, *How to Be an Antiracist*: "The only remedy to racist discrimination is antiracist discrimination. The only remedy to past discrimination is present discrimination. The only remedy to present discrimination is future discrimination."[15]

This could be interpreted as a justification for racist behavior in the name of antiracism—almost as a form of balancing out past (and future) grievances. In his book *The War on the West* (2022), Douglas Murray notes that philosophies like these are ultimately rooted in resentment and revenge.[16] As the saying goes, "Before you embark on a journey of revenge, dig two graves."[17]

Not surprisingly, divisive antiracist rhetoric is producing animosity and prejudice. In the same way that "equality" can morph into inequality, "antiracism" can morph into racism. For instance, at a talk delivered by a female psychiatrist at Yale's Child Study Center in 2021 titled "The Psychopathic Problem of the White Mind," she recounted a story: "I had fantasies of unloading a revolver into the head of any white person that got in my way, burying their body, and wiping my bloody hands as I walked away relatively guiltless with a bounce in my step." She also stated, "This is the cost of talking to white people at all. The cost of your own life, as they suck you dry. There are no good apples out there. White people make my blood boil."[18] Similarly, a bishop with nearly 200,000 Twitter followers tweeted the following in 2022: "Whiteness is an unrelenting, demonic, force of evil."[19]

A dance school in the United Kingdom decided in 2022 to remove ballet from its audition requirements because of its connection with "white European ideas." The change came after the school decided on an initiative aiming to "decolonise [sic] the curriculum."[20] **Even mathematics has been called racist.** For instance, a professor at the University of Illinois argued in 2017: "On many levels, mathematics itself operates as Whiteness. Who gets credit for doing and developing mathematics, who is capable in mathematics, and who is seen as part of the mathematical community is generally viewed as White." An article in *Campus Reform* continues by noting that the professor "also worries that algebra and geometry perpetuate privilege, fretting that 'curricula emphasizing terms like Pythagorean theorem and pi perpetuate a perception that mathematics was largely developed by Greeks and other Europeans.' Math also helps actively perpetuate white privilege too, since the way our economy places a premium on math skills gives math a form of 'unearned privilege' for math professors, who are disproportionately white."[21] Furthermore, an environmental activist in 2021 argued for the removal of dairy products from the school menu because, she says, **"Arguably, there is a racist element to serving dairy too much because 65 percent of the world's population are lactose intolerant, many from the BAME (black, Asian and minority ethnic) community."**[22] [emphasis added]

A company's firing decisions also sought to include racial factors. The CEO of Twilio announced layoffs in 2022 that would be "carried out through an 'Anti-Racist/Anti-Oppression' lens." His rationale was that "layoffs like this can have a more pronounced impact on marginalized communities."[23]

Division and prejudice become permissible under the guise of "compassionate" antiracism. It is reminiscent of George Orwell's fictional novella *Animal Farm*. After taking over Manor Farm, the animals created seven commandments, one of which was: "All animals are equal."[24] But eventually the animals' leadership became corrupt, and they altered the language of the commandment. It was changed to the following: **"All animals are equal. But some animals are more equal than others."**[25] [emphasis added]

Competitive Victimhood

Alleviating "oppression" often accompanies discussions about equality, fairness, and antiracism. The field known as *intersectionality* is associated with the work of Kimberlé Williams Crenshaw, a former UCLA law professor. Greg Lukianoff and Jonathan Haidt summarize her key insight:

> In a 1989 essay, Crenshaw noted that a black woman's experience in America is not captured by the summation of the black experience and the female experience. She made her point vividly by analyzing a legal case in which black women were victims of discrimination at General Motors even when the company could show that it hired plenty of black people (in factory jobs dominated by men) and plenty of women (in clerical jobs dominated by white people). So even though GM was found not to have discriminated against black people or women, it ended up hiring hardly any black women.[26]

In order to understand discrimination, as the theory goes, one has to look at the *intersection*. Kathryn Pauly Morgan, a professor of philosophy at the University of Toronto, elaborated on this notion with fourteen axes of privilege and oppression in her 1996 analysis. What follows are the fourteen axes, and each individual may vary in the extent to which he or she embodies the characteristic of each axis. This is "identity politics" to the extreme.

Privilege	Oppression
Able-bodied	Disabled
Cisgender	Transgender
Heterosexual	Gay/lesbian
White	Non-white
Male	Female
Upper class	Poor
Fertile	Infertile
Gender-typical	Deviant
Young	Old

European	Non-European
Credentialed	Non-literate
Anglophone	English as a second language
Light	Dark
Gentile	Jew

Note: This table is based on Lukianoff and Haidt's rendition of Morgan's diagram. Her version is shaped differently and shows axes; the above is a simplification.[27]

Lukianoff and Haidt note that "since 'privilege' is defined as the 'power to dominate' and to cause 'oppression,' these axes are inherently *moral* dimensions."[28] The privileged are "bad," and the oppressed are "good." Lukianoff and Haidt continue: "There is no escaping the conclusion as to who the evil people are. The main axes of oppression usually point to one intersectional address: straight white males."[29] [emphasis added]

This mentality leads to an effective competition for who can be viewed as the most oppressed. Sometimes this is referred to as the "Oppression Olympics."[30] Moreover, as discussed in Vivek Ramaswamy's book *Nation of Victims* (2022), oppression-focused thinking glorifies victimhood and demonizes excellence. Weakness, in a strange sense, becomes strength. Sowell puts it another way: "In the language of the politically correct, achievement is equated with privilege."[31]

Unfortunately, some leftists can become zealous in their defense of the oppressed and ferocious in their animosity toward those with perceived privilege. They want to be heroes and save victims from the villains. But their enthusiasm can sometimes lead to inconsistent, and even hypocritical, applications of intersectional principles. Lukianoff and Haidt tell a revealing story:

> An illustration of this way of thinking happened at Brown University in November of 2015, when students stormed the president's office and presented their list of demands to her and the provost....At one point in the video of the confrontation, the provost, a white man,

says, "Can we just have a conversation about—?" but he is interrupted by shouts of "No!" and students' finger snaps. One protester offers this explanation for cutting him off: "The problem they are having is that heterosexual white males have always dominated the space." The provost then points out that he himself is gay. The student stutters a bit but continues on, undeterred by the fact that Brown University was led by a woman and a gay man: "Well, homosexual…it doesn't matter…white males are at the top of the hierarchy."[32]

A toxic mentality starts to build quickly—and it's heightened when combined with oversensitivity to "microaggressions." As cited in the journal *Perspectives on Medical Education*, microaggressions are "everyday subtle put-downs directed towards a marginalized group which may be verbal or non-verbal and are typically automatic."[33] Lukianoff and Haidt note that "call-out culture" develops in which people "gain prestige for identifying small offenses committed by members of their community, and then publicly 'calling out' the offenders." They see this as a problem on college campuses in particular[34] and comment: "Imagine an entire entering class of college freshmen whose orientation program includes training in…intersectional thinking…along with training in spotting microaggressions. By the end of their first week on campus, students have learned to score their own and others' level of privilege, identify more distinct identity groups, and see more differences between people."[35]

Once again, a concept that on the surface might sound "compassionate" results in division and strife. It also stifles the free flow of ideas. Lukianoff and Haidt note that "reports from around the country are remarkably similar: students at many colleges today are walking on eggshells, afraid of saying the wrong thing, liking the wrong [social media post], or coming to the defense of someone whom they know to be innocent, out of fear that they themselves will be called out by a mob on social media." They quote a student who commented, **"I probably hold back 90 percent of the things that I want to say due to fear of being called out.…People won't**

call you out because your opinion is wrong. People will call you out for literally anything."[36] [emphasis added]

Violence through Words

The leftist, oppression-focused mentality has also led to the increasingly pervasive idea that speech is violence. Lukianoff and Haidt call it an example of ***concept creep***, a term used in 2016 by the Australian psychologist Nick Haslam. They summarize Haslam's findings: "[He] examined a variety of key concepts in clinical and social psychology—including abuse, bullying, trauma, and prejudice—to determine how their usage had changed since the 1980s. He found that their scope had expanded in two directions: the concepts had crept 'downward,' to apply to less severe situations, and 'outward,' to encompass new but conceptually related phenomena."[37]

Lukianoff and Haidt apply concept creep to new uses of the word *violence*:

> In just the last few years [as of 2018], the word "violence" has expanded on campus and in some radical political communities beyond campus to cover a multitude of nonviolent actions, including speech that this political faction claims will have a negative impact on members of protected identity groups....[Typically,] the word "violence" refers to *physical* violence....However, now that some students, professors, and activists are labeling their opponents' *words* as violence, they give themselves permission to engage in ideologically motivated *physical* violence. The rationale, as an essay in the [University of California at Berkeley's] op-ed series argued, is that physically violent actions, if used to shut down speech that is deemed hateful, are "not acts of violence" but, rather, "acts of self defense."[38]

In fact, actual violent protests broke out in 2017 at UC Berkeley— in response to an upcoming speech by Milo Yiannopoulos, who had been invited by campus Republicans. One of the university op-eds suggested that if Yiannopoulos had been allowed to speak, the conservative ideas he promotes would allegedly have resulted in "broken bodies." The speech was canceled due to the riots.[39]

Increasingly, free speech is being thwarted using this sort of logic. Thomas Sowell likens the twisted thinking to believing that a match *is* a forest fire. Certainly, matches can *result in* forest fires, but matches don't *start* forest fires on their own.[40]

Making nonviolent speakers responsible for the physical violence committed by other people is a slippery slope. Then anyone, due to purely subjective judgments, can declare a speaker violent. People could be silenced for expressing opinions that others disagree with—because, under this line of reasoning, the speech would simply be called "violent."

This manner of thinking takes away responsibility from those who truly commit violent acts. As economist Ryan McMaken argues, people "have the freedom to reject" words that they hear. He adds, "The reality is that people *do* have a choice."[41]

Along these lines, the concept of violent "hate speech" is inherently problematic. It's subjective. What is considered hateful to one person might not be considered hateful to another. Accusations of "hate" can thus be levied to criminalize *anyone*.

The same goes for "offensive" speech. What's offensive? Who makes that determination? Being offended is a subjective feeling, so how could a third party know if another person truly feels offended? In fact, Will Witt, from the conservative nonprofit "PragerU," dressed up in classical Chinese attire on a college campus and was told by non-Chinese college students that the outfit was offensive (he was accused of exhibiting "cultural appropriation"). But when he went to Chinatown dressed in that attire, the Chinese people said they liked his outfit and were not offended.[42] The same thing happened when he ran the experiment dressed up in traditional Mexican garb.[43]

Moreover, it's a personal choice to be offended. People are capable of regulating their own emotions like mature adults. To believe otherwise is to view humans as mere machines who take in inputs and have no control over the output. That's the patronizing view of humanity held under the leftist ideology.

These common-sense notions are not so common, unfortunately. Leftist thinking teaches that victimhood is king. This leads society in a dangerous direction in which mental gymnastics can be used to justify nonsensical ideas. And it typically begins with the premise of wanting a more caring and tolerant society that values things like "equality," "fairness," and protecting against "oppression." **This is why the Great Reset's cultural goals aren't so innocuous.**

Parasitic Ideas

Professor Gad Saad likens these toxic ideas to parasitic pathogens in his book *The Parasitic Mind* (2020). He writes: "I inhabit the world of academia. This is an ecosystem that has been dominated by leftist thinking for many decades....The idea pathogens that I discuss...stem largely if not totally from leftist academics."[44] He claims that "mind viruses take hold of one's neuronal circuitry, [and] the afflicted victim loses the ability to use reason, logic, and science to navigate the world. Instead, one sinks into an abyss of infinite lunacy best defined by a dogged and proud departure from reality, common sense, and truth."[45]

An example of an idea pathogen for Saad is *postmodernism*, which he calls "intellectual terrorism masquerading as faux-profundity."[46] It "posits that all knowledge is relative."[47] Postmodern thought is thus skeptical of objective truth. On its face, this idea is problematic because the statement "There is no objective truth" is *itself* a statement claiming an objective truth.[48] But in a world without objectively true ideas, the truth is whatever someone—or society—wants it to be at any given moment. Biology doesn't matter. For instance, Saad references the Canadian Cancer Society's ad campaign showing "a photo of a trans woman ([a] biological male) to represent a demographic group at risk for cervical cancer."[49] Similarly, men are now said to be capable of menstruation (as discussed, for example, in the 2016 *Daily Beast* article "Yes, Men Can Have Periods and We Need to Talk About Them").[50]

However, postmodern ideas seem to be applied selectively, depending on what the prevailing leftist ideology supports. For instance, consider some of the things that are permitted regarding gender identity: People can change their gender from day to day, regardless of their biological birth sex—and society is expected to uphold that identity. It's part of being a compassionate society that values "equality." Not upholding this view is sometimes punishable. As Saad reports, "In a California school [in 2017], a student was investigated and sent to the principal's office for innocently misgendering a classmate."[51] In 2022, a biological male, who identifies as a female, was allowed to compete in Ivy League swimming competitions and became a champion when competing against biological women—and even set a record time for women's swimming.[52] **Biologically female teammates felt uncomfortable changing with a biological male in the locker room but feared speaking out because they could be called "transphobic."**[53] Also in 2022, Rachel Levine, a senior U.S. government health official—a biological male who now identifies as a female—was named one of *USA Today*'s "Women of the Year."[54] The satirical news outlet The Babylon Bee then named Levine its "Man of the Year" and was subsequently suspended from Twitter.[55] Additionally, a biological male in prison, who identifies as a female, raped a female in the women's section of the jail (and pleaded guilty).[56]

However, this ability to self-identify based on one's internal feeling is not universal. Society does not allow unvaccinated people to self-identify as "vaccinated" against COVID-19 unless they have actually taken the vaccine. Imagine if a person tried to enter an establishment that required proof of vaccination and said, "I identify as vaccinated, so you have to let me in."

Saad also references *social constructivism*, which "proposes that the great majority of human behaviors, desires, and preferences are not formed by human nature or our biological heritage but by society, which means, among other things, that there are no biologically determined sex differences, but *only* culturally imposed 'gender roles.'"[57] [emphasis added]

These parasitic ideas result in what Saad calls "science denialism": scientific evidence will be rejected if the results put into question the prevailing leftist preferences.[58] He writes, "Scientific data cannot be used to question a politically correct narrative."[59]

Saad also references the case of Alessandro Strumia, a physics professor at the University of Pisa, who delivered a lecture at the inaugural event organized by CERN (the European Organization for Nuclear Research) in 2018. The talk was titled "Workshop on High Energy Theory and Gender." As summarized by Saad, Strumia "presented several bibliometric analyses that questioned the prevailing...narrative in physics, namely that women were discriminated against....**It would be perfectly reasonable to challenge his conclusions if one had competing data to present**, but he was condemned, essentially, as a blasphemer and metaphorically burned at the stake."[60] [emphasis added]

Several thousand scientists then signed a condemnatory statement. One of its points, in bold, was: "We write here first to state, in the strongest possible terms, that the humanity of any person, regardless of ascribed identities such as race, ethnicity, gender identity, religion, disability, gender presentation, or sexual identity is not up for debate."[61] Saad comments: "This is a grotesquely dishonest tactic, as Strumia did not question anyone's humanity let alone mention any of the listed identities."[62]

A physicist published a rebuttal in *Areo* magazine, in defense of Strumia. However, it was published anonymously because the author feared that "attaching my name could harm my career and relationships....The social atmosphere is toxic."[63] **In Saad's opinion, "That this physicist felt the need to publish his rebuttal anonymously is the most important take away from this whole debate."[64]** [emphasis added]

But if ideas *are* deemed to be in line with the prevailing leftist ideology, they are perfectly acceptable scientifically. This can lead to some crazy outcomes. Saad gives an example:

In 2017, James Lindsay [a PhD] and Peter Boghossian [a former assistant professor of philosophy at Port-land State University]…published a hoax paper (using pseudonyms) wherein they argued that the human penis was a conceptual construct that was a driving force behind climate change. I challenge the readers to go through the paper in question without bursting into uncontrollable laughter. I tried to do so on camera but failed. Once the hoax was publicized, an associate editorial director put out a statement that explained: "Two reviewers agreed to review the paper, and it was accepted with no changes by one reviewer, and with minor amends by the other. On investigation, although the two reviewers had relevant research interests, their expertise did not fully align with this subject matter, and we do not believe that they were the right choice to review this paper." Apparently, had the proper experts been used to review an utterly nonsensical paper that linked human penises to climate change, the outcome might have been different. I am unaware of any experts in phallic-based climatology, but perhaps I did not look hard enough.[65]

Saad notes that this journal, *Cogent Social Sciences*, was a pay-to-play publication. So detractors used this fact to claim that such absurd ideas wouldn't make it past the review of relatively more prominent outlets. The authors then decided to write twenty nonsensical papers that they submitted to more prestigious journals. *Seven* of them were accepted. The project is known as "the Grievance Studies affair" and was led by Lindsay, Boghossian, and Helen Pluckrose. What follows is a summary of the articles that were accepted.[66]

Title of the Paper	Brief Description	Journal That Accepted the Paper
"Human Reactions to Rape Culture and Queer Performativity in Urban Dog Parks in Portland, Oregon"	Saad comments that this paper "examines rape culture in dog parks via the use of black feminist criminology."	*Gender, Place, and Culture*
"Going in Through the Back Door: Challenging Straight Male Homohysteria and Transphobia through Receptive Penetrative Sex Toy Use"	The paper's abstract states: "This study seeks to explore, 'Do men who report greater comfort with receptive penetrative anal eroticism also report less transphobia, less obedience to masculine gender norms, greater partner sensitivity, and greater awareness about rape?'"[67]	*Sexuality & Culture*
"Our Struggle Is My Struggle: Solidarity Feminism as International Reply to Neoliberal and Choice Feminism"	Saad notes that this paper "involves a rewriting of Adolf Hitler's *Mein Kampf* using feminist buzzwords."	*Affilia: Journal of Women and Social Work*
"Who Are They to Judge?: Overcoming Anthropometry and a Framework for Fat Bodybuilding"	The paper's abstract states: "The author introduces fat bodybuilding as a means of challenging the prevailing assumptions of maximally fat-exclusionary (sports) cultures while raising fundamental ontological questions about what it means to 'build a body.'"[68]	*Fat Studies*

"When the Joke Is on You: A Feminist Perspective on How Personality Influences Satire"	The paper's abstract states: "The two functions of humor are clarified: as a tool of subversion that fosters social-justice aims when coming from marginalized groups and a tool of superiority/disparagement... when used by privileged ones against social-justice aims."	*Hypatia*
"An Ethnography of Breastaurant Masculinity: Themes of Objectification, Sexual Conquest, Male Control, and Masculine Toughness in a Sexually Objectifying Restaurant"	The authors write that the paper is best summarized as: "A gender scholar goes to Hooters to try to figure out why it exists." [69] The paper's abstract states: "The present study is based on a 2-year participant-observer ethnography of a group of men in a "breastaurant" to characterize the unique masculinity features that environment evokes. Currently, whereas some research examines sexually objectifying restaurant environments regarding their impacts upon women in those spaces, no known scholarly attention has been given to men and masculinities in these environments."[70]	*Sex Roles*

| "Moon Meetings and the Meaning of Sisterhood: A Poetic Portrayal of Lived Feminist Spirituality" | The authors give a summary statement in an *Areo* article titled "Academic Grievance Studies and the Corruption of Scholarship." They remark that this piece is "a rambling poetic monologue of a bitter, divorced feminist, much of which was produced by a teenage angst poetry generator before being edited into something slightly more 'realistic,' which is then interspersed with self-indulgent autoethnographical reflections on female sexuality and spirituality written entirely in slightly under six hours."[71] | *The Journal of Poetry Therapy* |

Note: The format here (other than the descriptions) is adapted from Gad Saad's presentation of the information on pages 78–79 of his book *The Parasitic Mind: How Infectious Ideas Are Killing Common Sense.*

The ridiculousness has even penetrated society's reluctance to define what a woman is. Matt Walsh's 2022 documentary, *What Is a Woman?*, revealed that many people—including credentialed professionals—could not (or would not) give a formal definition. Likewise, in her 2022 confirmation hearings, current Supreme Court Justice Ketanji Brown Jackson was asked to define what a woman is, and she replied that she is "not a biologist."[72] This is particularly ironic given the historic nature of her appointment— she is the first black *woman* on the bench (which implies that society generally *does* know what a woman is). It's also ironic given that the Left claims to so greatly value *women's* rights.

On a similar note, in a 2022 U.S. Senate hearing about abortion, a UC Berkeley professor was testifying as an expert in race and reproductive rights. She used the term *people with a capacity for pregnancy*, and Senator Josh Hawley asked her if she meant "women." She responded, "Many women, cis women—[that is, biological women who identify as women]—have the capacity for pregnancy. Many cis women do not have the capacity for pregnancy. There are also trans men who are capable of pregnancy as well as nonbinary people who are capable of pregnancy."[73] When Hawley then asked if abortion is a women's-rights issue, she responded: "We can recognize that this impacts women while also recognizing that it impacts other groups. Those things are not mutually exclusive....I want to recognize that your line of questioning is transphobic....It opens up trans people to violence by not recognizing them."[74]

Summary

If not monitored with a discerning eye, The Great Reset's sociocultural aims could wreak havoc on society. It's already happening through distorted leftist notions of "equality," "fairness," "anti-racism," and "oppression." Conveniently, these sorts of ideas often lack an end point—meaning that we don't even know what the markers are for reaching the final stage of a "fair and just society." This means that destructive activism can continue in perpetuity.

Furthermore, pathogenic ideas are becoming commonplace, victimhood is being glorified, and objective truth is only objective when convenient to proponents of the prevailing leftist preferences.

In fact, what's happening isn't all that new. A survivor of Mao Zedong's communist China said in a 2021 interview with political commentator Dan Bongino: **"I have been really paying close attention to what's going on in America, and I said, 'This is it: This is [the] Cultural Revolution I experienced when I was a little girl in China, and I have to do something [about it].'"**[75] An estimated 65 million people were murdered in communist China.[76] [emphasis added]

Similarly, in 2021, Chinese artist and political activist Ai Weiwei said on the PBS show *Firing Line* with Margaret Hoover: "Many things happening today in [the] U.S. can be compared to [the] Cultural Revolution in China....Like people trying to be unified in a certain political correctness. That is very dangerous." He added, "In many ways, you're already in the authoritarian state. You just don't know it."[77]

The seemingly intentional turmoil that's being created is often likened to "cultural Marxism" (for instance, as described in James Lindsay's 2022 book, *Race Marxism*). In simplified terms: Karl Marx's focus was on class struggles, whereas now the struggles are extended to include races, genders, and more. This creates division. **And divided people who are quibbling among themselves will be so preoccupied with their disputes that they might miss the bigger picture: society is becoming less free and more controlled by government.** And that leads us to our next discussion on the role of government in the Great Reset.

CHAPTER 5
POLITICS

Klaus Schwab and Thierry Malleret are explicit in their book *COVID-19: The Great Reset*: they foresee "the return of 'big' government."[1] However, the leftist vision of a benevolent government that's needed to manage—or perhaps micromanage—the population poses a serious threat. This chapter is a summary of reasons why bigger, more centralized government power is detrimental to society, whereas a smaller and less centralized government should be preferred. The related notion of the government's role in the economy will be covered in the next chapter. (Note: For further information on these political and economic topics, see my book *An End to Upside Down Liberty* [2021][2]).

Power over Freedom

Let's start with the basics. We have governments in society because we're taught to believe that if we didn't have them, there would be complete chaos. As the thinking goes: humans are too irresponsible, untrustworthy, and warlike to be left unchecked. A monopolistic government is the solution, almost like a responsible parent. When problems inevitably arise in society, government is always there to solve our problems.

But "government" is merely a group of humans—not gods. Once in government, those humans gain effective unilateral decision-making authority over the population. Why, then, would we assume that irresponsible, untrustworthy, and warlike humans should be trusted just because they're put together in a construct labeled "government"?

The argument often made is that these humans are *elected* into that position of power (in nondictatorial governments, at least). Because they're chosen by the people, it's okay for them to be in power. But who does the electing? And who runs the elections? Humans. If humans are deemed to be irresponsible, untrustworthy, and warlike, how would they temporarily snap out of it and become qualified to elect the right humans into power? And why should humans be trusted to run fair elections?

Essentially, the argument in favor of government control goes something like this: "We don't trust humans to have freedom, but when we put humans in a position of power, magically, we trust them more." It's backward.[3]

If anything, some people who seek government positions do it because they crave power. Those types of individuals might even be *more* dangerous than the average person.

Thus, the Great Reset's vision of *increased* government control over populations discounts the fact that human beings in power are dangerous. And, in fact, our checkered human history proves this: Governments have repeatedly inflicted harm. They've murdered, enslaved, and brainwashed countless people.

From this lens, consider the implications of gun control—an idea that the World Economic Forum (WEF) seems to support.[4] Gun control doesn't mean gun control for *everyone*, it means gun control for law-abiding citizens but not the government (or criminals who break the law). The government gets to keep its unfettered access. Gun control is simply the act of neutering some humans so that other humans can have a monopoly on high-tech violence. As economist Hans-Hermann Hoppe often says sarcastically about government cries for more gun control, "It's as if governments are saying 'give us your guns…so that we can protect you.'" Those in power have a strong incentive to disarm the masses.

Checks and Balances and Centralization

One might contend that governments are certainly imperfect, but with appropriate checks and balances, the danger can be managed. However, the "checking" occurs *within* the government. So if all branches of government—consisting of naturally flawed humans—become corrupt, what happens then? There isn't an external body that formally "checks" an individual nation.

And this is one of the points made by Schwab and Malleret. They state: "We live in a world in which nobody is really in charge,"[5] so they believe in "improved global governance."[6] However, even if an external global government had dominion over all other governments, the same problem would arise: there wouldn't be an external body who could check *that* global government.

Schwab further argues that "governments should improve coordination" with regard to regulations.[7] This means that unchecked governments would have an ability to control citizens in unison.

So, centralized, consolidated, and unchecked power structures are inherently dangerous to the masses. Yet the Great Reset seems to advocate more centralization, not less. As economist Ryan McMaken aptly points out in his book *Breaking Away* (2022), "Regimes…see decentralization as a threat. And they are right. Decentralization *is* a threat to state power."[8]

Social Contract

Schwab and Malleret devote an entire subsection of a chapter in their book to the "social contract." What follows is an excerpt that gives color to their views:

> It is almost inevitable that the pandemic will prompt many societies around the world to reconsider and redefine the terms of their social contract. We have

already alluded to the fact that COVID-19 has acted as an amplifier of pre-existing conditions, bringing to the fore long-standing issues that resulted from deep structural frailties that had never been properly addressed. This dissonance and an emergent questioning of the status quo is finding expression in a loudening call to revise the social contracts by which we are all more or less bound. Broadly defined, the "social contract" refers to the (often implicit) set of arrangements and expectations that govern the relations between individuals and institutions. Put simply, it is the "glue" that binds societies together; without it, the social fabric unravels.[9]

The keys words in this paragraph are "more or less bound" and "implicit."

Put another way, the social contract isn't an actual contract. And herein lies an essential problem with the Great Reset and the traditional government structure of our world, more broadly: **government institutions rule over citizens in their given geographic jurisdictions without explicit, contractual consent**. The whole discussion of revising the social contract under the Great Reset is really irrelevant—since it's always been an abstraction, there isn't a formal document, to which every citizen has voluntarily agreed, that can be revised. Citizens don't have mutually agreed-upon contracts with their governments. Consent is just *implicit*. As Judge Andrew Napolitano says, "Do you know anybody that's consented to the [United States] Constitution? I don't."[10]

Think about it this way: Governments provide services to citizens —court systems, road servicing, police and military services, and more.[11] But when citizens interact with *non*government service providers in society, an explicit contract is often signed— especially if the service provider is performing an important duty. For instance, when an adviser (such as a consultant or an attorney) is engaged to provide services, the customer *hires* that adviser and often formalizes the agreement with a written, signed contract. The contract specifies the services that the service provider will deliver, what will happen if the service provider fails to deliver properly (including the potential to terminate the relationship), what the pricing structure will be, and so on.

By contrast, as Hoppe puts it, the government "unilaterally fixes the rules of the game—the laws—and can change them by legislation during the game."[12] [emphasis added]

Moreover, citizens don't *hire* the government. It's imposed on them by virtue of their being physically located within a certain jurisdiction. Citizens could "terminate" their relationship with their government if they have the means to leave the jurisdiction. But then they'd simply find themselves under the rule of a different government. They might also still owe taxes to the original government because of expatriation challenges.

Governments also get paid no matter how they perform. In fact, sometimes poor performance within an area of government can be used to justify the need for *more* dollars in that area.[13] And they can pay for it with tax collections or by effectively printing money through a central bank (such as the Federal Reserve in the United States). True service providers don't have these luxuries: they have to perform well in order to survive financially. Governments don't have that same incentive or accountability.

The point is that citizens aren't truly customers. And that means governments don't formally work for the citizens they verbally purport to "serve." The social contract is not a real contract.

Taxation

Taxation is not always voluntary. Some people might be happy to pay taxes, but others might not be. And if they don't pay, they could be fined, taken to jail, have their assets seized, and so on. Payment here is more like extortion or coercion versus the voluntary payments made in an explicit service-provider contract.

So, taxation is a problematic concept on its face. But under the Great Reset, "taxation will increase."[14]

This is in line with leftist ideology, which often favors high taxes, particularly on the wealthy. The claim is that the "rich" need to pay their "fair" share. Who defines what "fair" is? It's arbitrary. Economist Thomas Sowell comments on this: "Since this is an era when many people are concerned about 'fairness' and 'social justice,' what is your 'fair share' of what someone else has worked for?"[15]

Under the Great Reset, something like this could be in order. Schwab and Malleret mention "massive wealth redistribution, from the rich to the poor."[16] The authors don't specify taxation here, but typically the word *redistribution* means taking money from some people and giving it to others—because the government decides that it will be beneficial.

Sowell explains why "redistribution" is really a euphemism for something much less wholesome: "In the plain, straightforward sense, most income is not *distributed* at all, either justly or unjustly. Most income in a market economy is *earned* directly by providing something that someone else wants."[17] In other words, "redistribution" is the process in which someone first *earns* money, and then the government *distributes* that money elsewhere. It's really a unilateral distribution of wealth, not a *re*distribution.

Another problem with taxation is that people can be forced to fund activities that they find immoral. If the government decides to fund something, the citizens' own morality means nothing. They still have to pay taxes. In this regard, the government determines morality on its own, and then imposes it on citizens.

Democracy

Taxation and other unsavory aspects of government are sometimes brushed aside within democratic nations because "democracy" is placed on a pedestal. The WEF echoes this typical leftist sentiment and expresses concern about "the decline of democracy."[18]

However, the various forms of democracy practiced around the world today are *compulsory* democracies. They aren't fully voluntary democracies.

Democracy involves allowing the majority to decide what happens to the group (through representatives, for instance). If this isn't explicitly agreed upon by all participants beforehand—that is, with a written contract—then a group of people gets an ability to *force* its will on others. The majority can thus become tyrannical against the defenseless minority. And the majority might make harmful decisions. As stated by Murray Rothbard in his famous critique of government titled *Anatomy of the State*: "If 70 percent of the people decided to murder the remaining 30 percent, this would still be murder and would not be voluntary suicide on the part of the slaughtered minority."[19]

Economist Ludwig von Mises levied a similar critique: "Democracy seems like oppression to the minority. Where…the choice is…to suppress or be suppressed, one easily decides for the former." So Mises regarded democracy as "subjugation under the rule of others."[20] The irony here is that leftists claim to oppose "oppression," and yet they value compulsory "democracy."

McMaken further remarks: "Those on the winning side, of course, don't see any problem here. What the minority thinks of as 'oppression' is really—according to the winners—just 'modernization,' 'progress,' 'decency,' 'common sense,' or simply 'the will of the majority.' The fact that the enforcement of that will of the majority is founded on state violence [or aggression against private property] is of little concern."[21] He adds that those in favor of democracy "often prefer to indulge in comforting fictions, and politely refrain from acknowledging that democracies can just as often produce disgruntled minority groups locked out of power by the majority."[22] **So when we hear cries from leftists that conservatives are a "threat to democracy," what they really mean is that democracy is good as long as they are in charge.**

Summary

Government is an organization that gives certain humans special privileges over other humans. It can impose its will on involuntary subjects—even in "democracies"—and force them to do things that they didn't explicitly sign up for. The structure naturally lends itself to tyranny, and governments around the world have steadily ratcheted up their power. As Patrick Deneen writes in his book *Why Liberalism Failed* (2018): "The 'limited government' of liberalism today would provoke jealousy and amazement from tyrants of old, who could only dream of such extensive capacities for surveillance and control of movement, finances, and even deeds and thoughts."[23]

All of this makes the Great Reset's call for big and centralized global power structures incredibly worrisome. McMaken calls out the obvious: **"Totalitarian states require bigness."**[24] [emphasis added]

CHAPTER 6

ECONOMICS

Alongside the push for big and centralized government under the Great Reset is the related leftist notion of a controlled—rather than a free—economy. Schwab and Malleret state in *COVID-19: The Great Reset*, "In general, there will be more regulation."[1] That begs multiple questions: Who will regulate the economy? Why should those people be trusted? What makes them capable of managing something so complex?

Furthermore, Schwab declares that "we need a 'Great Reset' of capitalism"[2]—an economic system "driven by selfish values."[3] He argues, instead, for "stakeholder capitalism." This chapter will discuss what these plans entail and why they're concerning.

Free-Market Capitalism

The term *capitalism* is often maligned in the modern era and blamed for many of the world's problems. And yet it has contributed to many positive developments, such as lifting much of the world's population out of poverty, increasing global per capita income, improving standards of living, adding to life expectancy, and contributing to higher levels of life satisfaction.[4] But what is capitalism, exactly?

Murray Rothbard provided an explanation in 1973:

> In order to discuss the "future of capitalism," we must
> first decide what the meaning of the term "capitalism"
> really is. Unfortunately, the term "capitalism" was coined
> by its greatest and most famous enemy, Karl Marx. We
> really can't rely upon him for correct and subtle usage.
> And, in fact, what Marx and later writers have done
> is to lump together two extremely different and even
> contradictory concepts and actions under the same
> portmanteau term. These two contradictory concepts
> are what I would call "free-market capitalism" on the
> one hand, and "state capitalism" on the other.
>
> The difference between free-market capitalism and state
> capitalism is precisely the difference between, on the
> one hand, peaceful, voluntary exchange; and on the
> other, violent expropriation. An example of a free-
> market exchange is my purchase of a newspaper on the
> corner for a dime; here is a peaceful, voluntary exchange
> beneficial to both parties. I buy the newspaper because
> I value the newspaper more highly than the dime that
> I give up in exchange; and the newsdealer sells me the
> paper because, he, in turn, values the dime more highly
> than the newspaper. **Both parties to the exchange ben-
> efit.** And what we are both doing in the exchange is
> the swapping of titles of ownership: I relinquish the
> ownership of my dime in exchange for the paper, and
> the newsdealer performs the exact opposite change of
> title. This simple exchange of a dime for a newspaper
> is an example of a unit free-market act; it is the market
> at work.
>
> The free market is really a vast network, a latticework, of
> these little, unit exchanges…. At each step of the way,
> there are two people, or two groups of people, and these
> two people or groups exchange two commodities, usu-
> ally money and another commodity; at each step, each
> benefits by the exchange, otherwise they wouldn't be

making it in the first place. If it turns out that they were mistaken in thinking that the exchange would benefit them, then they quickly stop, and they don't make the exchange again.

Another common example of a free market is the universal practice of children swapping baseball cards—the sort of thing where you swap "two Hank Aaron[s]" for "one Willie Mays." The "prices" of the various cards, and the exchanges that took place, were based on the relative importance that the kids attached to each baseball player....**We might put the case this way: liberals are supposed to be in favor of any voluntary actions performed, as the famous cliché goes, by "two consenting adults." Yet it is peculiar that while liberals are in favor of any sexual activity engaged in by two consenting adults, when these consenting adults engage in trade or exchange, the liberals step in to harass, cripple, restrict, or prohibit that trade. And yet both the consenting sexual activity and the trade are similar expressions of liberty in action....But the government, especially a liberal government, habitually steps in to regulate and restrict such trade.**[5] [emphasis added]

Free-market capitalism is a really simple concept: it is allowing people to make exchanges on their own, without interference. That is not the system under government structures today. We have some elements of it, but we really have "state capitalism," in which the government intervenes to varying degrees—some governments do it more than others.

Implicit in governments' intervention is their belief that they know what is best for other people. As Rothbard put it: "It is very much as [though] I were about to exchange two Hank Aaron [baseball cards] for one Willie Mays [baseball card], and the government, or some other third party, should step in and say: 'No, you can't do that; that's evil; it's against the common good. We hereby outlaw this proposed exchange; any exchange of such baseball cards must be one for one, or three for two'—or whatever other terms the government, in its wisdom and greatness, arbitrarily wishes to impose. By what right do they do this?"[6] This sort of intervention in the economy—and in the lives of people more generally—lacks humility.

Why does it lack humility? The answer is provided by the "Austrian School" of economics—featuring economists like Rothbard, Ludwig von Mises, Friedrich Hayek, Hans-Hermann Hoppe, Walter Block, Joseph Salerno, Thomas DiLorenzo, Mark Thornton, and others; and the lineage continues today at the Mises Institute in Auburn, Alabama. This school of thought argues that governments are *incapable* of knowing how to manage economies because there is far too much complexity and unpredictability in human behavior. By intervening anyway, governments exhibit intellectual arrogance, and in the process, they can damage the lives and finances of citizens in ways that those citizens didn't ask for. Nobel Prize–winning economist Friedrich Hayek thus called government central planning "the fatal conceit," stating: "The curious task of economics is to demonstrate to men how little they really know about what they imagine they can design."[7]

Consider the following: In free-market exchanges, human beings are reflecting their subjective preferences. They buy and sell things based on what they want or need at that moment. Those "wants" can *change* over time. And—even more important—they can change *in unpredictable ways*. Why? Because humans are complicated. They aren't robots. Humans have emotions, consciousness, and complex biology that influences their preferences, and they have varied life circumstances.

For some other person, or a group of people in government, or even an advanced algorithm to try to *predict* what is best for *all* of the complex people within an economy…is simply impossible.[8] That would be true even if the government regulators had the absolute best intentions for everyone, and even if they were the smartest people on the planet. By unilaterally pulling the levers in the economy—with *any* policy or regulation—governments inevitably hamstring certain people's activities, thereby damaging their lives. Put another way, government interventions inherently end up distorting the natural flow of the market.

On a related note, governments have an ability to alter the money supply, which can result in inflation. So without asking for it, people's money can be reduced in value whereby they can't buy as much with the money they have. Schwab and Malleret even discuss this risk (and the associated mechanics of Modern Monetary Theory).[9]

In his 2021 article titled "The 'Great Reset' is about Expanding Government Power and Suppressing Liberty," former congressman Ron Paul summarizes the broader problem from the perspective of Austrian economics: "Government interference in the marketplace disturbs the signals sent by prices, leading to an oversupply of certain goods and services and an undersupply of others."[10]

Profit through Service

Those who produce things of high value in a capitalistic society can become very wealthy. Profit is sometimes a focus for market actors, and anticapitalists don't like this. It's often regarded as selfish or greedy. In fact, Schwab expresses concern about "selfish values" that can arise from "short-term profit maximization."[11]

However, what is "profit"? Mathematically speaking, it is just "the revenue earned *minus* the cost required to gain that revenue." What is revenue? It is the *price* of goods and services sold multiplied by the *number* (that is, quantity) of goods and services sold. What is "selling" in a free-market system? It means that other people in the economy value the product or service and voluntarily trade their own resources (such as money) in order to acquire it.

In short, selling something in a free-market economy means that you've provided something of value. So you've *served* another party by going through the time and effort to create that product or service so that someone else can have it. The price and quantity—that is, the components of revenue—involved in sales provide insights into how much value has been provided to the buyers. Profit, from this lens, is thus a measure of service to others. And in exchange for that service, the service provider gets compensated. **Critics of capitalism often focus exclusively on the compensation and ignore the service.**

Think about it another way: People need lots of things for their survival. It can be cumbersome to manage all of those things on their own. For example, a man might need tomatoes for his meals, but he's too busy with his job and family to grow tomatoes on his own. And even if he wanted to do it, his local climate would add an additional challenge. So *someone else* harvests tomatoes and sells them to the man who needs them. The harvester—the seller—is thereby doing a service by providing tomatoes to someone who wants them. If the seller does a good job, he or she will profit greatly as a by-product of this service.

And if there are multiple sellers of tomatoes, there will be competition: each seller will want to produce the best and most accessible tomatoes; otherwise, buyers will buy from someone else. Competition encourages better production, which means more value to the buyers—that is, greater service to the buyers.

Competition is also a good thing in terms of the labor market. People who have skills (workers) can "sell" their skills to companies ("buyers") who need those skills. In a competitive marketplace with lots of companies, those companies will be incentivized to create positive conditions for workers. If they don't, which is certainly possible, those workers will be incentivized to take their skills somewhere else. Companies that treat employees badly might face greater difficulty in attracting talent, which will hurt their ability to produce and serve customers. Furthermore, having lots of workers in the market incentivizes those workers to engage in their own improvement, striving toward more personal excellence. The competitive free market for labor helps workers as well as the profit-seeking companies.

However, "competition" is one of the areas that Schwab feels needs to be governed under the Great Reset—to "promote more equitable outcomes."[12]

Income Inequality and Unfairness

Anticapitalists seem to resent these notions of profit and competition. Perhaps part of it derives from envy of those who are successful. However, that's not typically the outward emotion expressed because it doesn't reflect well on the envy-holder. Instead, we often hear cries that capitalism leads to inequality and unfairness—two of the concepts discussed in the Great Reset and within leftist ideology more generally.

Schwab and Malleret consider inequality to be a possible "next disaster"[13] in society. They also comment: "The policy tools to fight unacceptable levels of inequality do exist, and they often lie in the hands of governments."[14]

Inequality, in an economic sense, typically refers to the difference in wealth between the rich and the poor (however one chooses to define those terms—which, in itself, is a complicated discussion[15]). The Gini Coefficient is an economic metric used to show this differential. However, closer examination reveals that metrics like this aren't what they are often made out to be.

For example, would it be a good thing if everyone were equally poor? Then there wouldn't be inequality. Would this resolve the Great Reset's concerns?

Furthermore, imagine a world in which the lowest income bracket lived like kings, but they had much less wealth *relative to* the highest income brackets? In that case, there would be blatant "inequality." Would that still be a problem under the Great Reset's vision for the world?

Those who honestly care about the well-being of others wouldn't care about income inequality. They would care about the overall *well-being* of each individual. And if certain individuals are poor and struggling in that society, they'd focus their attention on helping those people through charitable work or otherwise. Instead, they often point the finger at individuals they consider to be wealthy. To them, the solution is to take from the wealthy and give to the poor in order to equalize the imbalance. That's their subjective version of "fairness." They often advocate this solution because, as economist Milton Friedman said, they fall for the economic fallacy of "[assuming] that there is a fixed pie, that one party can gain only at the expense of another."[16]

This method of *redistribution*—perhaps more accurately labeled *coerced distribution*—is just involuntary charity. Those who advocate for it are forcing their morality on others and not allowing people to utilize their legitimately earned wealth as *they* see fit. What entitles some people to decide what other individuals should do with their wealth? How could they possibly know what the best solution is? Why is their solution better than the wealth-holder's solution?

Ultimately, policies like compulsory "redistribution" seek to control people and limit liberty—under the belief that those in power know what is best for society.

Environment and Regulation

Some opponents of capitalism argue that businesses create "negative externalities" such as environmental damage. Therefore, they argue, the government is needed to regulate businesses. Otherwise, they'll pollute and destroy nature. Schwab explicitly echoes this concern.[17]

However, this line of thinking assumes that governments are capable of managing the problem through central planning. And it assumes that they will use their power to "defend nature" rather than promote their own political advancement.

Consider the example of the Soviet Union. It was a tightly managed, communistic/socialistic nation. But it destroyed its environment (in addition to murdering approximately 20 million people[18]). Authors Murray Feshbach and Alfred Friendly Jr. document this in their 1991 book *Ecocide in the USSR: Health and Nature Under Siege*. They write: **"When historians finally conduct an autopsy on the Soviet Union and Soviet Communism, they may reach the verdict of death by ecocide....No other great industrialized civilization so systematically and so long**

poisoned its land, air, water and people. None so loudly proclaiming its efforts to improve public health and protect nature so degraded both."¹⁹ [emphasis added]

(Note: Supporters of socialistic philosophies often suggest that disastrous outcomes—like those experienced in the Soviet Union—aren't accurate representations because they "simply didn't do it right," whereas places like modern Scandinavia are better comparisons. Denmark's prime minister rebutted this notion in 2015, saying, "Denmark is far from a socialist planned economy. Denmark is a market economy."²⁰ Further misconceptions about Scandinavia are explained by the Kurdish-Swedish author Dr. Nima Sanandaji in his 2021 book *Debunking Utopia: Exposing the Myth of Nordic Socialism.*²¹)

Regardless of societal structure, pollution and environmental degradation are risks that humans and businesses naturally impose by virtue of their existence on this planet. Managing this is inherently a challenge. **But the existence of a challenge doesn't mean that government is automatically the solution.** People in society might ultimately need to take the reins themselves.

For instance, a solution described by Rothbard is to make ecological issues a matter of private property: a polluting company that does damage to someone's land (and even the air over that land), could be sued by the landowner. The legal risk for polluting companies creates a natural financial incentive for companies to engage in better environmental practices. As Rothbard put it: "When we peel away the confusions and the unsound philosophy of the modern ecologists, we find an important bedrock case against the existing system, but the case turns out to be not against capitalism....It is a case against the failure of government to allow and to defend the rights of private property against invasion."²²

This subject ties in with a broader problem—something deeply embedded in modern psychology—particularly among leftists: There is often an implicit, unstated belief that the government is uniquely qualified to handle things. Yes, government is made of humans. But somehow—from their perspective—humans in government are *different.*

This bias came through clearly during podcaster Joe Rogan's October 2022 interview with Jann Wenner, the cofounder of *Rolling Stone* magazine. What follows is a segment from that conversation:[23]

Rogan: Do you want the government to regulate the internet?

Wenner: Absolutely.

Rogan: You trust the people who got us into the Iraq War on false pretenses to regulate the internet? [Rogan is referring to the U.S.'s justification for invading Iraq, which was that Saddam Hussein had "weapons of mass destruction." As it turned out, he did not, and many lives were lost.]

Wenner: The people who got us into the Iraq war [were] the politicians.

Rogan: It's the government...

Wenner: Who else is going to regulate?

Rogan: If they're gonna be in power and they're regulating the internet, they're gonna regulate the internet in a way that suits their best interest. The same way they do with the banking industry, the same way they do with the environment, the same way they do with energy, the same way they do with everything....We need to move forward collectively...with an ethic that respects truth and that appreciates opinions and reality and an understanding of things that are not necessarily possible with corporate interests involved in the dissemination of information....

Wenner: There's no way that you can do that except through the government....Human nature's not gonna change.

Rogan: But the government's not gonna change either.

Wenner: But the government is capable of change. Look…the government regulates the food supply.

Rogan: The food supply? Why would they let [the toxic herbicide] glyphosate infestate [*sic*] all of our foods?

Wenner: Then we better get better politicians.…Let's take…the Food and Drug Administration, which regulates Big Pharma. On the one hand, we've got a very safe supply of drugs.

Rogan: Safe?

Wenner: Drugs are tested.…You don't get too many bad drugs.

(Note: This was not included in the interview, but what follows is a list of almost forty FDA-approved drugs that were later pulled from the market because of safety concerns: Accutane, Baycol, Belviq/Belviq XR, Bextra, Cylert, Darvon & Darvocet, DBI, DES, Duract, Ergamisol, Hismanal, Lotronex, Meridia, Merital & Alival, Micturin, Mylotarg, Omniflox, Palladone, Permax, Pondimin, Posicor, Propulsid, PTZ & Metrazol, Quaalude, Raplon, Raptiva, Raxar, Redux, Rezulin, Selacryn, Seldane, Trasylol, Vioxx, Xigris, Zantac, Zelmid, and Zelnorm.[24])

Wenner—a big player in the media—reflects a typical leftist bias: the belief that humans in government are somehow endowed with special qualities. But as discussed in the previous chapter, if governments do a bad job, they don't go out of business. They continue to collect taxes, and they can essentially print money as needed through central banks. If a regular company performs poorly, its livelihood is at stake. Serving customers is required for companies' survival, whereas governments can survive without truly serving citizens' interests. That is one key difference between governments and companies comprised of regular people.

Another difference is this: People in government can compel regular citizens to do things against their will. If regular citizens do that, they're potentially criminals.

How would a futuristic economy without government oversight handle drug regulation, for example? Creative entrepreneurs, rather than politicians and bureaucrats, would have to come up with innovative solutions. Customers desire safe products, so entrepreneurs would have to find ways to demonstrate safety—and their performance in the marketplace (that is, their ability to attract and serve buyers) would act as the effective "regulation." For instance, they could create private regulation firms that get paid based on their performance. Drug companies would have an incentive to get approval from such private "regulators" if they want to attract buyers of their products: a product that has a "stamp" of credibility —from a trusted firm with a proven track record—might be more appealing to buyers than products without it. And if a regulation firm makes lots of mistakes, it risks going out of business and losing to competitors who do better. (Note: The potential privatization of government functions is discussed by many Austrian economists, including Murray Rothbard in his book *For a New Liberty* [1973].[25] Similarly, Hans-Hermann Hoppe has proposed a "private law society."[26])

Capitalism with little or no government is, of course, imperfect —because humans are imperfect. But at least free markets have corrective mechanisms with real financial accountability that governments lack. If citizens make mistakes in the free market, which is inevitable, those mistakes are being made on citizens' own terms. That is, the government isn't dictating what risks citizens can take in their personal lives. And by allowing citizens to make their own risk assessments, they can learn when they make mistakes. That stimulates personal—and collective—evolution.

Capitalism under the Great Reset

The alternative to modern capitalism ultimately proposed under the Great Reset is "stakeholder capitalism." Traditionally, companies are controlled by their financial owners—their shareholders. The Great Reset's "stakeholder capitalism" posits that companies are responsible not only to their shareholders but to other parties in society, such as customers, employees, suppliers, lenders, the economy, the state, and society.[27]

Shareholders represent a defined quantity, whereas determining what constitutes a stakeholder is much more abstract and nebulous. That's the first issue.

But more important, the Great Reset's architects don't see this as a voluntary activity: they want *governments* to influence how businesses engage with stakeholders. **It's compulsory or coerced stakeholder capitalism rather than fully voluntary stakeholder capitalism—and the rules are set by those in power.**

Schwab and Malleret elaborate on this in their 2022 book titled *The Great Narrative: For a Better Future*: "Contrary to shareholder capitalism that always saw government as the source of all 'evils,' stakeholder capitalism welcomes the idea of legislative action to define with precision the benchmarks."[28] **This means that they want the government to directly influence companies. By the way, economic *fascism* entails a close relationship between government and businesses.**[29]

Under the Great Reset, this is regarded as perfectly acceptable. As Schwab and Malleret put it: "There is nothing wrong with governments creating the right incentives and issuing appropriate norms for responsible behavior."[30] Who determines what are "appropriate norms" and "responsible behavior"? What is considered "appropriate and responsible" could vary drastically from person to person. Couldn't these terms just be defined however the government wants, based on its own preferences, and to enhance politicians' lives? As Murray Rothbard said, "Placing the government in charge of moral principles is equivalent to putting the proverbial fox in charge of the chicken coop."[31]

Schwab and Malleret feel that this is okay because governments "represent the choice expressed by citizens in free elections. This then gives them the authority to determine societal rules."[32] That might be true if governments engaged with their citizens in a truly voluntary manner. But citizens don't sign a formal, explicit, and mutually agreed-upon contract with governments giving them permission to determine for them what is "appropriate and responsible." This is particularly troubling for people who voted for a candidate who lost the election—the winning candidate, the person they didn't vote for—could determine the "societal rules" for them.

Under the Great Reset, many of these rules will be influenced by "Stakeholder Capitalism Metrics" of the World Economic Forum. So the WEF can directly influence how governments set rules for companies. It's like dictatorship by proxy—the masterminds at the WEF dictate how governments dictate business operations.

In a market free of government influence, this wouldn't happen. If citizens in the marketplace didn't like the way a company was acting toward stakeholders, they'd have every right to boycott that brand and choose another company (or start a better business themselves). People have an ability to make voluntary choices as to which businesses they engage with and buy from. The people's collective choices in a marketplace reflect a form of voluntary "democracy"—they vote with their dollars. Companies adjust to meet the needs of customers.

Schwab and Malleret do acknowledge this aspect, however. They comment that "in parallel" with government influence, "societal pressure and rising activism will accelerate the pace at which companies embrace stakeholder value and will 'force' the reluctant ones to convert to the cause."[33]

If the market has this natural ability to sway corporate behavior, then why does the government need to intervene as well? It's telling that Schwab and Malleret *start* their discussion with government influence, and then, almost as an addendum, say that "in parallel," the market will also have an influence. This is a demonstration of an elitist mentality, and they might not even realize it—it's as if they're saying, "Because we are enlightened, we know what is 'appropriate and responsible.' And by the way, the masses will probably agree with us."

Environmental, Social, and Governance (ESG)

A central part of this stakeholder capitalism is the integration of ESG—standards that companies will need to adhere to. Schwab and Malleret write:

> In the same way that companies have an obligation to report their financial results (quarterly or annually, depending on the countries and whether they are listed or not), in the not-too-distant future they will have a similar obligation to report on ESG metrics. Several initiatives have been undertaken to determine the best way to achieve this. The "Stakeholder Capitalism Metrics" of the World Economic Forum is a major one. They will converge toward a standardized ESG performance metric that works across industries and countries and that is supported by global standard-setters. Such initiatives tend to be led by business, but a globally accepted system of sustainability reporting will be a concerted effort of business, governments, regulators, the official accounting community, and voluntary standard-setters. In the end, governments will make the last call for setting the legal obligations, targets, and incentives around ESG standards and performance proposed by business. They will also ensure that stakeholder value is compatible with a rigorously defined concept of "societal and planetary value."[34]

How has this worked in practice? The nation of Sri Lanka had one of the highest ESG "scores" in the world. And things didn't go so well for its citizens. As reported by The Committee to Unleash Prosperity in July 2022: "You've probably heard that Sri Lanka is in a state of total economic collapse....The schools and businesses are shut down. The nation has run out of fuel. Last weekend, violent demonstrators stormed the official residence of the President and then set fire to the residence of the Prime Minister. Both officials have announced they will resign. There are many factors behind Sri Lanka's demise, but green policies [that is, ESG-related policies] are one of them."

As Al Jazeera reported in its headline: "Sri Lanka faces 'man-made' food crisis as farmers stop planting."[35] If we give the government in this situation the benefit of the doubt and assume that the politicians had a benign intent, then the government tried to "do good" with ideas that "sounded good"…but the results were far from good. And *citizens* suffered the consequences of their politicians' irresponsible actions.

The article by The Committee to Unleash Prosperity continues: "Sri Lanka was self-sufficient in food production until 2021. Then–President Gotabaya Rajapaksa issued an overnight ban on all synthetic fertilizers and pesticides….The production of rice, a staple of the Sri Lankan diet, fell by between 40 and 50% nationwide. Food prices rose by over 80%, and now there are severe shortages, which has led to malnutrition and widespread hunger. Michael Shellenberger, a liberal analyst who specializes in environmental issues, reported that Sri Lankan leaders 'fell under the spell of Western green elites.'"[36]

So what exactly do the components of ESG—"environmental, social, and governance"—include? The United Nations, another unelected body, has influence over this with its seventeen "Sustainable Development Goals," which are summarized in the table that follows:

Area	Sustainable Development Goal
People	No Poverty. End poverty in all its forms everywhere.
	Zero Hunger. End hunger, achieve food security, and improve nutrition and promote sustainable agriculture.
	Good Health & Well-Being. Ensure healthy lives, and promote well-being for all at all ages.
	Quality Education. Ensure inclusive and equitable quality education, and promote lifelong learning opportunities for all.
	Gender Equality. Achieve gender equality, and empower all women and girls.

Planet	Clean Water and Sanitation. Ensure availability and sustainable management of water and sanitation for all.
	Affordable and Clean Energy. Ensure access to affordable, reliable, sustainable, and modern energy for all.
	Climate Action. Take urgent action to combat climate change and its impacts.
	Life Below Water. Conserve and sustainably use the oceans, seas, and marine resources for sustainable development.
	Life on Land. Protect, restore, and promote sustainable use of terrestrial ecosystems; sustainably manage forests and combat desertification, halt and reverse land degradation, and halt biodiversity loss.
Prosperity	Decent Work and Economic Growth. Promote sustained, inclusive, and sustainable economic growth, full and productive employment, and decent work for all.
	Industry, Innovation and Infrastructure. Build resilient infrastructure, promote inclusive and sustainable industrialization, and foster innovation.
	Responsible Consumption and Production. Ensure sustainable consumption and production patterns.
Peace	Reduced Inequalities. Reduce inequality within and among countries.
	Sustainable Cities and Communities. Make cities and human settlements inclusive, safe, resilient, and sustainable.
	Peace, Justice, and Strong Institutions. Promote peaceful and inclusive societies for sustainable development, provide access to justice for all; and build effective, accountable, and inclusive institutions at all levels.
Partnership	Partnership for the Goals. Strengthen the means of implementation, and revitalize the Global Partnership for Sustainable Development.

This table has been adapted from a 2018 article by the law firm Davis Polk & Wardwell LLP posted on the Harvard Law School Forum on Corporate Governance.[37]

Many of these concepts, of course, "sound" good and use popular buzzwords, but many of them are vague and subject to interpretation. The idea that we should generally improve environmental, social, and governance issues is certainly an admirable goal. But a specific version of it is now being imposed by people who get to arbitrarily shape what those things mean. They can use all of this to micromanage global activities in the process.

For that reason, their implementation hasn't always received a warm welcome. One such vocal critic is Vivek Ramaswamy, a Harvard graduate and successful businessman. In his book *Woke, Inc.* (2021), he explains that powerful people support these initiatives using the following "trick": "*Pretend you care about something other than profit and power, precisely to gain more of each....*Today's captains of industry do it by promoting progressive social values. Their tactics are far more dangerous...than those of the older robber barons: their do-good smoke screen expands not only their market power but their power over every other facet of our lives."[38] He adds, "They are using the private sector to effectuate a left-wing social agenda that they could not directly effectuate through Congress."[39]

Ramaswamy elaborates on his personal journey, emphasizing the impact of stakeholder capitalism and ESG in America, specifically:

> I am a traitor to my class....As a young twenty-first-century capitalist myself, the thing I was supposed to do was shut up and play along: wear hipster clothes, lead via practiced vulnerability, applaud diversity and inclusion, and muse on how to make the world a better place at conferences in fancy ski towns. Not a bad gig.

> The most important part of the trick was to stay mum about it. Now I'm violating the code by pulling back the curtain and showing you what's really going on....

> Why am I defecting? I'm fed up with corporate America's game of pretending to care about justice in order to make money....It demands that a small group of investors and CEOs determine what's good for society....It's

not just ruining companies. It's polarizing our politics. It's dividing our country to a breaking point. Worst of all, it's concentrating the power to determine American values in the hands of a small group of capitalists rather than in the hands of the…citizenry at large, which is where the dialogue about social values belongs.[40]

He also views this veneer of altruism as a means for companies to win "favors…from the government over the long run—favorable legislative treatment, lenient prosecutorial discretion, fiscal grants, and other forms of corporate welfare."[41]

Along these lines, an ESG focus allows companies to change the way they are perceived amid a sensitive social culture. Ramaswamy elaborates, using the term *woke* to describe leftist activism:

The marriage of big business and woke culture was made in hell….It was arranged by necessity. Wokeness needed money. Wall Street need a moral imprimatur. So Wall Street eagerly embraced the new identity-based hierarchy and used wokeness to shield itself from the harsh glare the [2008] financial crisis had shed on it. That was the dowry of this arranged marriage.

By adopting these new "woke" values, America's business leaders stumbled upon a once-in-a-generation opportunity to leap from heresy to sainthood. Corporations were no longer the oppressors. Instead, corporate power—if wielded in the right way—could actually empower the new disempowered classes who suffered not at the hands of evil corporations but instead at the hands of straight white men—the real culprits who had exploited their power not only since the birth of the corporation but throughout all of modern human history.

Enter woke capitalism—or, more elegantly, the "multi-stakeholder model" of the corporation. The corporation would no longer exist to serve just shareholders but instead the interests of society at large, including those who deserved the kind of special protections that the rest of society had failed to afford. Women. "People of color." LGBTQ people. Victims of climate change. The tailwinds of this new conception of capitalism could not have been better timed to serve the objectives of the new class of corporate titans who readily espoused this new model.[42]

Summary

Capitalism allows consenting adults to freely exchange as they wish. The Great Reset's plan for more regulation and government intervention allows power structures to alter the natural flow of the market in whatever direction they please. Even if they wanted to create what they consider to be beneficial change, the inherent complexity of human consciousness makes this an impossibility— even for the smartest people with the best economics degrees. Yet the Great Reset aspires to create more intervention to enact its subjective ideals. As Ramaswamy concisely summarizes the situation: "Stakeholder capitalism pretends to be a milder form of capitalism, but it's actually capitalism gone wild: it encourages capitalism's winners to wield greater power....Ordinary [people] who vote at the ballot box...are like the poor devotees who wait in the long line at the temple. Meanwhile, CEOs and investors issuing moral fiats from Davos are the rich devotees who get to cut the line."[43]

CHAPTER 7

ENVIRONMENT

Klaus Schwab and Thierry Malleret mention climate change as a possible "next disaster."[1] Furthermore, they write in *The Great Narrative: For a Better Future* (2022): "Our current apparent inability to end the critical environmental and climate crisis (they are one and the same as nature and climate are inextricably linked) or to at least keep it under control, is the greatest collective action problem we've ever been confronted with. Humanity has never faced an endeavour [*sic*] more complex, ambitious, and far-reaching than arresting the collapse of our ecosystem and stabilizing the climate."[2]

Most people tend to agree that the climate is changing and that human activity is affecting it. But opinions differ as to the nature of the changes, how dangerous they are, and the extent to which humans are impacting them relative to the natural climate variability of Earth and other factors. Even among those who agree on these issues, there can be disagreement on what measures should be taken in response—and how much control should be exerted over people's lives in order to execute those measures.

In one sense, the desire for humans to take better care of the environment is a great thing. But the questions become: At what cost?

Who gets to make those decisions? What assumptions are those decisions based on? How precise is the data? What actions should be taken? Should "excessive consumption"[3] be limited (as Schwab and Malleret imply)? Who gets to define what is "excessive"?

This chapter explores those matters. It also considers how climate-related panic could be weaponized to further centralize power and increase controlling measures placed on the global population. Climate is emphasized here over other important environmental matters because that issue is having a particularly significant impact on our world today—and it's a primary focus of the Great Reset.

COVID-19 and Climate-Change Parallels

Although COVID-19 and climate change have different objective qualities, they have the potential to be weaponized in similar ways. As stated by Thomas Schomerus, a professor of public law at Leuphana University in Germany: "Both corona virus [sic] and the climate crisis require freedom-limiting measures. The earlier and more vigorously these are defined and implemented, the sooner the success that is vital for survival can be expected. In this respect, corona and climate protection measures do not differ in principle, but only on the time axis."[4]

A related sentiment emerged from a media insider. In April of 2021, a CNN technical director was secretly videotaped by an undercover Project Veritas journalist at a restaurant—while COVID-19 was still the major focus of people's attention around the world. He revealed, "I think there's just, like, a COVID fatigue. So...whenever a new story comes up, they're going to latch onto it. They've already announced in our office that once the public... will be open to it, we're going to start focusing mainly on climate....Climate, like global warming, and that's going to be our next...focus. Like our focus was to get Trump out of office, right? Without saying it, that's what it was, right? So our next thing is going to be climate change awareness." He added, "I have a feeling it's just going to be like constantly showing videos of... decline in ice and weather warming up, and the effects it's having on the economy." He also commented that it will be like the next "pandemic-like story, that we'll beat to death, but that one's got longevity....[The] climate thing is going to take years. **So, they'll probably be able to milk that for quite a bit....Be prepared, it's coming." When asked about whether the stories would be related to fear about the climate, he said, "Yeah. Fear sells."**[5] [emphasis added]

In fact, he turned out to be right. As the public became more accustomed to living with COVID-19, discussions about climate change became central. It represented the next crisis in focus.

President Barack Obama's chief of staff, Rahm Emanuel, offered useful insights that can be applied here. Speaking at a conference hosted by the *Wall Street Journal* in 2008, he mentioned: "You never want a serious crisis to go to waste. And what I mean by that is an opportunity to do things that you think you could not do before."[6] **In other words, crises—or the perception of crises—can be utilized by those in power to justify dictatorial action that otherwise wouldn't be acceptable.**

During the COVID-19 era of 2020–2022, governments locked people in their homes, shut down businesses, kept children out of school, mandated or coerced people into taking a vaccine that hadn't been tested for long-term side effects, and more. They ratcheted up their power, and many citizens gladly gave their freedoms away.

Schwab and Malleret even comment on the opening that this presented: **"We should take advantage** of this unprecedented opportunity to reimagine our world."[7] In other words, the crisis provided a chance to enact ideals that might not have been possible before the crisis. Actress Jane Fonda put it well in October of 2020: "I just think COVID is God's gift to the Left."[8] [emphasis added]

With regard to COVID-19 and climate matters, the mainstream narrative seems to *encourage* paranoia about the future, while *punishing* those who question whether things are as bad as they're made out to be. It's as if extreme levels of fear are being valued rather than pathologized. **Conveniently, fear also tends to make people more controllable.**

Climate Socialism

U.S. congresswoman Alexandria Ocasio-Cortez stated in 2019: "The world is gonna end in 12 years if we don't address climate change."[9] The belief in a near-term, civilization-ending climate catastrophe has impacted legislative aims. Governments—influenced by the World Economic Forum and others—have decided to take action. However, in some cases they seem to be using the opportunity to enact leftist policies that are in line with other aspects of the Great Reset.

For instance, U.S. House Resolution 109, introduced on February 7, 2019, labeled "Recognizing the duty of the Federal Government to create a Green New Deal," describes a focus well beyond climate change. It talks about "adequate health care, housing, transportation, and education"; "wage stagnation"; "socioeconomic mobility"; "the erosion of the earning and bargaining power of workers in the United States"; "the greatest income inequality since the 1920s"; "a large racial wealth divide amounting to a difference of 20 times more wealth between the average white family and the average black family"; "a gender earnings gap that results in women earning approximately 80 percent as much as men, at the median"; "guaranteeing a job with a family-sustaining wage, adequate family and medical leave, paid vacations, and retirement security to all people of the United States"; and more.[10]

Former Harvard physicist Luboš Motl commented in 2020 on the fact that the Green New Deal mixes climate-change issues "with tons of other topics that have nothing to do with it and with each other....So we learn that the goal of this 'Green Deal' is actually the standard Marxist garbage plan to 'erase inequalities.'"[11]

Author Marc Morano offers a similar perspective: "The premise of the Green New Deal is very simple: if you pay more taxes, regulate industry, drive up the cost of energy, micromanage every aspect of your life—we can then control the climate in order to avoid a climate emergency....What criteria will the overlords of the Green New Deal use to say, 'Okay, that's enough taxes spending and regulations; the climate has been fixed?' Or is it just an endless parade of money, regulations, bureaucracy, loss of freedom, redistribution of wealth, and enforced mandates on people?"[12] He adds that the climate panic "is merely a premise for achieving the political goals that the Left has sought for decades."[13]

For this reason, Morano says that climate policy is "a watermelon: green on the outside, red on the inside"[14] (because socialism/communism are associated with the color red). Meteorologist Eric Holthaus made this explicit in a 2018 tweet, responding to a recently released United Nations climate report: "The world's top scientists just gave rigorous backing **to systematically dismantle capitalism** as a key requirement to maintaining civilization and a habitable planet."[15] And in 2022, teenage climate activist Greta Thunberg expanded her focus beyond climate change to defeating the West's "oppressive" and "racist" capitalist system "built on the exploitation of people and the planet" and "defined by colonialism, imperialism, oppression, and genocide."[16] [emphasis added]

Climate Colonialism

Climate concerns can also be used to deprive developing nations of the energy they need to flourish.[17] This is, of course, justified as necessary because of an impending catastrophe. And it assumes that humans have an ability to reverse it.

But it also raises ethical questions. Let's say the most apocalyptic climate estimates are correct, but it's unclear whether humans can avoid the coming catastrophe. Would that give permission to a small group of powerful individuals to tell others that they can't freely enjoy their potentially short time remaining on the planet? Who gets to make those decisions? What sorts of restrictions are appropriate?

As discussed in the previous chapter, Sri Lanka's environmental measures might have sounded good, but in practice they were demonstrably disastrous for people's lives. Along similar lines, climate author Michael Shellenberger writes: "The idea that you would get poor countries not to use fossil fuels is imperialistic."[18] Put another way by UCLA economist Anthony Downs: "The elite's environmental deterioration is often the common man's improved standard of living."[19]

Furthermore, as reported by Al Jazeera in June 2022, the president of Niger said, "Africa is being 'punished' by the decisions of Western countries to end public financing for foreign fossil-fuel projects by the end of 2022."[20] Steven Koonin, a former Caltech provost and physicist, and a climate author, opined on this matter: "It is immoral for the developed world to deny the developing nations the energy they need. And it is the height of ecocolonialism to restrain their development by mandating ineffective energy systems, especially when the developed world has neither the will nor the capacity to pay their green premium."[21] [emphasis added]

The great irony here is that the Left is typically critical of colonialism, and its racial implications, and yet leftist global climate policies could be interpreted as a modern form of colonialism. But because it is cloaked in a benevolent desire to save the planet, this criticism doesn't come up very often. Leftists have a psychological incentive to ignore their own implicit advocacy of colonialism—it would be very painful for them to admit their hypocrisy.

Morano adds: "The underlying reality, which is lost on many today, is that fossil fuels—coal, oil, and natural gas—have been one of the greatest liberators of mankind in the history of our planet. Is it greedy to want heat, air conditioning, lower infant mortality, and longer life expectancy?"[22] Or as stated by actor Clifton Duncan, "Wanting cheap food and fuel is not a threat to democracy."[23]

Climate Antihumanism

The subject of trade-offs between living in the present and sacrificing for the future introduces an ideological undercurrent that often goes unstated: much of the climate movement carries with it an antihuman perspective.

In a 2022 interview, philosopher and climate author Alex Epstein summarized this antihuman outlook:

> It's immoral for humans to impact nature—that's a core belief. It's sort of a primitive religion: "Thou shalt not impact nature" [is] their core commandment. And you see that with the idea of "being green"—green really means minimize or eliminate our impact. And the logical end goal of that is we don't impact anything, and we either die or we try to live primitively...which... doesn't work for eight billion people. So that's just total mass murder...if you follow that....So the ultimate goal, then, if you want to call it a goal, is eliminating human impact and having an unimpacted planet. So [that's] really...the ideal planet to the modern environmental thought leaders:...the earth that would exist had human beings never existed....I think of that as apocalyptic, but I think...when people talk about [it] like, "We've destroyed the environment, destroyed the planet," even though it's way better for us now—what they're implying is the best planet is the one where human beings had never been here, where we had no impact....What's the number one moral goal in the world right now?....Eliminating our impact on climate: "[carbon] net zero." I'm sure you hear this in the finance world with ESG....Net zero has totally dominated as a moral goal, [and] what does net zero mean? It means eliminating our impact on climate is our number one goal....But notice, [the messaging is] not, "Make the climate more livable."[24]

Stated another way by Princeton physicist William Happer: "To call carbon dioxide a pollutant is really Orwellian. You are calling something a pollutant that we all produce. Where does that lead us eventually?"[25]

The antihuman perspective implies that the needs of people—or at least the needs of the masses—are secondary to the planet's needs. And that can lead to some strange proposals with the potential to hurt humans in ways that we can't even comprehend. For instance, CNBC wrote in October of 2022 that the U.S. government is looking to "cool Earth by reflecting back sunlight":

> The Office of Science and Technology Policy is coordinating a five-year research plan to study ways of modifying the amount of sunlight that reaches the Earth in order to temporarily temper the effects of global warming. There are several kinds of sunlight-reflection technology being considered, including stratospheric aerosol injection, marine cloud brightening, and cirrus cloud thinning....Stratospheric aerosol injection involves spraying an aerosol like sulfur dioxide into the stratosphere, and because it has the potential to affect the entire globe, [it] often gets the most attention....While arguments of moral hazard have handicapped research efforts, the idea is getting more urgent attention in the worsening climate crisis.[26]

Farming is under fire as well. Author George Monbiot said in a 2022 interview that farming is a form of land use that humans "inflict" on the planet. He suggested shutting down farming, to which the Irish interview host said, "I can hear farmers all over the small country of ours shocked and perhaps screaming at their television because they're saying, 'Are you saying all animal farming...really needs to stop?'" Monbiot's reply was, "Yes, it does. It really does."

Political commentator Matt Walsh takes a cynical view on these comments, calling Monbiot's perspective "a genocidal ideology." Walsh adds that this mentality isn't new, but "usually [the activists are] not as open about it." He continues with a more detailed criticism:

> [Monbiot] subscribes to a murderous ideology....Climate alarmists...are anti-human, anti-civilization. They see all of humanity—well most of it anyway, with the exception of themselves—as a blight, a stain, a parasite on the face of the Earth....[Monbiot] obviously

knows that we can't produce cricket energy bars and tofu burgers quickly enough—and distribute them widely enough—to feed everybody. [Monbiot] says that livestock farming, eating eggs, and drinking milk [are] mere indulgence[s] that the planet can't afford to support any longer. Yet billions of people in the world depend on...livestock farming to survive, especially in poor countries. The Maasai [people of Africa] subsist almost entirely on goats and cows. Take those away and they'll all starve to death. Billions of people will starve along with them. Environmentalists know this, and they're just okay with it—more than okay, it's what they want. Mass starvation is, as they say, "a feature, not a bug." You really can't be anti-farming without being anti-civilization. Human civilization is based on agriculture. It was born from and by agriculture.... People like Monbiot literally want to bring us back to the Stone Age. They want to reverse the clock by about 10,000 years, give or take.[27]

In a similar vein, a government-funded report was produced in 2019 by academics from six universities in the United Kingdom called *Absolute Zero*. It proposes limitations on basic aspects of human living in an effort to deliver "net-zero emissions by 2050." The report states that people need to "stop doing anything that causes emissions regardless of its energy source." Their "key message for individuals" is: "Travel less distance, travel by train or in small (or full) electric cars and stop flying; use...heating less and electrify the boiler when next upgrading; lobby for construction with half the material for twice as long; stop eating beef and lamb. Each action we take to reduce emissions, at home or at work, creates a positive ripple effect."[28]

Morano worries that "they're going after everything it means to be a free person and turning it over to the administrative state." He believes "they're going after freedom of movement."[29] For instance, as *Forbes* reports: "The French government has become the first large economy to ban short-haul flights where a train or bus alternative of two and a half hours or less exists—a move which was voted on in 2021 and comes into effect in April 2022."[30] Morano also references former political candidate Andrew Yang's 2019 suggestion that by 2050, "we might not own our cars" because they are "really inefficient and bad for the environment." The replacement would be a "constant roving fleet of electric cars."[31] Additionally, in 2022, the state of California finalized regulations to ban gasoline-powered vehicles by 2035. And yet days later, it told people to hold off on charging electric vehicles to avoid blackouts.[32]

The press even introduced the notion of lockdowns as it relates to climate. For instance, *The Guardian* summarized a study suggesting that "carbon dioxide emissions must fall by the equivalent of a global lockdown roughly every two years for the next decade for the world to keep within safe limits of global heating."[33]

However, the most diabolical aspect of the antihuman perspective is the belief that there are too many people on the planet—an idea endorsed by the World Economic Forum.[34] As the thinking goes: "Sure, micromanaging people's lives can help us save the planet by reducing emissions, but it would be even better if most people weren't here anymore."

This raises questions about the mechanisms by which depopulation might be enacted. Theoretically, the following avenues could be used: war; sterilization; euthanasia (which was the sixth-leading cause of death in Canada as of August 2022[35]); mass abortion; preventing and/or controlling new births; starvation (for example, by limiting or disrupting the food supply); freezing (for example, by limiting or disrupting the energy supply); inducing disease (for example, by toxifying food, water, and the air; administering harmful medications; increasing exposure to electric and magnetic fields [EMFs]; and unleashing bioweapons); and a long list of other unsettling possibilities.

Climate Predictions

Many of the fears about climate change come from predictions that are derived from models. And the actions taken to prevent climate-related problems are also influenced by models. **But as stated by ex–Caltech physics professor Steven Koonin—who was also the former undersecretary for science in the U.S. Department of Energy under the Obama Administration: "Projections of future climate and weather events rely on models demonstrably unfit for the purpose."**[36] Happer from Princeton adds: "Aside from the human brain, the climate is the most complex thing on the planet. The number of factors that influence climate—the sun, the earth's orbital properties, oceans, clouds, and yes, industrial man—is huge and enormously variable."[37] Similarly, Shellenberger cautions about **"false precision."**[38] [emphasis added]

It's important to acknowledge just how sensitive weather-related models are. This was demonstrated famously by meteorologist and mathematician Edward Lorenz in 1961. During one of his weather-prediction exercises, he rounded one of the numbers in his mathematical equations from 0.506127 to 0.506. This seemingly insignificant difference yielded wildly different results.[39] In other words, weather-related models can be highly responsive to initial conditions. If those conditions change, even by a tiny bit, the eventual outcome can change in a disproportionate—that is, a nonlinear—manner.[40] The climate is influenced by many factors, so we have to wonder: What might we be missing if assumptions in our models are even slightly off? And how might our models be impacted by limitations in our ability to measure climate-related factors—for the present time, and also looking back at Earth's much earlier history?

With COVID-19, we saw just how powerful mathematical models can be in terms of influencing policy. A model developed by Imperial College in London exaggerated COVID-19 death estimates. For instance, it forecasted 2.2 million deaths in the United States alone and was also wrong about its projections in other countries.[41] The model's predictions ramped up fear and helped justify draconian policies that limited freedom and harmed people's lives around the globe. A few months into the pandemic, the model was regarded by some as "totally unreliable"—but the damage was already done.[42]

Projections about overpopulation have been wrong as well. For instance, Stanford professor Paul Ehrlich published an apocalyptic book in 1968 called *The Population Bomb*, which has the subtitle *While You Are Reading These Words Five People, Mostly Children, Have Died of Starvation—and Forty More Babies Have Been Born*. He took an alarmist perspective, writing, for example: "The encouragement of high death rates through political interference is now the most important role of the Church in the population crisis."[43]

People—even "experts"—who use complex reasoning to develop their views, are capable of getting things very wrong. The climate space hasn't been immune from such erroneous predictions, either. But we don't often hear about them. This is not to imply that every current environmental prediction is automatically wrong. It's simply a reminder to remain humble. **Additionally, it's worth keeping in mind Koonin's observation that sometimes forecasts are intentionally exaggerated to serve a purpose: "Some people argue that there's no harm in a bit of misinformation if it helps 'save the planet.'"**[44] [emphasis added]

What follows is an exemplary list of climate-related predictions that proved to be wrong:

- ○ The 1977 book *The Weather Conspiracy: The Coming of the New Ice Age* made incorrect predictions about global cooling. Interestingly, as noted by Morano, many of the suggestions made in that book are similar to the ones proposed today to combat global warming.[45]

- ○ As reported in the *New York Times* in 1982: "Mostafa K. Tolba, executive director of the United Nations environmental program, told delegates that if the nations of the world continued their present policies, they would face by the turn of the century 'an environmental catastrophe which will witness devastation as complete, as irreversible, as any nuclear holocaust.' In his opening address, Mr. Tolba said that the nations should 'begin now to use the world's resources rationally and fairly.'"[46]

○ According to a 1989 Associated Press article, a senior United Nations environmental official said, "Entire nations could be wiped off the face of the Earth by rising sea levels if the global warming trend is not reversed by the year 2000."[47]

○ As reported in *The Independent* in the year 2000, David Viner, a senior research scientist at the climate research unit at the University of East Anglia, said that "within a few years, winter snowfall will become 'a very rare and exciting event....Children just aren't going to know what snow is.'"[48]

○ As presented in *The Guardian* in 2004, quoting a Pentagon report: "European cities will be plunged beneath rising seas as Britain is plunged into a Siberian climate by 2020."[49]

○ Al Gore's 2006 climate documentary *An Inconvenient Truth* emphasized the negative impact of global warming on polar bears.[50] The young climate activist Greta Thunberg was inspired into activism in part because she saw images of starving polar bears.[51] Zoologist Dr. Susan Crockford, a former adjunct professor at the University of Victoria, found that the fears were unwarranted. **In her 2019 book *The Polar Bear Catastrophe That Never Happened*, she explains her finding that polar-bear populations are thriving. In fact, they now threaten human populations in northern Canada.[52] Crockford was then fired by the university.[53]**

○ In 2006, the *HuffPost* reported that "93 Percent Of The Great Barrier Reef Is Practically Dead: Climate change is destroying Earth's largest coral ecosystem."[54] In 2017, *The Guardian* reported: "Great Barrier Reef at 'terminal stage': scientists despair at latest coral bleaching data."[55] **Then the messaging reversed: in 2022, CNN reported the headline: "Parts of Great Barrier Reef record highest amount of coral in 36 years."[56] Meanwhile,**

Dr. Peter Ridd, a thirty-year faculty member at James Cook University in Queensland, Australia, had been protesting apocalyptic views about the Great Barrier Reef and climate change. He was given a gag order by the university and then was fired. The more recent findings seemingly vindicate his views, however.[57]

○ In 2009, at the beginning of the new presidential term, NASA scientist James Hansen told President Obama that he had four years to save Earth.[58]

○ An August 2022 paper published by physicist Nicola Scafetta in *Climate Dynamics* revealed incorrect past modeling. As summarized in the *Daily Sceptic*: "A major survey into the accuracy of climate models has found that almost all the past temperature forecasts between 1980 and 2021 were excessive compared with accurate satellite measurements....Scafetta attributes the inaccuracies to a limited understanding of Equilibrium Climate Sensitivity (ECS)." Scafetta concluded in the paper that "the projected global climate warming over the next few decades could be moderate and probably not particularly alarming."[59]

Climate Consensus and Dissenters

Incorrect predictions can cause cognitive dissonance—emotional discomfort—especially for those who firmly believe in science. Author Charles Eisenstein notes that "for many people, especially liberals and progressives, science is the only trustworthy institution remaining in our society."[60] But, in fact, science is designed to challenge existing beliefs. Being wrong and revising hypotheses are part of the scientific process.

All too often, however, there is a religious rigidity whereby the current scientific views cannot be challenged. They are treated as irrefutable fact. Any dissenters are heretics and are often accused of spreading "misinformation"—that is, any information that the establishment disagrees with or doesn't want publicized.

That occurred frequently during the COVID-19 era. A November 2022 article published in the journal *Minerva* titled "Censorship and Suppression of Covid-19 Heterodoxy: Tactics and Counter-Tactics" explained: "Our findings point to the central role played by media organizations, and especially by information technology companies, in attempting to stifle debate over COVID-19 policy and measures. In the effort to silence alternative voices, widespread use was made not only of censorship, but of tactics of suppression that damaged the reputations and careers of dissenting doctors and scientists, regardless of their academic or medical status and regardless of their stature prior to expressing a contrary position."[61] Moreover, the leading medical figure in the United States, Dr. Anthony Fauci, stated that attacks on him are "attacks on science."[62]

Climate science has a similar feel. At a World Economic Forum event called "Sustainable Development Impact Meetings 2022," the United Nations Secretary of Global Communications said, "If you Google 'climate change'…at the top of your search you will get all kinds of UN resources. We started this partnership [with Google] when we were shocked to see that when we Googled 'climate change,' we were getting incredibly distorted information right at the top.…We own the science, and we think that the world should know it."[63] Who defines what is distorted? How can one group "own" the science?

It is similarly heretical in climate science to make claims that dispute the "invisible enemy" of a coming apocalypse.[64] There is a cultural belief that a consensus on these matters has already been established. However, even if that were true, a consensus opinion does not automatically imply a correct opinion. Human history is full of examples in which the majority ended up being wrong. Also, full consensus does *not* actually exist: there are many scientists who challenge the prevailing narrative in various ways.

One noteworthy example is that of Judith Curry, PhD, the former chair of the School of Earth and Atmospheric Sciences at the Georgia Institute of Technology. After voicing her dissenting opinions about climate change, she says she became "essentially unhirable," remarking, "Academically, they pretty much finished me off."[65] She comments on the impact of a perceived consensus: "The skewed scientific 'consensus' does indeed act to reinforce itself, through a range of professional incentives: ease of publishing results, particularly in high-impact journals; success in funding; recognition from peers in terms of awards, promotions, etc.; media attention and publicity for research; appeal of the simplistic narrative that climate science can 'save the world'; and a seat at the big policy tables."[66]

Contrarian opinions are simply not as well publicized. Steven Koonin experienced this firsthand, even with his stature in academia and government. After *Scientific American* criticized his 2021 book titled *Unsettled*, he submitted a rebuttal, and the magazine refused to publish it.[67]

The number of dissenters is probably difficult to estimate because many of them keep quiet. Koonin recalls after outlining climate-science uncertainties in the *Wall Street Journal* in 2014, that he received many positive comments. However, the academic response wasn't so positive. He writes: "As the chair of a highly respected university earth sciences department told me privately, 'I agree with pretty much everything you wrote, but I don't dare say that in public.'"[68]

Making matters more challenging is a lack of transparency in climate science. The infamous "ClimateGate" emails leaked in 2009 from the University of East Anglia revealed disturbing behavior. The iconic example often cited is that one of the world's leading climate scientists mentioned a "trick" he used to "hide the decline" (because declining temperatures threatened the global-warming narrative—at least that's how some analysts interpreted it).[69] The leaked emails had a major impact on Curry, and she wrote an open letter that was published in the *New York Times*:

> Based upon feedback that I've received from graduate students at Georgia Tech, I suspect that you are confused, troubled, or worried by what you have been reading about ClimateGate. After spending

considerable time reading the hacked emails and other posts in the blogosphere, I wrote an essay that calls for greater transparency in climate data and other methods used in climate research....

What has been noticeably absent so far in the Climate-Gate discussion is a public reaffirmation by climate researchers of our basic research values: the rigors of the scientific method (including reproducibility), research integrity and ethics, open minds, and critical thinking. Under no circumstances should we ever sacrifice any of these values; the...emails, however, appear to violate them.[70]

Even though the ClimateGate emails were released years ago, they offered insights into the possible suppression of information *today*. We can't possibly know what is being hidden now—not just in the climate space, but in all realms of science. This is especially true given that science has become political.

Therefore, it can be difficult to develop a firm opinion on climate issues. In his book *Climate: A New Story* (2018), Charles Eisenstein remarks on what he's experienced in trying come to a view on climate change: **"I am probably unable to make my choice of belief on purely evidentiary grounds. When I pursued the question of temperature readings...I got mired in a morass of technical minutiae about atmospheric physics, statistical methods, and so forth that I lack the scientific background to easily understand. Mind you, I am scientifically literate and have a degree in mathematics from Yale University. If I can't judge the issue on its merits, how can the average citizen?"[71]** [emphasis added]

So, understandably, this challenge leaves many people simply trusting the media and the supposed "experts." That gives those parties—and whoever controls them—an ability to drastically skew public opinion in the direction of whatever they want people to believe.

Credentialed dissenters like Steven Koonin, however, present some thought-provoking ideas. He writes in his book *Unsettled*:

"Both the research literature and government reports that sum-marize...the state of climate science say clearly that heat waves in the US now are *no more common* than they were in 1900, and that the warmest temperatures in the US have not risen in the past fifty years. When I tell people this, most are incredulous. Some gasp. And some get downright hostile."[72] Koonin mentions additional facts that typically surprise people, and they are "drawn directly from recent published research or the latest assessments of climate science published by the US government and the UN." He pro-vides several examples: "Humans have had no detectable impact on hurricanes over the past century. Greenland's ice sheet isn't shrinking any more rapidly than it was eighty years ago. The net economic impact of human-induced climate change will be min-imal through at least the end of this century."[73] Koonin continues:

> If you're like most people, after the surprise wears off, you'll wonder *why* you're surprised. Why haven't you heard these facts before?...Most of the disconnect comes from the long game of telephone that starts with the research literature and runs through the assessment reports to the summaries of the assessment reports and on to the media coverage. There are abundant oppor-tunities to get things wrong—both accidentally and on purpose—as the information goes through filter after filter to be packaged for various audiences. The public gets their climate information almost exclusively from the media; very few people actually read the assessment summaries, let alone the reports and research papers themselves. That's perfectly understandable—the data and analyses are nearly impenetrable for non-experts, and the writing is not exactly gripping. As a result, most people don't get the whole story.[74]

Michael Shellenberger provides some additional examples. Pre-viously, he was a mainstream climate activist and even cocreated the predecessor to the Green New Deal. However, upon further investigation into climate matters, he changed his views and wrote a book titled *Apocalypse Never: Why Environmental Alarm-ism Hurts Us All* (2020), which contends that "climate change is real but it's not the end of the world. It is not even our most serious environmental problem."[75] His nonprofit organization, Environmental Progress, provides a significant amount of data to back up his now-contrarian opinions (available at https://environmentalprogress.org/the-case-against-environmental-alarmism). Furthermore, in the 2020 short documentary *Religion of Green*, he comments:

> Natural disasters aren't getting worse, in fact they're getting better. The number of people that die from natural disasters has declined over 90 percent over the last 100 years. They've declined over 80 percent over the last 40 years. We should be celebrating this fact. It's mostly occurred because our infrastructure is more hardened, we're more prepared for natural disasters, [and] we have better weather forecasting systems. So when a hurricane comes to…Florida or Haiti or Bangladesh, we can…get ourselves into safe environments, so that's great news. Damage to property has increased, but it's entirely explained by the fact that we're just much wealthier than we were. So if you look at a picture of Miami Beach in 1920 [versus] a picture of Miami Beach today, there's a lot more buildings on it, so when a hurricane hits them there's more damage. So that's great news. There is no scenario, in the Intergovernmental Panel on Climate Change, which oversees all the science of this, for that trend to reverse itself. In other words, it's not to say it's impossible, but there's no science suggesting that climate change is going to become so bad that the number of deaths from natural disasters stops going down and starts going back up again.[76]

Alex Epstein, another climate contrarian, cites data in his book *Fossil Future* (2022), suggesting, "Over the last century, the rate of climate-related disaster deaths has fallen by 98 percent."[77] He writes: "'Climate emergency' and 'climate crisis' are no longer treated as predictions about the future. They are treated as descriptions of the present—even though in the present we are safer from climate than any human population has ever been."[78] Additionally,

Epstein notes that "deaths from cold far exceed deaths from heat,"[79] which muffles the narrative about the dangers of global warming. (Note: It's interesting that around 2010, the branding changed from "global warming" to "climate change"—now *any* change can be viewed as a concern. Because natural climate change is always likely to occur to some degree, there will always be an ability for leaders to point to a climate-change-related crisis—whether or not it is truly there.[80])

As a philosopher, Epstein's approach is to encourage an examination of both the benefits and the downsides of each energy solution. For solutions that are not in vogue with the mainstream narrative, the benefits are often ignored, and the downsides are catastrophized. For instance, fossil fuels are generally regarded as exclusively "bad," and yet they've helped humanity with what Epstein calls "climate mastery": an ability to withstand climate much better than we could at earlier times in our history. Similarly, renewable energy sources like solar energy are often regarded as "good" because they're a clean source of energy. But Epstein notes that many solar panels are made in China, which are produced with coal under low environmental standards. They also use slave labor.[81]

Summary

The climate picture is much more complex than what is typically presented by leftists. There is a prevailing alarmist position about climate change, which is often disseminated to the public with certainty—in spite of modeling limitations, a history of incorrect predictions, and noteworthy dissenting opinions.

And, in fact, it is detrimentally affecting mental health and leading to some disturbing activism. For instance, in 2022, climate activists threw tomato soup on a Van Gogh painting at the National Gallery in London and then glued their hands to the wall. One of the activists said, "What is worth more, art or life? Is it worth more than food? Worth more than justice? Are you more concerned about the protection of a painting or the protection of our planet and people?"[82]

Climate is also being brought into discussions where previously it likely would have been considered irrelevant. A 2022 study on childhood obesity was reported in the media as showing that climate change is causing obesity—because kids are staying indoors due to the heat.[83] Moreover in 2021, an elderly Canadian woman had breathing problems and was diagnosed as "suffering from climate change."[84]

Just like the perceived crisis of COVID-19, climate matters can be used to centralize power and control the population. They can also be used as an excuse to bring about leftist, socialistic ideals. Therefore, the climate focus of the Great Reset could be seen as another piece of the puzzle to mold society as desired by the World Economic Forum and its allies. And, as will be discussed in the next chapter, technological improvements make dystopian, Orwellian control systems real possibilities.

CHAPTER 8

TECHNOLOGY

Klaus Schwab states in his 2016 book *The Fourth Industrial Revolution*: **"Of the many diverse and fascinating challenges we face today, the most intense and important is how to understand and shape the new technology revolution, which entails nothing less than a transformation of humankind."**[1] He adds, "The fourth industrial revolution, however, is not only about smart and connected machines and systems. Its scope is much wider. Occurring simultaneously are waves of further breakthroughs in areas ranging from gene sequencing to nanotechnology, from renewables to quantum computing. It is the fusion of these technologies and their interaction across the physical, digital, and biological domains that make the fourth industrial revolution fundamentally different from previous revolutions."[2] [emphasis added]

The question is: Will such technological advancements be used to benefit humanity or enslave it? This chapter will consider the risks. Schwab, to his credit, is open about these risks. He writes: "There is the very real danger that governments might employ combinations of technologies to suppress or oppress actions of civil society organizations and groups of individuals who seek to create transparency around the activities of governments and businesses and promote change....The tools of the fourth industrial revolution enable new forms of surveillance and other means of control that run counter to healthy, open societies."[3]

A Totalitarian, Social-Credit-Control System

COVID-19 provided an opportunity to apply advanced technologies, outwardly for the purpose of "public health." The flip side is that many such technologies can be used to monitor and micromanage citizens' lives. For that reason, technologies like the implantable microchip used by some people in Sweden for COVID-19 vaccine verification could be considered scary.[4] As stated by Yuval Noah Harari, a World Economic Forum adviser and the influential author of *Sapiens*: "COVID is critical because this is what convinces people to accept, to legitimize, total biometric surveillance....We need not just monitor people, we need to monitor what's happening under their skin."[5]

In *COVID-19: The Great Reset*, Schwab and Malleret elaborate:

> Contact tracing and tracking are...essential components for our public-health response to COVID-19....A tracking app gains insights in real time by, for example, determining a person's current location through geodata via GPS coordinates or radio cell location. By contrast, tracing consists in gaining insights in retrospect, like identifying physical contacts between people using Bluetooth....
>
> The most effective form of tracking or tracing is obviously one powered by technology: it not only allows backtracking all the contacts with whom the user of a mobile phone has been in touch, but also tracking the user's real-time movements, which in turn affords the possibility to better enforce a lockdown and to warn other mobile users in the proximity of the carrier that they have been exposed to someone infected.[6]

The potential limitations on freedom here are frightening. And, in fact, similar technology is being planned for climate change as well. At a WEF event, the Alibaba Group president stated: "We're developing through technology an ability for consumers to measure their own carbon footprint. What does that mean? That's: Where are they traveling? How are they traveling? What are they eating? What are they consuming on the platform? So, [an] individual carbon-footprint tracker. Stay tuned; we don't have it operational yet, but this is something we are working on."[7]

Along these lines, Mastercard and the Swedish startup Doconomy announced in 2019 "the world's first credit card with a carbon limit."[8] The description states: "The launch of this premium card marks the first milestone in the support that Doconomy provides to the UN Climate Change secretariat (UNFCCC) to encourage global climate action. DO Black not only helps users track and measure CO_2 emissions associated with their purchases, but also puts a limit to the climate impact of their spending."[9]

What could that mean? If you "overconsume" (which is one of the big concerns often described in the Great Reset), then you could be prohibited from buying certain things. It's a potential mechanism to control people's lives. What happens if measures like these become mandatory? Could one's carbon footprint affect the ability to get loans, for example? Could it affect one's ability to buy food?[10]

This starts to move in the direction of a "social credit score," which essentially means that if you are a "good" citizen, then you can do whatever you like. But if you're "bad," then you'll be restricted. China has faced criticism for enacting policies along these lines, and citizens all over the world have expressed concern that COVID-19 measures might move other countries in a similar direction.

The big issue is: Who defines what is "good" or "bad"? The government does. Or more precisely, whoever it is that controls the government.

The social credit score could be applied not only to whether people are "good" with regard to the government's climate or COVID-19 standards, but it could extend into other areas too. For instance, if you say something that the government doesn't like on social media, could that be used as a negative for your social credit score? What if you act in a way that the government says promotes "inequality" or "unfairness"? What if your company doesn't hire enough people of a certain ethnicity or sexual orientation? What if you "offend" someone? These could be grounds for punishing people. In the worst-case scenario, people might have no choice but to obey if they want to be able to feed themselves and have a temperature-controlled roof over their heads.

Events in Canada turned this notion from a far-out science-fiction story to something much more real for citizens in Western nations. In early 2022, Canadian truckers were protesting COVID-19 vaccine mandates and restrictive COVID-19 measures imposed by the government. Author Dr. Naomi Wolf describes what happened:

> [The] Deputy Prime Minister…gave chilling proof of how far the global elites would go to enforce absolute compliance to their diktats by the citizenry. "As of today, a bank or other financial service provider will be able to immediately freeze or suspend an account without a court order," she announced. "In doing so, they will be protected against civil liability for actions taken in good faith….If your truck is being used in these illegal blockades, your corporate account will be frozen. The insurance on your vehicle will be suspended." Police shattered truck windows, arrested a hundred protesters, including the demonstration's leaders, and Prime Minister Justin Trudeau invoked an emergency order. For a time, representative government was suspended in the nation of Canada.[11]

The government was basically saying, "If you protest against us, we'll cut off your ability to pay for things." If people have cash on hand or other assets that they can use for barter, they might be able to temporarily get around the inconvenience. But imagine if there were *only* digital payments? Then the government could not only track every transaction, but it could literally wipe out the ability to buy anything.

That's what makes the "central bank digital currency" (CBDC) —a government digital currency—so concerning. In particular, it would be dangerous if it is programmed to restrict buying based on the government's decrees. Programmable digital currencies are in fact being taken seriously. In 2021, *The Telegraph* published an article titled "Bank of England tells ministers to intervene on digital currency 'programming'" which explained, "Digital cash could be programmed to ensure it is only spent on essentials, or goods which an employer or Government deems to be sensible."[12] The Federal Reserve's website also features a lengthy 2021 article on the possibilities for programmable money.[13] The danger could be amplified if "Universal Basic Income" is adopted, whereby people's dependence on the government would increase. The WEF even posted an article explaining why Universal Basic Income is "the answer" to inequalities (in the context of COVID-19).[14]

Along similar lines, COVID-19 policies demonstrated that people's ability to participate in society could be dictated by whether they allow a government-sponsored foreign substance into their bodies (that is, a vaccine). In her book *The Bodies of Others: The New Authoritarians, COVID-19 and the War Against the Human*, Naomi Wolf elaborates on what this means:

> By the end of 2021, "vaccine passports" in many states and nations effectively became the passports to human life. Imposed worldwide…they gave tech companies an all-encompassing historic advantage over human beings. In essence, all human experience, fellowship, and joy was put behind a paywall.
>
> Do you want to worship? See family at Thanksgiving? Have a job and need your family? Go to the theater? Get on a long-distance train?
>
> Not without your vaccination subscription. And your "booster" every five to eight months…is the renewal of the subscription.

> Your body is your credit card. It's what you pay with. Vaccine passports are at the heart of the transition to a world where humans are at the mercy of Big Tech and a few oligarchs....
>
> In China, the [Chinese Communist Party] can find any dissident in five minutes because of the 360-degree surveillance of the social credit system....The vaccine passports being rolled out in the West could enable the same platform.[15]

Governments also made it clear that dissent would not be tolerated—which is ironic in Left-controlled nations that claim to value "tolerance." For instance, Canada's prime minister, Justin Trudeau, made a generalization about those who strongly oppose vaccination, claiming that they "do not believe in science [and] are often misogynists, often racists....[A] decision needs to be made as a leader, as a country: Do we tolerate these people?" (December 2021).[16]

Similarly, France's president, Emmanuel Macron, said that he intended to make life difficult for unvaccinated individuals, "limiting as much as possible their access to activities in social life." He suggested that such individuals are "irresponsible" and that "an irresponsible person is no longer a citizen" (January 2022).[17] And the chief minister of Australia's Northern Territory ordered a four-day lockdown period for unvaccinated individuals, declaring that they would only be allowed to leave their homes, within a thirty-kilometer radius, for three reasons: (1) medical treatment, (2) essential goods and services (such as groceries), and (3) providing care and support for people who cannot support themselves. He clarified: "Work is not a reason to leave the home for the unvaccinated...[and] one hour of exercise for the next four days is not essential" (January 2022).[18] The media assisted with this rhetoric, such as CNN's Don Lemon, who said: "The people who are not getting vaccines, who are believing the lies on the internet instead of science, it's time to start shaming them or leave them behind" (September 2021).[19] The Left went along with this—nearly half of U.S. Democrats polled agreed that "federal governments should be allowed to either fine or imprison those who publicly question COVID-19 vaccine efficacy" (January 2022).[20]

The message in these situations is clear: play by our rules, or else. Whether it's COVID-19, climate change, or whatever additional perceived crises emerge in the future, a precedent has been established.

Authoritarianism is nothing new, however. It's gone on throughout human history. What *is* unique about the modern era is technology's ability to enhance this dictatorial capacity.

Transhumanism and the Metaverse

Klaus Schwab states that "the mind-boggling innovations triggered by the fourth industrial revolution, from biotechnology to AI [artificial intelligence], are redefining what it means to be human."[21] AI on its own poses potential dangers. Schwab considers the possibility that "autonomous warfare, including the deployment of military robots and AI-powered automated weaponry, holds out the prospect of 'robo-war,' which will play a transformative role in future conflict."[22]

The dystopian possibilities extend to the merging of AI with humans, known as *transhumanism*. The idea is that technology will help humans reach new levels as a species—to become something different altogether. An example is an implantable chip that improves brain functioning (such as Elon Musk's Neuralink product). Genetic editing is another example.

As stated by Yuval Noah Harari, "Now humans are developing even bigger powers than ever before. We are really acquiring divine powers of creation and destruction. We are really upgrading humans into gods....Humans are now hackable animals.... There's a common view that humans...have this soul or spirit... that's over."[23] He also delivered a talk for the WEF called "Will the Future Be Human?"[24]

Furthermore, Schwab and Malleret acknowledge in their book *The Great Narrative: For a Better Future* (2022) the potential power of synthetic biology, pointing to the COVID-19 vaccine mRNA technology: "[They] insert synthetic strings of genetic code that are computer-modelled into our bodies."[25] They consider the "potential" of "transforming our health care so that personalized treatments and predictive health issue modeling become possible."[26] But this leaves open questions about how customized treatments of the future could alter what we are as humans—at the level of our genetic blueprint. Although the possibilities of synthetic biology are great, Schwab and Malleret do list many concerns as to "what could go wrong."[27]

Related to the notion of transhumanism is the metaverse—a digital playground for the mind and a way to disconnect from the physical world. In Schwab and Malleret's words: "The metaverse will contain environments where we will earn money, forge relationships, and have all sorts of different experiences that could enrich our lives or quite the opposite....The distinction between being offline and online will become increasingly blurred and harder to identify, and the meaning of reality itself will evolve (it might become extended—XR—combining augmented, virtual and mixed realities)."[28] Taken to an extreme—and if the technology ever became so advanced—one wonders if humans could end up like the people in *The Matrix* movie series. In that science-fiction world, people's bodies existed in pods, but they weren't even aware of it because from birth, their minds were hooked up to an entirely virtual world.

Even in less extreme forms, the metaverse could drastically alter the basic nature of the human experience. Schwab mentions that technology is enabling "family structures [to be] redefined. No longer bound by space, they often stretch across the world, with constant family dialogue, reinforced by digital means. Increasingly, the traditional family unit is being replaced by the trans-national family network."[29] With the advent of the metaverse, Schwab's statements might be taken to a whole new level: family relationships could become much more virtual—which is a concerning notion for those who value the traditional family unit.

Overall, these technologies risk impacting the basic notion of "human connection"—as Schwab rightly points out. He states: "The more digital and high-tech the world becomes, the greater the need to still feel the human touch, nurtured by close relationships and social connections. There are growing concerns that, as the fourth industrial revolution deepens individual and collective relationships with technology, it may negatively affect our social skills and ability to empathize."[30]

Summary

The fourth industrial revolution could enable new conveniences, but it could also enable invasive surveillance and totalitarian control. In addition, it could transform the basics of what a human being is and how we connect with one another. Thus, technology under the Great Reset carries with it—in Schwab and Malleret's own words—"the risk of dystopia."[31]

Schwab summarizes the situation well: "The fourth industrial revolution has the potential to robotize humanity, and thus compromise our traditional sources of meaning—work, community, family, identity. Or we can use the fourth industrial revolution to lift humanity into a new collective and moral consciousness based on a shared sense of destiny. It is incumbent on us all to make sure that the latter is what happens."[32]

CHAPTER 9

METAPHYSICS

Conspicuously absent from the Great Reset literature and commentary is the acknowledgment that human beings exist within an inherently spiritual reality. As the saying goes: "We aren't human beings having a spiritual experience, we are spiritual beings having a human experience." That is not the mentality explicitly advocated under the Great Reset, nor is it part of the typical leftist creed.[1] Instead, the leftist mindset aligns more closely with World Economic Forum adviser Yuval Noah Harari's sentiment quoted in the previous chapter: "The whole idea that humans have this soul or spirit...that's over."[2]

This chapter will briefly examine some of the scientific evidence to counter that perspective—and why it's so important. I've written about this extensively elsewhere, particularly in my book *An End to Upside Down Thinking* (2018), so what follows will be a summary with noteworthy source material in the endnotes.

The Significance of a Spiritual Worldview

The mainstream view in science and academia is that life is fundamentally random and meaningless. We exist because humans evolved through random evolutionary processes. Furthermore, when the human body dies, that's the end of our sense of experiencing life (that is, our *consciousness* no longer exists).

With that worldview—known as *scientific materialism* or, alternatively, *physicalism*—the often-unstated implication is that there is no meaning built into the fabric of reality itself. Meaning is an arbitrary construct that an individual can create in his or her own life. Also, there are no consequences to one's actions, metaphysically speaking. This belief system thereby allows people to make up their own morality.

It also makes people apt to find their "religion" elsewhere. Many of the leftist causes supported within the Great Reset indeed do become their own form of religion. For instance, John McWhorter, an associate professor of English and comparative literature at Columbia University, wrote a book called *Woke Racism: How a New Religion Has Betrayed Black America* (2021). As a black man himself, he is disturbed by the way in which "woke" culture is impacting society. He sees it as a religion that has all of the typical qualities you'd expect: the equivalents of superstition, clergy, original sin, evangelism, an apocalyptic mindset, a tendency to ban the heretic, and a desire to supplant older religions.[3]

Also, climate alarmism can take on similarly religious qualities. The belief in compulsory government (known as *statism*) can take on religious characteristics too.

We've seen the negative consequences that can result from attaching to these faux religions. They often end up causing great anxiety, narcissism, and conflict. The dynamics can lead to brainwashing and a "stickiness" of belief due to cognitive biases.

If there *is* a deeper metaphysical meaning to life, however, that would be important to know about. It might help to break the cultlike behavior that can emerge in leftist movements associated with the Great Reset. And, indeed, there is an abundance of scientific evidence supporting the idea that we exist within an innately meaningful universe.

Scientific Evidence of Spiritual Phenomena

The science of "spiritual" phenomena is considered heretical. It's similar to what was discussed regarding COVID-19 and climate science: the scientists in the domain of spiritual phenomena are largely shunned within mainstream circles. Some traditional academics let these researchers know privately that they agree, but they won't do it publicly because they fear reputational damage.[4]

The science here relates to consciousness. Not just traditional neuroscience and philosophy, but rather the study of "anomalies"— phenomena that don't fit the mold of the mainstream worldview. More specifically, this taboo science challenges the view that consciousness comes from the brain. The alternative perspective that emerges is that the brain is like an antenna/receiver that taps into the "cloud" of consciousness, so to speak. Another analogy is to view the brain as a filtering mechanism that processes something from outside the body. In other words, the brain is like a blindfold that gets in the way of a broader reality that we can't ordinarily perceive. Our vision, hearing, and other senses are severely limited relative to what actually exists. Also, consider the possibility that there are other dimensions of reality that we normally don't access.

That's what studies on consciousness "anomalies" examine—using traditional, rigorous scientific methods. For example, various "psychic" phenomena include: the ability to have mind-to-mind communications with another person (telepathy); the ability to know or sense the future before it happens (precognition); the ability to see or otherwise sense something that is far away in space and/or time, using the mind alone (remote viewing); and the ability for the mind to impact physical matter without any physical contact (psychokinesis).

Scientific studies suggest that humans have these abilities, but most often the effects are small and subtle. From a statistical standpoint, however, they're massively significant. For instance, Dean Radin, PhD, the chief scientist at The Institute of Noetic Sciences (founded by Apollo 14 astronaut Dr. Edgar Mitchell), aggregated the "six-sigma" statistical results for the aforementioned psychic phenomena. That means the odds that the results were due to chance alone were more than a billion to one.[5]

The following quotation from Jessica Utts, PhD, the 2016 president of the American Statistical Association, encapsulates the strength of the data. She analyzed statistical evidence of psychic phenomena, including work done in the U.S. government's previously classified psychic spying program (for which there are now declassified documents explicitly validating the reality of the phenomena).[6] Utts's summary of her review—from 1995—is as follows:

> **Using the standards applied to any other area of science, it is concluded that psychic functioning has been well established. The statistical results of the studies examined are far beyond what is expected by chance.** Arguments that these results could be due to methodological flaws in the experiments are soundly refuted. Effects of similar magnitude to those found in government-sponsored research…have been replicated at a number of laboratories across the world. Such consistency cannot be readily explained by claims of flaws or fraud. [emphasis added]
>
> The magnitude of psychic functioning exhibited appears to be in the range between what social scientists call a small and medium effect. That means that it is reliable enough to be replicated in properly conducted experiments, with sufficient trials to achieve the long-run statistical results needed for replicability....
>
> Precognition…appears to work quite well. [Recall that precognition is a phenomenon in which people know or sense the future before it happens.] Recent experiments suggest that if there is a psychic sense then it works much like our other five senses, by detecting change. Given that physicists are currently grappling with an understanding of time, it may be that a psychic sense exists that scans the future for major change, much as

our eyes scan the environment for visual change or our ears allow us to respond to sudden changes in sound.

It is recommended that future experiments focus on understanding how this phenomenon works, and on how to make it as useful as possible. There is little benefit to continuing experiments designed to offer proof, since there is little more to be offered to anyone who does not accept the current collection of data.[7]

Another noteworthy study was conducted by Lund University's Dr. Etzel Cardeña. His 2018 paper was published in *American Psychologist*, the official peer-reviewed academic journal of the American Psychological Association. It showed positive statistical results for multiple psychic phenomena, covering studies across many researchers and decades.[8] Additionally, the journal *Frontiers in Psychology* published a paper in 2022 that challenged mainstream models of consciousness. Its title—"What if consciousness is not an emergent property of the brain? Observational and empirical challenges to materialistic models"—was written by Helané Wahbeh, Dean Radin, Cedric Cannard, and Arnaud Delorme from the Institute of Noetic Sciences.[9] The paper received lots of attention, accumulating more than 20,000 views in just a few months.

The fact that mainstream journals are starting to publish *some* of this material is significant because historically they rejected certain papers simply because of the topic. That is, those rejections weren't necessarily tied to the quality of the research, but rather the domain is one that journals don't want to be associated with.[10]

Unfortunately, scientists who venture into this domain publicly are sometimes branded as "pseudoscientists." That's what consciousness researcher and former Cambridge biochemist Dr. Rupert Sheldrake's Wikipedia bio says about him. The page is marked "semi-protected," which means editing is restricted.[11]

Furthermore, neuroscientist Mario Beauregard, PhD, has experienced active suppression of science that relates to spirituality. As he put it during a 2022 interview on the *Skeptiko* podcast: "It's part of a social engineering program, clearly." He was even told by a "famous" woman at a neurological institute in Canada that such research would not be permitted. In Beauregard's words:

> She told me: "As long as I'm alive and I'm controlling [this neurological institute], you'll never do neuroscience studies on spirituality. Never." So she organized something with all the members of the committees—the ethics research committee and the scientific committees—to prevent me from doing these studies. I had earned a grant from the Templeton Foundation based in the United States, but I was not allowed [to pursue the research]. They blocked me....I asked them, "What is the reason?" And when I started to argue [with] them regarding spiritual experiences, they were becoming berserk....And then I knew that it was...a war between two contrasting [and] totally different paradigms: dark and light.[12] [emphasis added]

Consciousness after Death

Quintuple-blind studies have been conducted to research people claiming they can communicate with the deceased (performed at the Windbridge Research Center in Tucson, Arizona). Analyses have also been done on other alleged "afterlife" communications. There are, in fact, some positive results.[13]

A related domain that has received a significant amount of attention is research on the "near-death experience." **These are instances in which people are close to death, sometimes clinically dead. They're even reported when patients are under general anesthesia.** When these individuals are resuscitated, they bring back vivid memories that are described as being *more real than real life*. While some experiences are frightening or hellish, the majority are overwhelmingly positive. They often include the feeling of interconnectivity with all of life and being immersed in "unconditional love" (among other features that are difficult to describe using language).[14] They are reported all over the world, in adults and children, and have a long history. A landmark study was published in *The Lancet* medical journal in 2001 showing that many people who were resuscitated following cardiac arrest had memories of stunning near-death experiences.[15]

In the most compelling near-death-experience cases, people say that their consciousness was hovering outside their body and perceiving things, for instance, in their hospital room (and sometimes even outside the operating room where they had surgery). After the resuscitation, when they tell doctors or family members what they saw or heard, the reaction is typically something like this: "That's impossible! We know what your brain was doing at that time, and it was not in a condition that should have been able to produce an experience so complex. And, by the way, the thing you perceived was from a vantage point outside of your body. How could you have seen it from that perspective? Even if you had a fully functional brain, which you didn't, you shouldn't have been able to perceive that!" These are known as *veridical out-of-body experiences*, which means the memories are verified. If the memories are verified, then, by definition, they are *not* hallucinations.[16]

The University of Virginia's Division of Perceptual Studies (DOPS) is a rare instance of a mainstream institution that studies topics like these. It exists because one of its highly credentialed researchers, Dr. Ian Stevenson, founded it in 1967, and it continues today. Psychiatrist Bruce Greyson, MD, is a researcher at DOPS, and, like other doctors and scientists who've examined near-death experiences closely, he's perplexed. He comments: **"We're left with this paradox that at a time when the brain isn't functioning, the mind is functioning better than ever."**[17] [emphasis added]

A series of detailed, lengthy books have been published by DOPS researchers, and their colleagues, which summarize the evidence for these sorts of phenomena, including *Irreducible Mind* (2007), *Beyond Physicalism* (2015), and *Consciousness Unbound* (2021). The lead editor and coauthor is DOPS's Edward Kelly, who holds a PhD from Harvard.

Research has also been conducted on people who've had similar experiences to what near-death experiencers describe—except there's one key difference: they weren't the ones dying. They were healthy family members or bystanders who somehow co-experienced the dying process *with* the dying person—almost like they'd entered another dimension of consciousness. Their brain was normal, so it wasn't just a "hallucination caused by a dying brain"—which is what many skeptics try to use to "explain away" near-death experiences. This phenomenon is known as the *shared-death experience*, and it has been examined by Dr. Raymond Moody[18] and more recently by William Peters. A paper on shared-death experiences, written by Peters and his colleagues, was published in the peer-reviewed *American Journal of Hospice and Palliative Care* (2021).[19]

One of the phenomena that emerges often in near-death experiences, and is also sometimes reported in shared-death experiences, is known as a *life review:*[20] **People relive the events of their lives in a compressed amount of time, sometimes starting from birth. In those events, they literally *become* the people that they impacted, and sometimes they even become third parties who feel the effects of the original interaction.** They get to experience the ways in which they made people feel good and the ways in which they didn't make people feel good. Their message is often that the seemingly little things in life—interactions that we wouldn't consider all that meaningful—are often the big things in the life review.[21]

Life-review experiencers generally come back forever changed. Afterward, they often have trouble reintegrating into their routines. As a result, they sometimes change jobs or get divorced. Greyson adds, "Even though [near-death experiences] are not influenced by prior religious beliefs or religiosity, they do seem to affect subsequent religious preferences, religiosity, and spirituality. Near-death experiencers describe themselves as more spiritual than they were before."[22] Likewise, many of them believe in God following their experience, even if they didn't previously (as studied by radiation oncologist Jeffrey Long, MD).[23]

The life review suggests that there is in fact a moral imperative built into the fabric of reality. Greyson finds, after speaking to many survivors of these experiences, that it is "natural law" and "as inescapable as gravity." The implication is that the things we do in life are significant on a metaphysical level. The way we treat people matters, and our actions have real consequences.[24]

Moreover, the accumulated research suggests that there's an inherent interconnectedness of everything. That comes through clearly in the life review, but it also makes psychic phenomena seem more plausible. For example, if our minds are somehow connected in ways we can't see, then a telepathic ability—no matter how subtle it may be—is completely within the realm of possibility. This also ties in with the notion of quantum entanglement. In fact, Radin wrote a book, *Entangled Minds* (2006), to explore this connection. As stated by Brian Josephson, the Nobel Prize–winning physicist from Cambridge University: "Yes, I think telepathy exists… and I think quantum physics will help us understand its basic properties."[25]

These spiritual notions are compatible with a wide variety of religions—even though the various traditions might disagree about details. The fundamental concepts are often consistent. For example, "The Golden Rule"—"Treat others as you want to be treated" (since we're all interconnected)—is a core lesson in the life review and appears in religious traditions all over the world.[26] Also, the existence of a transcendent consciousness/intelligence of which we are a part—what some call *God*—is a theme that emerges from such metaphysical explorations.

But these essential concepts are not part of the Great Reset. And they're not part of the leftist ideology that underpins it. So, arguably, our society is being pushed in a direction that ignores the most important things: the basic nature of reality itself, who we are innately, and hints about the deeper meaning of life.

Schwab and Malleret do talk about our interconnected (and interdependent) world, but not in an explicitly metaphysical sense.[27] The deeper moral imperative related to our being a part of something literally interconnected appears to be absent.

Metaphysics and Transhumanism

With this spiritual lens in mind, transhumanism takes on a whole new meaning—and potentially a whole new threat. If the human body is like a vessel for a spiritual energy that inhabits it (some would call it a *soul*), then the design and DNA of that vessel are likely important. Perhaps altering our genetics or merging the body with artificial intelligence disrupts or pollutes the body's innate spiritual connection.

For those who deny the reality of anything spiritual, alterations to the body wouldn't matter. Humans get to "play God" and design whatever they want without repercussions. But if that's wrong, transhumanistic changes could be more detrimental than we realize.

Similarly, an aspect of the transgender movement can be examined through this lens. The acceptance of questioning one's gender identity is in some cases morphing into an acceptance of questioning one's species. There are reports of people identifying as various animals, for example.[28] If this becomes normalized, rather than pathologized, it could be regarded as a step toward denying one's physical identity as a human. Quite literally, it's transhumanism.[29] And it's a rejection of biology (which is ironic given that leftists claim to revere science). One might also wonder if the denial of the vessel that houses the soul could be metaphysically harmful in ways that we don't fully understand.

Also, the metaverse—if it ever becomes sufficiently sophisticated—could keep people spiritually disconnected. Perhaps there are metaphysical dangers associated with keeping one's consciousness overly focused on a fake world. In any event, spiritual ramifications need to be considered as the technology advances. This aspect of Schwab's fourth industrial revolution is being overlooked.

Metaphysical Evil and Children

In my book *An End to Upside Down Contact* (2022), I examined evidence suggesting that humans "are not alone"—of which there is an abundance. For example, in transcendent consciousness experiences (like near-death and shared-death experiences) people report encountering various species of intelligent beings. Some of them are apparently multidimensional and nonphysical, such as "beings of light." Also, there is evidence of contact related to UFOs. The former head of psychiatry at Harvard, Pulitzer Prize winner John Mack, MD, studied this (among many other researchers) and felt there was reality to many of the contact allegations. Encounters with nonhuman intelligences have in fact been reported throughout history, by cultures all over the world.

One of the findings across the various domains of "contact" is that some of the nonhuman intelligences are benevolent, others are clearly malevolent, and others are in between. Some even masquerade as benevolent, but in reality, they are tricksters. The point is: a spectrum of "good" and "evil" appears to be a metaphysical reality.

The antihuman mentality might literally be a manifestation of evil metaphysical energies. This is an important consideration for the direction of society.

Furthermore, a concept that emerges in contact experiences with malevolent entities is that they feed off of fear and suffering. In particular, they seem to enjoy the destruction of innocence and the abuse of children.[30] In the most extreme cases, this can manifest through the horrific practices of ritual torture and sacrifice (with the intent of invoking dark spirits); pedophilia; and child sex-trafficking—as discussed, for example, in Sean Stone's *Best Kept Secret* docuseries (2021).[31] Thus, the emerging far-Left notion of being "tolerant" to pedophiles by calling them "minor attracted persons" is particularly troubling.[32]

More generally, there seems to be a leftist trend toward sexualizing children—marketed as simply being "progressive" and "open-minded." But from the lens of metaphysical evil, it is pernicious. There is even a group called "Gays Against Groomers," which describes itself as "a coalition of gay people who oppose the recent trend of indoctrinating, sexualizing and medicalizing children under the guise of 'LGBTQIA+.' Our community that once preached love and acceptance of others has been hijacked by radical activists who are now pushing extreme concepts onto society, specifically targeting children."[33] After speaking out against the Left's narrative, the group's Twitter account was suspended, its Google account was disabled, and it was banned from PayPal and Venmo.[34]

Concern has also emerged over the trend of bringing young children to drag-queen shows, for example.[35] Also, consider what this parent from Virginia reported in 2021, published in the *Washington Examiner*:

> Since my appearance at the Fairfax County Public Schools [FCPS] board meeting on Sept. 23, [2021], a national conversation has begun. I went that night after seeing two reports in early September about parents finding pornographic materials in their children's schools.
>
> I checked out two titles from my son's library at Fairfax High School. What I found was more shocking than I could have ever imagined: The two books, *Gender Queer: A Memoir* by Maia Kobabe, and *Lawn Boy* by Jonathan Evison, contain explicit descriptions and illustrations of X-rated pornographic sex and, even worse, pedophilia.
>
> The books were not only in Fairfax High School but many other high schools within FCPS, including Robinson Secondary School, which is a combined middle school. So these books describing pedophilic acts were accessible to children as young as 12.
>
> The *Gender Queer* book was actually found on the shelf in the comic-book section, next to titles such as *The Black Panther*, *The Avengers*, *Superman*, etc.[36]

The transgender movement among children fits in here too. Within schools and culture more broadly, there isn't just a "tolerance" for questioning one's gender, but there seems to be a trend to actively encourage and celebrate it. Like many leftist cultural movements, merely "accepting" often isn't enough—if you aren't exuberantly in favor of their actions, you risk being called a "bigot" (or some similar term).

For individuals with true gender dysphoria, who have no choice as to how they feel, the movement is indeed compassionate—as it should be. However, not everyone has true gender dysphoria, especially children who are in an imaginative and impressionable phase of life. Abigail Shrier's book *Irreversible Damage* (2020) chronicles these disturbing matters deeply.

In addition to the mental trauma that could result from a child's confusion about gender identity, the problem is made even more serious because of what's physically involved in the "transition" process. If a vulnerable child is inappropriately encouraged to have a sex change, only to realize later that it was a mistake, that's truly awful—and perhaps a manifestation of metaphysical evil.

Puberty-blocking drugs and hormone-therapy drugs are used, and they carry with them potential harms and unknown long-term risks.[37] Lupron—a chemical castration drug given to sex offenders—is one of the drugs used for gender transitions, for instance.[38] And the "gender-affirming" surgeries are perhaps more severe than is often acknowledged. "Gender-affirming" could be regarded as a euphemism for genital mutilation (an act that's strongly condemned in other contexts). On its website, the Johns Hopkins School of Medicine summarizes what these surgeries entail:

> Penile construction (phalloplasty/metoidioplasty): This surgical procedure can include removal of the vagina (vaginectomy), reconstruction of the urethra and penile reconstruction. Surgeons may use either vaginal tissue or tissue from another part of the body to construct the penis.
>
> Vaginal construction (vaginoplasty): This surgical procedure is a multistage process during which surgeons may remove the penis (penectomy) and the testes (orchiectomy), if still present, and use tissues from the

penis to construct the vagina, the clitoris (clitoroplasty) and the labia (labiaplasty).

Top surgery is surgery that removes or augments breast tissue and reshapes the chest to create a more masculine or feminine appearance for transgender and nonbinary people.[39]

An essential protective mechanism against such troubling trends is the family unit (at least among families that interpret the trends as harmful). Parents can shield their children; society isn't going to do it for them. Schwab's discussion about a technology-assisted version of the family that could replace the traditional family unit sounds potentially problematic in this regard.[40]

Likewise, schools have become havens for programming children with leftist ideology. As President Joe Biden said in 2022 when speaking to teachers, "They're all our children....They're not somebody else's children. They're like yours when they're in the classroom."[41] Government-sponsored schools give governments direct access to children's malleable minds. In a society like the one envisioned under the Great Reset, with "big government," the risk of attempted indoctrination is accentuated.

Summary

The Great Reset misses perhaps the most important aspect of what's needed as society advances: a metaphysical revolution. Because of this omission, societal movements aren't being viewed from a spiritual lens, and therefore significant dangers might be overlooked. This is especially concerning as it relates to children, who are the future of our civilization.

SOCIETAL EVOLUTION

The Great Reset poses great dangers. It impacts all aspects of society, including culture, politics, economics, the environment, technology, and metaphysics. And it's driven by an underlying leftist ideology so deeply engrained in modern thinking that adherents are at risk of being totally blindsided. A dystopian surveillance police state with a social credit system and a technologically altered, brainwashed, divided, and spiritually blocked populace is not out of the question if the Great Reset takes hold fully. In such an "upside down" society, an elitist and antihuman mentality will drive policy while it masquerades as benevolent.

The question then arises: If the Great Reset, in its current construction, isn't the best way forward, then what is? Philosopher Ken Wilber's model of holistic, "integral" development is a useful framework in this regard. In essence, he suggests that moving from one stage of development to a more advanced stage involves "transcending" the current one but not leaving everything behind. **So, to him, the process is to both "transcend" and "include." That entails keeping the beneficial parts of the previous stage and *integrating* them into the new, more advanced stage.**[1]

On a societal level, that's perhaps what we need. Leftism, and its implementation in the Great Reset, isn't *all* bad. For example, it includes a strong focus on being kind, caring, and compassion-ate. That's a good thing. It's also aligned with spiritual values that emerge from the life review in near-death experiences (among other spiritually transformative phenomena). But the desire to "do good" is inadequate when decoupled from the judgment, knowledge, and wisdom that are required to apply compassion appropriately.[2] The heart and the mind need to work in tandem; the heart, by itself, can be led astray. It can induce a bias toward what *feels* good rather than what *does* good. Therefore, blind com-passion isn't the solution, but rather *compassion with discernment*.[3]

This suggests that toughness and strength are required. However, these important qualities are being demonized and discouraged by leftism—especially through the growing sentiment that mas-culine qualities are bad (known as *toxic masculinity*). In 2019, the American Psychological Association even labeled "traditional masculinity" as "on the whole, harmful."[4] Also, as discussed earlier, college campuses, and leftist culture generally, are encouraging oversensitivity to anything subjectively deemed "offensive." This is contributing to a phenomenon that Greg Lukianoff and Jon-athan Haidt call *safetyism*, whereby the need for safety—which is in some ways essential for our survival—is being weaponized such that it "trumps everything else." Younger generations are thus "more fragile and less resilient."[5] The title of their book, *The Coddling of the American Mind*, says it all. These are the signs of a weakening culture, which is beneficial for those who want to exert control without facing resistance.

A related framework for societal progress is that of Wilber's "lines" of development. These are different axes along which we evolve. Wilber specifically refers to three major lines of devel-opment: "waking up," "cleaning up," and "growing up."[6] Some-one who is advanced in terms of waking up is highly spiritually advanced, embodies an "enlightened" state of unconditional love and joy, and prioritizes service to others and to "the divine" (as examined in my book *An End to Upside Down Living* [2020]). Cleaning up refers to the healing of past trauma and transmut-ing whatever darkness lies within us. Growing up, as I see it, is a form of maturation, accepting reality as it is, valuing personal responsibility rather than victimhood, and building toughness for the times that require it. These lines of development tend to be relatively independent of one another. So, for example, it's possible to be at a very high level of waking up without having done as much work on cleaning up and growing up. As I've argued in the past, evolving in *all three* of these areas—on personal and societal levels—is essential for the future of our civilization.

However, there's another developmental line in Wilber's framework that needs to be considered here: "showing up."[7] Without showing up to what life brings, it's possible to be highly evolved but also highly passive and disconnected from the world. And that's not a good thing given how actively society is being steered in a very particular direction.

Showing up, for instance, could involve the active rejection of evil. This means being *intolerant* of evil. In the words of Seth Dillon, CEO of the political satire website The Babylon Bee: "Some people think we're improving morally by making fun of fewer things. I think the opposite is true. We're more depraved than ever because we're accepting and affirming what should be ridiculed and rejected."[8]

Furthermore, showing up could entail not conforming to a broader group's behaviors. It also means being proactive in terms of setting boundaries as to what's acceptable for one's life and one's family. That means determining when to say no. Blindly going along with what society deems "good" isn't satisfactory in a world gone mad. Consensus doesn't necessarily imply virtue.

The efficacy of showing up can be enhanced by staying aware of what's happening in society; remaining intellectually humble; and using independent, critical-thinking skills—regardless of what the mainstream narrative says. This can allow individuals to break through the many unconscious psychological biases discussed in chapter 3, thereby enabling them to show up in a more informed manner.

"Waking up, cleaning up, growing up, and showing up" is a path to "transcending" the Great Reset. But this is about more than just the Great Reset. The Great Reset seems to be the latest iteration of a broader movement to control people and instill a toxic, leftist ideology for future generations. Today it's called the Great Reset, but in the future, it might be called something else and take on slightly different implementations. It could even be viewed as part of an ongoing process of spiritual evolution—what some call a "spiritual war." From this multidimensional lens, we don't know how high the stakes might be.

As daunting as all of this can seem, it's important to remember that the decision makers represent a relatively tiny number of people compared to the overall population. That means the ultimate choice as to how we live our lives—and direct our society—doesn't rest in *their* hands.

It rests in *ours*.

ACKNOWLEDGMENTS

Many thanks once again to my fabulous publishers, Bill and Gayle Gladstone of Waterside Productions. I also thank those who have supported me in the process of publishing this book: Jill Kramer (proofreading), Joel Chamberlain (design), Ken Fraser (cover art), Jennifer Uram (contract support), Sandi Schroeder (index), and Justin Levy (audiobook). Thank you to my friends and family for your encouragement and feedback.

ENDNOTES

OPENING QUOTATION

1   Hoffer, *The True Believer*, 80–81. This excerpt is also used in Levin, *American Marxism*, 23.

INTRODUCTION: THE GREAT RESET

1   World Economic Forum, "Klaus Schwab and Prince Charles on why we need a Great Reset – listen to the podcast," https://www.weforum.org/agenda/2020/06/the-great-reset-this-weeks-world-vs-virus-podcast/.

2   Ibid.

3   Schwab, "Now is the time for a "great reset,'" https://www.weforum.org/agenda/2020/06/now-is-the-time-for-a-great-reset/.

4   Bruce-Lockhart and Chainey, "'Normal wasn't working' – John Kerry, Phillip Atiba Goff and others on the new social contract post-COVID," https://www.weforum.org/agenda/2020/06/great-reset-social-contract-john-kerry-phillip-goff/.

5   Schwab and Malleret, *COVID-19: The Great Reset*, 12.

6   As cited in Ibid., 244: Klaus Schwab on March 3, 2020; see also World Economic Forum, "The Great Reset," June 3, 2020, https://www.facebook.com/worldeconomicforum/videos/189569908956561. Also quoted on the World Economic Forum's website: https://www.weforum.org/focus/the-great-reset.

7   *The World Economic Forum: A Partner in Shaping History 1971–2020*, https://www3.weforum.org/docs/WEF_A_Partner_in_Shaping_History.pdf. Also see https://www.weforum.org/about/history.

8   World Economic Forum, "History," https://www.weforum.org/about/history. The roughly 2,500-attendee figure is for the 2022

meeting and comes from https://www.weforum.org/agenda/2022/05/davos-2022-whos-coming-and-everything-else-you-need-to-know/.

9   World Economic Forum, "Our Mission," https://www.weforum.org/about/world-economic-forum.

10   World Economic Forum, "Leadership and Governance," https://www.weforum.org/about/leadership-and-governance.

11   The WEF's Young Global Leaders is searchable here: https://www.younggloballeaders.org/community?utf8=%E2%9C%93&q=&x=0&y=0&status=&class_year=&sector=&region=#results. Justin Trudeau and Vladimir Putin are not listed when their names are searched (as of November 2022), but Klaus Schwab has separately suggested that they were in fact part of the Young Global Leader's Program: https://www.youtube.com/watch?v=RxtiD8Z6g-BI&t=10s. The video is also available on Rumble: https://rumble.com/vtfrxk-klaus-schwab-of-world-economic-forum-boasting-of-his-infiltration-into-gove.html.

12   "KLAUS SCHWAB TRUDEAU AND OTHER YOUNG GLOBAL LEADERS PENETRATED CABINETS," https://www.youtube.com/watch?v=RxtiD8Z6gBI&t=10s. The video is also available on Rumble: https://rumble.com/vtfrxk-klaus-schwab-of-world-economic-forum-boasting-of-his-infiltration-into-gove.html.

13   As of November 11, 2022, listed at https://www.weforum.org/partners#J.

14   See screenshots of the video in Morano, *The Great Reset*, 2–3.

15   "World Economic Forum: "By 2030, you'll own NOTHING and you'll be happy about it," https://rumble.com/vdgi1h-world-economic-forum-by-2030-youll-own-nothing-and-youll-be-happy-about-it.html.

16   Auken, "Welcome To 2030: I Own Nothing, Have No Privacy And Life Has Never Been Better," https://www.forbes.com/sites/worldeconomicforum/2016/11/10/shopping-i-cant-really-remember-what-that-is-or-how-differently-well-live-in-2030/?sh=7d71814d1735.

17   Romeo, "Disinformation is a growing crisis. Governments, business and individuals can help stem the tide," https://www.weforum.org/agenda/2022/10/how-to-address-disinformation/.

18   Jezard, "Even as birth rates decline overpopulation remains a global challenge," https://www.weforum.org/agenda/2018/04/almost-everywhere-people-are-having-fewer-children-so-do-we-still-need-to-worry-about-overpopulation.

19   Kraychick, "WEF Adviser Yuval Harari: 'We Just Don't Need the Vast Majority of the Population' in Today's World," https://www.breitbart.com/economy/2022/08/10/wef-adviser-yuval-harari-we-just-dont-need-the-vast-majority-of-the-population-in-todays-world/.

20   Schwab and Malleret, *COVID-19: The Great Reset*, 18.

21   Ibid., 213.

22   Ibid., 244.

23   Ibid., 240–42.

24 Ibid., 96–97.

25 Ibid., 244.

26 Ibid., 171. The authors reference Evgeny Morozov's concern about "techno-totalitarian state surveillance" and write: "What Morozov perceives as the greatest and ultimate danger to our political systems and liberties is that the 'successful' examples of tech in monitoring and containing the pandemic will then 'entrench the solutionist toolkit as the default option for addressing all other existential problems—from inequality to climate change. After all, it is much easier to deploy solutionist tech to influence individual behavior than it is to ask difficult political questions about the root causes of these crises.'"

27 Ibid., 102.

28 Ibid., 89.

29 Ibid., 94.

30 Ibid., 113.

31 Ibid., 114.

32 Ibid., 95.

33 Ibid., 96.

34 For example, see Schwab and Malleret, *The Great Narrative*, 74–82.

35 Schwab and Malleret, *COVID-19: The Great Reset*, 94.

36 Schwab, "Now is the time for a 'great reset,'" https://www.weforum.org/agenda/2020/06/now-is-the-time-for-a-great-reset/.

37 Schwab, *Stakeholder Capitalism*, xv.

38 Ibid., 174–75.

39 Schwab and Malleret, *COVID-19: The Great Reset*, 171. The authors reference Evgeny Morozov's concern about "techno-totalitarian state surveillance" and write: "What Morozov perceives as the greatest and ultimate danger to our political systems and liberties is that the 'successful' examples of tech in monitoring and containing the pandemic will then 'entrench the solutionist toolkit as the default option for addressing all other existential problems—from inequality to climate change. After all, it is much easier to deploy solutionist tech to influence individual behavior than it is to ask difficult political questions about the root causes of these crises.'"

40 Ibid., 102.

41 Ibid., 89.

42 Ibid., 240.

43 *TODAY* show (NBC News), "Al Gore Talks Climate Crisis: 'This Is the Time for a Great Reset,'" June 19, 2020, https://www.youtube.com/watch?v=1iv6WkIZ2pI.

44 Schwab and Malleret, *COVID-19: The Great Reset*, 152.

45 Schwab, *The Fourth Industrial Revolution*, 8.

46 The science is summarized in chapter 9 of this book. For further detail, see Gober, *An End to Upside Down Thinking*, and the *Where Is My Mind?* podcast by Gober and Blue Duck Media.

47 Paul, "The 'Great Reset' is about Expanding Government Power and Suppressing Liberty," http://www.ronpaulinstitute.org/archives/featured-articles/2021/january/04/the-great-reset-is-about-expanding-government-power-and-suppressing-liberty/.

48 Anton, "Socialism and the Great Reset," in Walsh (Ed.), *Against the Great Reset*, 170.

49 Beck, *The Great Reset*, 31.

50 Ibid., 22.

51 Ibid., 153.

52 Ibid., 32

53 Ibid.

54 Ibid., 14.

55 Morano, *The Great Reset*, 32–33.

56 Hanson, "The Great Regression." in Walsh (Ed.), *Against the Great Reset*, 18.

57 For example, see Hare, *Without Conscience: The Disturbing World of the Psychopaths Among Us*.

58 Mind-control tactics could include techniques employed under MK-ULTRA, a U.S. government–sponsored mind-control program. For more on that subject, see Gober, *An End to Upside Down Liberty*, 57–65.

59 For more on this topic, see Prager, "If the Road to Hell Is Paved With Good Intentions, With What Do We Pave the Road to Heaven?" https://dennisprager.com/column/if-the-road-to-hell-is-paved-with-good-intentions-with-what-do-we-pave-the-road-to-heaven/.

60 Wolf, *The Bodies of Others*, 53.

61 The term *human flourishing* is often used by author Alex Epstein in the context of the antihuman worldview. He is discussed further in chapter 7 of this book.

CHAPTER 1: THE PSYCHOLOGICAL FOUNDATIONS OF LEFTISM

1 Andrews, "Where Did the Terms 'Left Wing' and 'Right Wing' Come From?" https://www.history.com/news/how-did-the-political-labels-left-wing-and-right-wing-originate.

2 Prager, "Leftism Is Not Liberalism," https://dennisprager.com/column/leftism-is-not-liberalism/.

3 See Pierre, "Demands for Segregated Housing at Williams College Are Not News," https://www.nationalreview.com/2019/05/american-colleges-segregated-housing-graduation-ceremonies/; and James, "More than 75 colleges host blacks-only graduation ceremonies," https://www.washingtonexaminer.com/red-alert-politics/more-than-75-colleges-host-blacks-only-graduation-ceremonies.

4 See Volokh, "UC teaching faculty members not to criticize race-based affirmative action, call America 'melting pot,'" https://www.washingtonpost.com/news/volokh-conspiracy/wp/2015/06/16/uc-teaching-faculty-members-not-to-criticize-race-based-affirmative-

action-call-america-melting-pot-and-more/. Also see Soave, "The University of California's Insane Speech Police," https://www.the dailybeast.com/the-university-of-californias-insane-speech-police and see The European Union Times, "University of California says you are a racist if you say 'the human race,'" https://www.eutimes.net/2015/08/university-of-california-says-you-are-a-racist-if-you-say-the-human-race/.

5   "PhilosophyInsights" YouTube channel, "Roger Scruton: Why Intellectuals are Mostly Left," https://www.youtube.com/watch?v=FYo4KM hUx9c.

6   Big Think, "Jordan Peterson: The fatal flaw in leftist American politics | Big Think," https://www.youtube.com/watch?v=8UVUnUnWfHI.

7   Rectenwald, *Beyond Woke*, 194.

8   Ibid., 195–96.

9   Kling, *The Three Languages of Politics*, 5.

10   Samuels, *The Psychopathology of Political Ideologies*, 4.

11   Lakoff, *Moral Politics*, 33.

12   Ibid., 35.

13   Haidt, *The Righteous Mind*, 211–16. I abbreviated the moral foundations for the purposes of simplicity. Haidt refers to them as follows: care/harm, fairness/cheating, liberty/oppression, loyalty/betrayal, authority/subversion, and sanctity/degradation.

14   Ibid., 212.

15   Schwab and Malleret, *COVID-19: The Great Reset*, 18.

16   See Gober, *An End to Upside Down Liberty*, 172–76. The dangers of collectivism have also been described by G. Edward Griffin, F.A. Hayek, and others.

17   This reflects my own assessment, and I'm not sure if formal psychological research has been done to test the hypothesis. If not, it is an area worthy of consideration for future exploration.

18   From an interview with Mike Shellenberger available at Shellenberger, "The Woke Grift," https://michaelshellenberger.substack.com/p/the-woke-grift.

19   Lakoff, *Moral Politics*, 31.

CHAPTER 2: THE DOMINANCE OF LEFTISM

1   Lukianoff and Haidt, *The Coddling of the American Mind*, 111.

2   Saad, *The Parasitic Mind*, 66–67.

3   Ibid., 63–64.

4   As cited in Ibid., 64.

5   As cited in Ibid.

6   The Best Schools Staff, "What is a Safe Space in College?" https://thebestschools.org/resources/safe-space-college/. Also see University of Missouri, "Bias Hotline."

7   Rectenwald, *Beyond Woke*, 19.

8   Ibid., 20.

9   Lukianoff and Haidt, *The Coddling of the American Mind*, 47–49.

10   Ibid., 49.

11   Prior, "The definitive proof critical race theory is being taught in our schools," https://www.foxnews.com/opinion/proof-critical-race-theory-taught-schools.

12   "Wikipedia co-founder: I no longer trust the website I created," https://unherd.com/thepost/wikipedia-co-founder-i-no-longer-trust-the-website-i-created/.

13   Fernandez, "Facebook CEO Mark Zuckerberg acknowledges Silicon Valley left-wing bias," https://www.foxbusiness.com/politics/facebook-ceo-mark-zuckerberg-acknowledges-silicon-valley-left-wing-bias.

14   Wilson, "Evidence Of FBI Meddling In 2020 Election Mounts After Zuckerberg's Hunter Biden Laptop Revelation," https://www.dailywire.com/news/evidence-of-fbi-meddling-in-2020-election-mounts-after-zuckerbergs-hunter-biden-laptop-revelation.

15   Miller, "Twitter CEO Admits Censoring Hunter Biden Story Was 'Wrong,'" https://www.westernjournal.com/twitter-ceo-admits-censoring-hunter-biden-story-wrong/.

16   Golding, "79% say 'truthful' coverage of Hunter Biden's laptop would have changed 2020 election," https://nypost.com/2022/08/26/2020-election-outcome-would-differ-with-hunter-biden-laptop-coverage-poll/.

17   Ramaswamy, *Woke Inc.*, 189. Bokhari, "Google Is Still Erasing Breitbart Stories About Joe Biden from Search," https://www.breitbart.com/tech/2020/11/03/google-is-still-erasing-breitbart-stories-about-joe-biden-from-search/. Alexander, "Google's right-wing blacklist: Ex-engineer at tech giant says glitch which blocked some conservative websites from appearing in their search may have exposed a secret internal list which suppresses certain outlets," https://www.dailymail.co.uk/news/article-8547049/Ex-engineer-Google-says-glitch-blocked-conservative-websites-exposed-secret-internal-list.html. Perlroth, "One Man's Fight With Google Over a Security Warning," https://archive.nytimes.com/bits.blogs.nytimes.com/2012/01/05/one-mans-fight-with-google-over-a-security-warning/. Epstein, "Why Google Poses a Serious Threat to Democracy, and How to End That Threat," https://www.judiciary.senate.gov/imo/media/doc/Epstein%20Testimony.pdf. Lee, "'Strongly biased in favor of liberals': Psychologist says Google manipulated content ahead of election that swayed votes," https://www.washingtonexaminer.com/news/strongly-biased-in-favor-of-liberals-psychologist-says-google-manipulated-content-ahead-of-election-that-swayed-votes.

18   Saad, *The Parasitic Mind*, 67.

19   Lukianoff and Haidt, *The Coddling of the American Mind*, 130–31.

20   Kline, "Alyssa Milano on why Hollywood is so politically left-leaning," https://www.aol.com/article/entertainment/2017/08/30/alyssa-milano-on-why-hollywood-is-so-politically-left-leaning/23188416/.

21   Gross, "Why Is Hollywood So Liberal?" https://www.nytimes.com/2018/01/27/opinion/sunday/hollywood-liberal.html.

22   Saad, *The Parasitic Mind*, 66–67.

23   McCarthy, "ESPN's own study indicates big chunk of viewers perceive network has liberal bias," https://www.sportingnews.com/us/other-sports/news/espn-political-bias-liberal-conservative-langer-research-associates-hank-williams-jr-colin-kaepernick-curt-schilling/5goo5xpn3hhd1eiwiqm9vmahl.

24   Donner, "The Sports Media: Just as Biased as Their 'News' Brethren," https://www.libertynation.com/sports-media-bias/.

25   Fleischer, *Suppression, Deception, Snobbery, and Bias*, 11–12.

26   Groseclose, *Turn Left*, 99.

27   Saad, *The Parasitic Mind*, 67.

28   Investor's Business Daily, "Media Bias: Pretty Much All Of Journalism Now Leans Left, Study Shows," https://www.investors.com/politics/editorials/media-bias-left-study/.

29   Groseclose, *Turn Left*, 111.

30   Ibid., 113.

31   Chris Rossini, Twitter post, September 26, 2022. https://twitter.com/ChrisRossini/status/1574431709701062657.

32   The Rubin Report, "Conservatives, Black Lives Matter, Racism | Larry Elder | POLITICS | Rubin Report" https://www.youtube.com/watch?v=IFqVNPwsLNo.

33   Groseclose, *Turn Left*, vii.

CHAPTER 3: THE STICKINESS OF LEFTISM

1   Nisbett, "2017: WHAT SCIENTIFIC TERM OR CONCEPT OUGHT TO BE MORE WIDELY KNOWN?" https://www.edge.org/response-detail/27014.

2   Kahneman, *Thinking, Fast and Slow*, 85.

3   Ibid., 86.

4   Ibid., 87.

5   Krueger and Dunning, "Unskilled and unaware of it: how difficulties in recognizing one's own incompetence lead to inflated self-assessments," https://www.semanticscholar.org/paper/Unskilled-and-unaware-of-it%3A-how-difficulties-in-to-Kruger-Dunning/f2c80eef3585e0569e93ace0b9770cf76c8ebabc?p2df. Also see *Psychology Today*, "Dunning-Kruger Effect," https://www.psychologytoday.com/us/basics/dunning-kruger-effect.

6   *Psychology Today*, "Dunning-Kruger Effect," https://www.psychologytoday.com/us/basics/dunning-kruger-effect.

7   Ibid.

8   Kahneman, *Thinking, Fast and Slow*, 88.

9   Ibid., 82–83.

10   Ibid.

11   Ibid., 119–20.

12 Ibid., 126.

13 Ibid., 66–67.

14 Ibid., 67.

15 Ibid., 129.

16 Ibid., 131.

17 Strack in *International Encyclopedia of the Social & Behavioral Sciences*, https://www.sciencedirect.com/topics/computer-science/availability-heuristic.

18 Haidt, *The Righteous Mind*, 105.

19 Levy, "Political Decision-Making" in Hewer and Lyons (Ed.), *Political Psychology*, 176.

20 Haidt, *The Righteous Mind*, 59.

21 Ibid., 98–99.

22 Ibid., 102.

23 Ibid., 102–03.

24 Ibid., 100.

25 As cited in Ibid.

26 As cited in Ibid.

27 Lukianoff and Haidt, *The Coddling of the American Mind*, 58.

28 Kahneman, *Thinking, Fast and Slow*, 131.

29 Rubin, *Don't Burn This Book*, 95.

30 Ibid., 89.

31 The Rubin Report, "Conservatives, Black Lives Matter, Racism | Larry Elder | POLITICS | Rubin Report" https://www.youtube.com/watch?v=IFqVNPwsLNo. Bracketed text inserted as shown in Rubin, *Don't Burn This Book*, 90.

32 Rubin, *Don't Burn This Book*, 90–91.

33 Ibid., 91.

34 Richardson, "Republican recall frontrunner Larry Elder called 'Black face of white supremacy,'" https://www.washingtontimes.com/news/2021/aug/20/los-angeles-times-column-larry-elder-black-face-wh/.

35 Rubin, *Don't Burn This Book*, 93.

36 Sky News Australia, "Dave Rubin on his 'wake-up call' to 'twisted, evil, woke cult,'" https://www.youtube.com/watch?v=sAte3bVhcnY.

37 Rubin, *Don't Burn This Book*, 14–15.

38 Larry Elder with Epoch Times, "Larry Elder SCHOOLS Woke Liberals | Larry Elder," https://www.youtube.com/watch?v=1xoDvfJK5yE. Also see Richardson, "No racial bias in police shootings, study by Harvard professor shows," https://www.washingtontimes.com/news/2016/jul/11/no-racial-bias-police-shootings-study-harvard-prof/.

39 Prager, "Does it Feel Good or Does it Do Good? Left vs. Right #2," https://www.prageru.com/video/does-it-feel-good-or-does-it-do-good-left-vs-right-2.

CHAPTER 4: CULTURE

1 Schwab and Malleret, *COVID-19: The Great Reset*, 244.

2   Rothbard, *Egalitarianism as a Revolt Against Nature*, 6–8.

3   As cited in Miltimore, "Hayek: Social Justice Demands the Unequal
        Treatment of Individuals," https://fee.org/articles/hayek-social-justice-
        demands-the-unequal-treatment-of-individuals/. Source video: https://
        www.youtube.com/watch?v=RnMd40dqBlQ.

4   Larry Elder, Twitter post, October 20, 2022, https://twitter.com/larry-
        elder/status/1583310284143267841?s=21&t=BMo2tvw3vPfARQUm
        ZVgnIA.

5   Rothbard, *Egalitarianism as a Revolt Against Nature*, 8.

6   Schwab, "Now is the time for a 'great reset,'" https://www.weforum.org/
        agenda/2020/06/now-is-the-time-for-a-great-reset/.

7   Sowell, *Dismantling America*, 210.

8   Ibid., 210–11. For studies about trends related to first borns and average
        IQ scores, see The University of Edinburgh, "First borns have mental
        edge, study shows," https://www.ed.ac.uk/news/2017/first-borns-
        have-mental-edge-study-shows. Also see the Daily Mail, "First-borns
        'really do have a higher IQ,'" https://www.dailymail.co.uk/news/
        article-463761/First-borns-really-a-higher-IQ.html and Wolke, "First-
        Borns May Have Higher IQ, But Sibling Bonds Are What Really
        Shape Our Future," https://www.sciencealert.com/first-borns-may-
        have-higher-iq-but-sibling-bonds-are-what-really-shape-our-future.

9   Ibid., 214.

10   Fox News, "Martin Luther King Jr.'s famous 'I Have a Dream' speech:
        Full text," https://www.foxnews.com/us/transcript-of-martin-luther-
        king-jr-s-i-have-a-dream-speech.

11   Borysenko, *Actively Unwoke*, 23.

12   Ibid.

13   DiAngelo, *White Fragility*, 51. Also cited in this context in Borysenko,
        Actively Unwoke, 23.

14   Ramaswamy, *Woke Inc.*, 218.

15   Kendi, *How to Be an Antiracist*, 19.

16   Murray, *The War on the West*, 204–05.

17   This quotation is often attributed to the Chinese philosopher Con-
        fucius, but its origin is disputed.

18   Weiss, "The Psychopathic Problem of the White Mind," https://www.
        commonsense.news/p/the-psychopathic-problem-of-the-white#details.

19   Bishop Talbert Swan, Twitter, October 14, 2022, https://twitter.com/
        talbertswan/status/1581103527585120257?s=21&t=YluSewgwo9hHM
        r8Yk5LnFQ.

20   Simpson, "Woke dance school drops ballet from auditions as it is
        'white' and 'elitist,'" https://www.telegraph.co.uk/news/2022/07/16/
        woke-dance-school-drops-ballet-auditions-white-elitist/.

21   Airaksinen, "Prof: Algebra, geometry perpetuate white privilege,"
        https://www.campusreform.org/article?id=10005.

22   Watson, "Environmental Activist Says Cheese is Racist, Dairy
        Shouldn't Be Served in Schools," https://summit.news/2021/04/14/

environmental-activist-says-cheese-is-racist-dairy-shouldnt-be-served-in-schools/.

23   Hathaway, "CEO announces 11% cut to staff, promises 'anti-racist' layoffs," https://www.theblaze.com/news/twilio-anti-racist-firings.

24   Orwell, *Animal Farm*, 25.

25   Ibid., 134.

26   Lukianoff and Haidt, *The Coddling of the American Mind*, 67.

27   Ibid., 69.

28   Ibid., 70.

29   Ibid.

30   Saad, *The Parasitic Mind*, xii.

31   Sowell, *Dismantling America*, 214.

32   Lukianoff and Haidt, *The Coddling of the American Mind*, 70.

33   Espaillat et al., "An exploratory study on microaggressions in medical school: What are they and why should we care?" https://www.ncbi.nlm.nih.gov/pmc/articles/PMC6565651/.

34   Lukianoff and Haidt, *The Coddling of the American Mind*, 71.

35   Ibid.

36   Ibid., 72.

37   Ibid., 25.

38   Ibid., 85–86.

39   Ibid., 84–85.

40   Sowell, *Discrimination and Disparities*, 130.

41   McMaken, "The Alex Jones Verdict Shows the Danger of Defamation Laws," https://mises.org/power-market/alex-jones-verdict-shows-danger-defamation-laws.

42   PragerU, "Students vs. Chinese: Cultural Appropriation," https://www.youtube.com/watch?v=GNXm7juuM-8.

43   PragerU, "Students vs. Mexicans: Cultural Appropriation," https://www.youtube.com/watch?v=IT2UH74ksJ4.

44   Saad, *The Parasitic Mind*, xiv.

45   Ibid., 17.

46   Ibid., 75.

47   Ibid., 69.

48   An argument made by the philosopher Ken Wilber, among others.

49   Saad, *The Parasitic Mind*, 74. Also see Fox, "Clown World: Canadian Cancer Society Claims Men Without Cervixes Can Get Cervical Cancer," https://pjmedia.com/news-and-politics/megan-fox/2019/09/11/clown-world-canadian-cancer-society-claims-men-without-cervixes-can-get-cervical-cancer-n68784.

50   Street, "Yes, Men Can Have Periods and We Need to Talk About Them," https://www.thedailybeast.com/yes-men-can-have-periods-and-we-need-to-talk-about-them.

51   Saad, *The Parasitic Mind*, 74. See Starnes, "First grader sent to office for 'misgendering' fellow student," https://www.foxnews.com/opinion/first-grader-sent-to-office-for-misgendering-fellow-student.

52   Miller, "Transgender swimmer Lia Thomas sets pool record in 500-yard freestyle win at Ivy League Championship," https://nypost.com/2022/02/18/trans-swimmer-lia-thomas-wins-500-yard-freestyle-at-ivy-league-championship/.

53   Reilly, "Teammates say they are uncomfortable changing in locker room with trans UPenn swimmer Lia Thomas," https://nypost.com/2022/01/27/teammates-are-uneasy-changing-in-locker-room-with-trans-upenn-swimmer-lia-thomas/.

54   Mancini, "Dr. Rachel Levine named as one of USA Today's Women of the Year," https://www.phillyvoice.com/rachel-levine-health-secretary-women-of-the-year-usa-today/.

55   Zilber, "Twitter suspends Babylon Bee for naming Rachel Levine 'Man of the Year,'" https://nypost.com/2022/03/21/twitter-suspends-babylon-bee-over-rachel-levine-man-of-the-year-title/.

56   Reilly, "Transgender Rikers inmate sentenced to 7 years for raping female prisoner," https://nypost.com/2022/04/25/transgender-rikers-inmate-gets-7-years-for-raping-female-prisoner/.

57   Saad, *The Parasitic Mind*, 69.

58   Ibid., 65.

59   Ibid., 35.

60   Ibid., 35–36.

61   Ibid., 36.

62   Ibid.

63   Ibid.

64   Ibid.

65   Ibid., 77.

66   Some of the papers were later retracted *after* they were determined to be a "hoax."

67   Smith, "Going in Through the Back Door: Challenging Straight Male Homohysteria, Transhysteria, and Transphobia Through Receptive Penetrative Sex Toy Use."

68   Baldwin, "Who are they to judge? Overcoming anthropometry through fat bodybuilding." Also see Pluckrose et al., "Understanding the 'Grievance Studies Affair' Papers and Why They Should Be Reinstated: A Response to Geoff Cole," https://journals.sagepub.com/doi/full/10.1177/00491241211009946.

69   Baldwin, "When the Joke Is on You: A Feminist Perspective on How Positionality Influences Satire," https://ia802809.us.archive.org/22/items/20181002-Mike_Nayna-Academics_expose_corruption_in_Grievance_Studies-kVk9a5Jcd1k/Papers/HoH2%20TYPESET.pdf.

70   Lindsay et al., "Academic Grievance Studies and the Corruption of Scholarship," https://areomagazine.com/2018/10/02/academic-grievance-studies-and-the-corruption-of-scholarship/.

71   Baldwin, "An Ethnography of Breastaurant Masculinity: Themes of Objectification, Sexual Conquest, Male Control, and Masculine Toughness in a Sexually Objectifying Restaurant," https://ia802809.us.archive.

org/22/items/20181002-Mike_Nayna-Academics_expose_corruption_
in_Grievance_Studies-kVk9a5Jcd1k/Papers/HootersPublished.pdf.

72   Keene, "Republicans baffled that Ketanji Brown Jackson can"t say
what a woman is: 'It is a simple question,'" https://www.foxnews.com/
politics/republicans-baffled-ketanji-brown-jackson-define-woman.

73   Moore, "Sen. Hawley called transphobic in heated exchange with
woke prof over pregnancy," https://nypost.com/2022/07/12/sen-
hawley-called-transphobic-in-heated-exchange-with-woke-prof-
over-pregnancy/.

74   Ibid.

75   The Freedom Records, "Growing Up In The Cultural Revolution,
Xi Van Fleet The Freedom Records," https://www.youtube.com/
watch?v=4wl0fS0aIDw.

76   Courtois et al., *The Black Book of Communism*, 4.

77   *Firing Line with Margaret Hoover* | PBS, "Ai Weiwei | Full Episode
11.12.21 | Firing Line with Margaret Hoover | PBS," https://www.
youtube.com/watch?v=OjYjhxGJ-sI.

CHAPTER 5: POLITICS

1   Schwab and Malleret, *COVID-19: The Great Reset*, 89.

2   My critiques of government reflect a synthesis from studying many
other thinkers in the field. For example, see Larken Rose, *The Most
Dangerous Superstition*; the work of Murray Rothbard, Ludwig von
Mises, Friedrich Hayek, Walter Block, Hans Hermann-Hoppe, Lew
Rockwell, Tom DiLorenzo, Joseph Salerno, Mark Thornton, Jeff Deist,
Tom Woods, Dave Smith, Michael Malice, and others who endorse
concepts generally associated with the Austrian School of Economics.
See the following website for free access to books on these topics, as
well: https://mises.org/books-library.

3   A similar argument is made in Rose, *The Most Dangerous Superstition*,
31.

4   Weller, "Gun control in four countries around the world," https://
www.weforum.org/agenda/2018/02/these-4-countries-have-nearly-
eliminated-gun-deaths-heres-what-the-us-can-learn/.

5   Schwab and Malleret, *COVID-19: The Great Reset*, 114.

6   Ibid., 113.

7   Schwab, "Now is the time for a 'great reset,'" https://www.weforum.org/
agenda/2020/06/now-is-the-time-for-a-great-reset/.

8   McMaken, *Breaking Away*, 61.

9   Schwab and Malleret, *COVID-19: The Great Reset*, 95–96.

10   "Taking Rights Seriously | Judge Andrew P. Napolitano," July 13, 2020.
https://www.youtube.com/watch?v=3QMSDJn2wSU.

11   The notion that government is a service provider has been explored by
political philosophers. For instance, see Rose, *The Most Dangerous Superstition*, 16.

12   "Society Without State: Private Law Society | Hans-Hermann Hoppe,"
     https://youtu.be/TlWGA9H5An4, May 17, 2012.
13   An argument made by economist Tom DiLorenzo, among others.
14   Schwab and Malleret, *COVID-19: The Great Reset*, 94.
15   Sowell, *Dismantling America*, 335.
16   Schwab and Malleret, *COVID-19: The Great Reset*, 78.
17   Sowell, *Discrimination and Disparities*, 145.
18   Barbier, "Transitioning to green energy is key to both tackling climate
     change and creating sustainable economies. Here's why," https://www.
     weforum.org/agenda/2022/07/green-energy-transition-democracy-
     economy/.
19   Rothbard, *Anatomy of the State*, 11, https://cdn.mises.org/Anatomy%20
     of%20the%20State_3.pdf.
20   As cited in Salerno, "Mises on Nationalism, the Right of Self-
     Determination, and the Prolem of Immigration," https://mises.org/wire/
     mises-nationalism-right-self-determination-and-problem-immigration.
21   McMaken, *Breaking Away*, 155.
22   Ibid., 154.
23   Deneen, *Why Liberalism Failed*, 7.
24   McMaken, *Breaking Away*, 49.

CHAPTER 6: ECONOMICS

1   Schwab and Malleret, *COVID-19: The Great Reset*, 94.
2   Schwab, "Now is the time for a 'great reset,'" https://www.weforum.org/
     agenda/2020/06/now-is-the-time-for-a-great-reset/.
3   Schwab, *Stakeholder Capitalism*, xv.
4   Mackey and Sisodia, *Conscious Capitalism*, 12–14.
5   Rothbard, *A Future of Peace and Capitalism*, https://www.lewrockwell.
     com/2020/08/murray-n-rothbard/a-future-of-peace-and-capitalism/.
6   Ibid.
7   Hayek, *The Fatal Conceit*, 76, https://mises.at/static/literatur/Buch/
     hayek-the-fatal-conceit.pdf.
8   Discussed in a similar manner by economist Tom DiLorenzo in "Ten
     Things You Should Know About Socialism | Thomas J. DiLorenzo,"
     July 22, 2019, https://www.youtube.com/watch?v=vFrrovr7GVs.
9   Schwab and Malleret, *COVID-19: The Great Reset*, 68.
10   Paul, "The 'Great Reset' is about Expanding Government Power
     and Suppressing Liberty," http://www.ronpaulinstitute.org/archives/
     featured-articles/2021/january/04/the-great-reset-is-about-expanding-
     government-power-and-suppressing-liberty/.
11   Schwab, *Stakeholder Capitalism*, xv.
12   Schwab, "Now is the time for a 'great reset,'" https://www.weforum.org/
     agenda/2020/06/now-is-the-time-for-a-great-reset/.
13   Schwab and Malleret, *COVID-19: The Great Reset*, 171.
14   Ibid., 89.
15   Sowell, *Economic Facts and Fallacies*, 150–57.

16   As cited in Palumbo, "Why Larry Summers Doesn't Under-
      stand Economic Inequality," https://mises.org/library/
      why-larry-summers-doesnt-understand-economic-inequality.

17   Schwab, *Stakeholder Capitalism*, xv. He writes, "I argue…that we can't
      continue with an economic system driven by selfish values, such as
      short-term profit maximization, the avoidance of tax and regulation, or
      the externalizing of environmental harm."

18   Courtois et al., *The Black Book of Communism*, 4.

19   Feshbach and Friendly Jr., *Ecocide in the USSR*, 1.

20   Yglesias, "Denmark's prime minister says Bernie Sanders is wrong to
      call his country socialist," https://www.vox.com/2015/10/31/9650030/
      denmark-prime-minister-bernie-sanders.

21   Also see, Paul, *The Case Against Socialism*.

22   Rothbard, *For a New Liberty*, 327.

23   The Joe Rogan Experience, "#1877-Jann Wenner," https://open.spotify.
      com/episode/4yb794L4eMgchIFx1dJtaW.

24   Britannica ProCon.org, *FDA-Approved Prescription Drugs Later
      Pulled from the Market*, https://prescriptiondrugs.procon.org/
      fda-approved-prescription-drugs-later-pulled-from-the-market/.

25   Rothbard's book has been made available for free by the Mises Institute
      at the following link: https://mises.org/library/new-liberty-libertarian-
      manifesto. Also see Gober, *An End to Upside Down Liberty*, chapter 5
      for more information on the potential privatization of government
      functions.

26   LibertyInOurTime, "Society Without State: Private Law Society |
      Hans-Hermann Hoppe," https://www.youtube.com/watch?v=
      TlWGA9H5An4.

27   Schwab, *Stakeholder Capitalism*, 174–75.

28   Schwab and Malleret, *The Great Narrative: For a Better Future*, 178–79.

29   DiLorenzo, "The Rise of Economic Fascism in America," https://www.
      lewrockwell.com/2021/09/thomas-dilorenzo/the-rise-of-economic-
      fascism-in-america/. DiLorenzo writes in summary: "When people
      hear the word 'fascism' they naturally think of its ugly racism and
      anti-Semitism as practiced by the totalitarian regimes of Mussolini and
      Hitler. But there was also an economic policy component of fascism,
      known in Europe during the 1920s and '30s as 'corporatism,' that was
      an essential ingredient of economic totalitarianism as practiced by
      Mussolini and Hitler. So-called corporatism was adopted in Italy and
      Germany during the 1930s and was held up as a 'model' by quite a few
      intellectuals and policy makers in the United States and Europe. A
      version of economic fascism was in fact adopted in the United States in
      the 1930s and survives to this day. In the United States these policies
      were not called 'fascism' but 'planned capitalism.' The word fascism may
      no longer be politically acceptable, but its synonym 'industrial policy' is
      as popular as ever."

30   Schwab and Malleret, *The Great Narrative: For a Better Future*, 178–79.

31   Rothbard, "Myth and Truth About Libertarianism," https://mises.org/
        library/myth-and-truth-about-libertarianism. The article notes: "This
        essay is based on a paper presented at the April 1979 national meeting
        of the Philadelphia Society in Chicago. The theme of the meeting was
        'Conservatism and Libertarianism.'"

32   Schwab and Malleret, *The Great Narrative: For a Better Future*, 178–79.

33   Ibid.

34   Ibid.

35   Rasheed and Kuruwita, "Sri Lanka faces 'man-made' food crisis as
        farmers stop planting," https://www.aljazeera.com/news/2022/5/18/
        a-food-crisis-looms-in-sri-lanka-as-farmers-give-up-on-planting.

36   The Committee to Unleash Prosperity, "The Tragedy of Sri Lanka:
        A Cautionary Tale On 'Going Green,'" https://committeetounleash
        prosperity.com/hotlines/the-tragedy-of-sri-lanka-a-cautionary-tale-
        on-going-green/. Also see Athas, Mogul, and Woodyatt. "Sri Lanka
        Prime Minister says he's willing to resign as protesters storm President's
        residence," https://www.cnn.com/2022/07/09/asia/sri-lanka-protest-
        president-saturday-intl-hnk/index.html.

37   Huber et al., UN Sustainable Development Goals—The Leading ESG
        Framework for Large Companies, https://corpgov.law.harvard.edu/
        2018/10/04/un-sustainable-development-goals-the-leading-esg-
        framework-for-large-companies/.

38   Ramaswamy, *Woke, Inc.*, 3.

39   As cited in Morano, *The Great Reset*, 313.

40   Ramaswamy, *Woke, Inc.*, 1–4.

41   Ibid., 121.

42   Ibid., 135.

43   Ibid., 54.

CHAPTER 7: ENVIRONMENT

1   Schwab and Malleret, *COVID-19: The Great Reset*, 102.

2   Schwab and Malleret, *The Great Narrative: For a Better Future*, 51.

3   Schwab and Malleret, *COVID-19: The Great Reset*, 238–40.

4   As cited in Morano, *The Great Reset*, 276.

5   Project Veritas, "PART 1: CNN Director ADMITS Network Engaged
        in 'Propaganda' to Remove Trump from Presidency," https://www.
        youtube.com/watch?v=Dv8Zy-JwXr4.

6   As cited in Beck, *The Great Reset*, 40.

7   Schwab and Malleret, *COVID-19: The Great Reset*, 19.

8   Concha, "Jane Fonda calls coronavirus 'God's gift to the left,'" https://
        thehill.com/homenews/media/520039-jane-fonda-calls-covid-19-gods-
        gift-to-the-left/.

9   Crowe, "Ocasio-Cortez: 'The World is Going to End In Twelve Years If
        We Don't Address Climate Change,'" https://news.yahoo.com/ocasio-
        cortez-world-going-end-150517060.html.

10   Congress.gov, "H.Res.109 - Recognizing the duty of the Federal Government to create a Green New Deal," https://www.congress.gov/bill/116th-congress/house-resolution/109/text. Also mentioned in Morano, *Green Fraud*, 71–72.

11   As cited in Morano, *Green Fraud*, 89.

12   Ibid., 4.

13   Ibid., 2.

14   Ibid., 127.

15   Eric Holthaus, Twitter, October 7, 2018. https://twitter.com/Eric Holthaus/status/1049339997827084295.

16   McTaggart, "Greta Thunberg: It's time to transform the West's oppressive and racist capitalist system," https://www.msn.com/en-gb/entertainment/music/greta-thunberg-its-time-to-overthrow-the-wests-oppressive-and-racist-capitalist-system/ar-AA13Ebby. Harris, "Greta Thunberg throws in her lot with the anti-capitalist Left," https://unherd.com/thepost/greta-thunberg-throws-her-lot-in-with-the-anti-capitalist-left/.

17   For example, see the article by McFarlane and Abnett, titled "African nations tell COP27 fossil fuels will tackle poverty." It states: "Echoing [comments] from other African nations, [Maggy Shino, who works within Namibia's] Ministry of Mines and Energy, said wealthy countries had failed to deliver promised funding that would help them to expand clean energy instead of exploiting their fossil fuel resources. 'If you are going to tell us to leave our resources in the ground, then you must be prepared to offer sufficient compensation, but I don't think anyone has yet come out to make such an offer,' she said." https://www.reuters.com/business/cop/african-hosted-climate-talks-give-fossil-fuel-voice-2022-11-10/.

18   Winston Marshall, Twitter, November 14, 2022, https://twitter.com/mrwinmarshall/status/1592236611898834944?s=21&t=ti6PMV0ysGvpjPPELiHp6A.

19   As cited by Steven Koonin in Rathnakumar S, "Andrew Dessler vs Steven Koonin: Climate Change Debate," https://www.youtube.com/watch?v=IGNSGyhK_z0.

20   Al Jazeera, "Africa being 'punished' by fossil fuel investment ban – Niger," https://www.aljazeera.com/news/2022/6/15/africa-punished-by-investment-clamp-on-fossils-says-niger.

21   Rathnakumar S, "Andrew Dessler vs Steven Koonin: Climate Change Debate," https://www.youtube.com/watch?v=IGNSGyhK_z0.

22   Morano, *Green Fraud*, 4.

23   Clifton Duncan, Twitter, October 20, 2022, https://twitter.com/cliftonaduncan/status/1583207340936830976?s=21&t=0AmkdAJNruC4IAXOXEYcfQ.

24   The Fort with Chris Powers, "Alex Epstein – The Future is Fossil Fuels," https://www.youtube.com/watch?v=TQUh9lsfRYc.

25   As cited in Morano, *Green Fraud*, 48.

26   Clifford, "White House is pushing ahead research to cool Earth by reflecting back sunlight," https://www.cnbc.com/2022/10/13/what-is-solar-geoengineering-sunlight-reflection-risks-and-benefits.html.

27   Matt Walsh, "Environmentalism Gets Even More Genocidal | Ep. 993," https://www.youtube.com/watch?v=HwxnWIgQEvM.

28   Icax, Absolute Zero Report, https://www.icax.co.uk/Absolute_Zero_Report.html.

29   Morano, *The Great Reset*, 308.

30   Ledsom, "France Travel: Many Short-Haul Flights Outlawed From April," https://www.forbes.com/sites/alexledsom/2022/04/03/france-travel-many-short-haul-flights-outlawed-from-april/?sh=71a0d2e27618.

31   Piro, "Yang: Climate Change May Require Elimination of Car Ownership," https://freebeacon.com/politics/yang-well-eliminate-car-ownership-to-fight-climate-change/.

32   Pollak, "Don't Charge that Electric Vehicle: California Braces for Energy Shortage Thru Labor Day," https://www.breitbart.com/economy/2022/08/31/dont-charge-that-electric-vehicle-california-braces-for-energy-shortage-thru-labor-day/.

33   Harvey, "Equivalent of Covid emissions drop needed every two years – study," https://www.theguardian.com/environment/2021/mar/03/global-lockdown-every-two-years-needed-to-meet-paris-co2-goals-study.

34   Jezard, "Even as birth rates decline overpopulation remains a global challenge," https://www.weforum.org/agenda/2018/04/almost-everywhere-people-are-having-fewer-children-so-do-we-still-need-to-worry-about-overpopulation.

35   Housman, "Euthanasia Is Now A Leading Cause Of Death In Canada, And Ethicists Are Freaking Out," https://dailycaller.com/2022/08/12/canada-euthanasia-disability-human-rights-mental-health/.

36   Koonin, *Unsettled*, 24.

37   As cited in Morano, *Green Fraud*, 42.

38   ReasonTV, "Russia and the Global Green Energy Crisis: Live With Michael Shellenberger," https://www.youtube.com/watch?v=H9qdQ1u_BDQ.

39   Gleik, *Chaos*, 3.

40   Britannica, "Edward Lorenz," https://www.britannica.com/biography/Edward-Lorenz.

41   Magness, "Imperial College Predicted Catastrophe in Every Country on Earth. Then the Models Failed," https://www.aier.org/article/imperial-college-predicted-catastrophe-in-every-country-on-earth-then-the-models-failed/.

42   Curl, "Experts Finally Declare Imperial College Coronavirus Model That Predicted 2.2M Dead In U.S. 'Totally Unreliable,'" https://www.dailywire.com/news/experts-finally-declare-imperial-college-coronavirus-model-that-predicted-2-2m-dead-in-u-s-totally-unreliable.

43   Ehrlich, *The Population Bomb*, 138.

44   Koonin, *Unsettled*, 7.

45   Morano, *Green Fraud*, 113–25.

46   Shabecoff, "U.N. ECOLOGY PARLEY OPENS AMID GLOOM," https://www.nytimes.com/1982/05/11/world/un-ecology-parley-opens-amid-gloom.html.

47   Kasprak, "Did UN Official Say Nations Would Vanish If Global Warming Not Reversed by 2000?" https://www.snopes.com/fact-check/nations-vanish-global-warming/.

48   Onians, "Snowfalls are now just a thing of the past," https://web.archive.org/web/20130422045937/http://www.independent.co.uk/environment/snowfalls-are-now-just-a-thing-of-the-past-724017.html.

49   As cited in Koonin, *Unsettled*, 9. Townsend and Harris, "Now the Pentagon tells Bush: climate change will destroy us," https://www.theguardian.com/environment/2004/feb/22/usnews.theobserver.

50   Bastasch, "Al Gore Was Wrong, Polar Bears Survived When The Arctic Was Ice-Free," https://thelibertarianrepublic.com/al-gore-was-wrong-polar-bears-survived-when-the-arctic-was-ice-free/.

51   CISION PRWeb, "Starving Polar Bear Images Inspired Climate Activist Greta Thunberg but Dr. Crockford Says Polar Bears are Thriving in a New Video from Friends of Science," https://www.prweb.com/releases/starving_polar_bear_images_inspired_climate_activist_greta_thunberg_but_dr_crockford_says_polar_bears_are_thriving_in_a_new_video_from_friends_of_science/prweb16267141.htm.

52   Ibid. Also see Cecco, "Polar bear numbers in Canadian Arctic pose threat to Inuit, controversial report says," https://www.theguardian.com/world/2018/nov/13/polar-bear-numbers-canadian-arctic-inuit-controversial-report. Lombard, *False Alarm*, 50-52. Paul, *The Case Against Socialism*, 260. Morano, *Green Fraud*, 52. Shellenberger, *Apocalypse Never*, 252-253. Shellenberger writes: "As for fossil fuel-funded climate denialists misleading people about polar bears, we couldn't find any. The main critic of polar bear exaggerations is a zoologist in Canada named Susan Crockford, who told me that she neither accepts money from fossil fuel interests nor denies that the planet is warming due to human activities."

53   Richardson, "Susan Crockford fired after finding polar bears thriving despite climate change," https://www.washingtontimes.com/news/2019/oct/20/susan-crockford-fired-after-finding-polar-bears-th/.

54   D'Angelo, "93 Percent Of The Great Barrier Reef Is Practically Dead," https://www.huffpost.com/entry/climate-change-destroying-great-barrier-reef_n_571918e6e4b0d912d5fde8d4.

55   Knaus and Evershed, "Great Barrier Reef at 'terminal stage': scientists despair at latest coral bleaching data," https://www.theguardian.com/environment/2017/apr/10/great-barrier-reef-terminal-stage-australia-scientists-despair-latest-coral-bleaching-data.

56   Subramanian, "Parts of Great Barrier Reef record highest amount of coral in 36 years," https://www.cnn.com/2022/08/04/australia/great-barrier-reef-high-coral-report-australia-climate-intl-hnk/index.html.

57   Moore, *Fake Invisible Catastrophes and Threats of Doom*, 27–30.

58   McKie, "President 'has four years to save Earth,'" https://www.theguardian.com/environment/2009/jan/18/jim-hansen-obama.

59   Scafetta, "CMIP6 GCM ensemble members versus global surface temperatures," https://link.springer.com/content/pdf/10.1007/s00382-022-06493-w.pdf. Also see Morrison, "Satellite Temperature Data Show Almost All Climate Model Forecasts Over the Last 40 Years Were Wrong," https://dailysceptic.org/2022/10/08/satellite-temperature-data-show-almost-all-climate-model-forecasts-over-the-last-40-years-were-wrong/.

60   Eisenstein, *Climate: A New Story*, 66.

61   Shir-Raz et al., "Censorship and Suppression of Covid-19 Heterodoxy: Tactics and Counter-Tactics," https://link.springer.com/article/10.1007/s11024-022-09479-4.

62   O'Neill, "Fauci says attacks on him are 'attacks on science,'" https://nypost.com/2021/06/09/fauci-says-attacks-on-him-are-attacks-on-science/.

63   Disclose.tv, Twitter, October 2, 2022, https://twitter.com/disclosetv/status/1576522107051446273?s=21&t=WnTR7d4uoO5gidDefbu9AA. Also see United Nations, https://www.un.org/en/climatechange/google-search-information.

64   Author Patrick Moore makes the point that many perceived crises are conveniently "invisible" in his book *Fake Invisible Catastrophes and Threats of Doom*.

65   BizNews Radio, "'There's no emergency' – dissident climatologist Dr Judith Curry on the 'manufactured scientific consensus' on climate change," https://podcasts.apple.com/us/podcast/theres-no-emergency-dissident-climatologist-dr-judith/id1441394221?i=1000581672289.

66   Curry, "The paradox of the climate change consensus," https://judith-curry.com/2016/04/17/the-paradox-of-the-climate-change-consensus/.

67   The Joe Rogan Experience, #1776-Steven E. Koonin (see 2:00:00 to 2:02:00), https://open.spotify.com/episode/76RdMG5Tne7H9ja P7mhkdk?si=VrAXD3pxTfeY4p-ygxVdbA&context=spotify %3Ashow%3A4rOoJ6Egrf8K2IrywzwOMk&nd=1.

68   Koonin, *Unsettled*, 5.

69   Lundgren, "Hide the Decline," https://www.epw.senate.gov/public/index.cfm/press-releases-all?ID=8F16552A-802A-23AD-465F-8858B EB85AC2.

70   Revkin, "A Climate Scientist Who Engages Skeptics," https://archive.nytimes.com/dotearth.blogs.nytimes.com/2009/11/27/a-climate-scientist-on-climate-skeptics/.

71   Eisenstein, *Climate: A New Story*, 65-66.

72   Koonin, *Unsettled*, 1.

73   Ibid., 1-2.

74   Ibid., 2.

75   Shellenberger, *Apocalypse Never*, inner flap hardcover quote.

76   PragerU, *Religion of Green*, https://www.youtube.com/watch?v=UTgN
     tvTuYRU. Also see https://environmentalprogress.org/the-case-against-
     environmental-alarmism.

77   Epstein, *Fossil Future*, ix.

78   Ibid., x. Also see Lomborg, "More people die of cold: Media's heat-
     death climate obsession leads to lousy fixes," https://nypost.com/
     2021/07/14/more-die-of-cold-medias-heat-death-climate-obsession-
     leads-to-lousy-fixes/.

79   Alex Epstein, Twitter, August 31, 2022, https://twitter.com/
     AlexEpstein/status/1565009174194446336.

80   Plumer, "Rebranding Global Warming," https://newrepublic.com/
     article/77820/rebranding-global-warming.

81   Steamboat Institute, "Should America Rapidly Eliminate Fossil Fuel
     Use to Prevent Climate Catastrophe?" https://www.youtube.com/
     watch?v=4AIVpK4oACs.

82   Kiderlin, "Oil protesters arrested after throwing tomato soup at Van
     Gogh painting," https://www.cnbc.com/2022/10/14/oil-protesters-
     arrested-after-throwing-tomato-soup-at-van-gogh-painting.html.

83   Harrington, "Climate change is not making children obese," https://
     unherd.com/thepost/climate-change-is-not-making-children-obese/.

84   Migdon, "Canadian woman becomes first person diagnosed as suffering
     from 'climate change,'" https://thehill.com/changing-america/
     sustainability/climate-change/580527-canadian-woman-becomes-first-
     person-diagnosed/.

CHAPTER 8: TECHNOLOGY

1   Schwab, *The Fourth Industrial Revolution*, 1.

2   Ibid., 8.

3   Ibid., 96.

4   Aitken, "Swedish COVID vaccine pass microchip maker addresses
     privacy concerns," https://www.foxbusiness.com/technology/swedish-
     covid-vaccine-pass-microchip-privacy-concerns.

5   As cited in Durden, "Doug Casey On The WEF's Plan For Mankind
     And What Comes Next," https://www.zerohedge.com/geopolitical/
     doug-casey-wefs-plan-mankind-and-what-comes-next. Also see,
     "'Covid is critical because this is what convinces people to accept, to
     legitimize, total biometric surveillance,'" https://www.youtube.com/
     watch?v=hm7lTEoTe_Q.

6   Schwab and Malleret, *COVID-19: The Great Reset*, 160–61.

7   Andrew Lawton, Twitter, May 24, 2022, https://twitter.com/
     andrewlawton/status/1529045188764921856?s=21&t=_OxrCqlGT
     guU2to_46w-2g.

8   Mastercard, "DO Black – the world's first credit card with a carbon limit," https://www.mastercard.com/news/europe/sv-se/nyhetsrum/pressmeddelanden/sv-se/2019/april/do-black-the-world-s-first-credit-card-with-a-carbon-limit/.

9   Ibid.

10   Imanuelson, "The credit card that tracks your CO2 emissions," https://petersweden.substack.com/p/card-co2-tracking.

11   Wolf, *The Bodies of Others*, 1.

12   Wallace, "Bank of England tells ministers to intervene on digital currency 'programming,'" https://www.telegraph.co.uk/business/2021/06/21/bank-england-tells-ministers-intervene-digital-currency-programming/.

13   FEDS Notes, "What is programmable money?" https://www.federalreserve.gov/econres/notes/feds-notes/what-is-programmable-money-20210623.htm.

14   Wignaraja and Horvath, "Universal basic income is the answer to the inequalities exposed by COVID-19," https://www.weforum.org/agenda/2020/04/covid-19-universal-basic-income-social-inequality/.

15   Wolf, *The Bodies of Others*, 215, 217.

16   Brimelow, "Prime Minister Justin Trudeau Says Unvaccinated Are Usually 'Racist' and 'Misogynist,'" https://timcast.com/news/prime-minister-justin-trudeau-says-unvaccinated-are-usually-racist-and-misogynist/.

17   Hart, "France's Macron Vows To 'Piss Off' Unvaccinated With New Restrictions," https://www.forbes.com/sites/roberthart/2022/01/05/frances-macron-stokes-outrage-after-vowing-to-anger-unvaccinated-with-tough-new-restrictions/?sh=117430ff2c0f.

18   Funnell, "Northern Territory placed into lockout until noon on Monday, unvaccinated residents to enter lockdown," https://www.skynews.com.au/australia-news/coronavirus/northern-territory-placed-into-lockout-until-noon-on-monday-unvaccinated-residents-to-enter-lockdown/news-story/85112b44c171b0196694c65807d1ed63.

19   Notheis, "'Don Lemon says unvaccinated people should be 'shunned' or 'left behind,'" https://news.yahoo.com/don-lemon-says-unvaccinated-people-175300636.html.

20   Rogers, "Nearly half of Dems say fines, prison time appropriate for questioning vaccines, poll says," https://katv.com/amp/news/nation-world/half-of-dems-believe-fines-prison-time-appropriate-for-questioning-vaccine-poll-says.

21   Schwab, *The Fourth Industrial Revolution*, 98.

22   Ibid., 85.

23   Stauffer, "Pfizer CEO Intros Horrifying Wireless 'Compliance' Device," https://www.westernjournal.com/pfizer-ceo-intros-horrifying-wireless-compliance-device/. Also see, "'The idea of a Soul, Free Will -- these are Over!' - Technocracy explained by Prof Yuval Harari," https://www.youtube.com/watch?v=NV0CtZga7qM and "Yuval Noah Harari | Why

Does Yuval Noah Harari Say 'We Are Upgrading Humans Into Gods?,'" https://rumble.com/v1cpnzj-yuval-noah-harari-non-human-world-new-gods-what-does-the-world-look-like.html.

24   World Economic Forum, "Will the Future Be Human? – Yuval Noah Harari," https://www.youtube.com/watch?v=hL9uk4hKyg4.

25   Schwab and Malleret, *The Great Narrative*, 102.

26   Ibid, 103.

27   Ibid.

28   Ibid., 95.

29   Schwab, *The Fourth Industrial Revolution*, 82.

30   Ibid., 101.

31   Schwab and Malleret, *COVID-19: The Great Reset*, 166.

32   Schwab, *The Fourth Industrial Revolution*, 114–15.

CHAPTER 9: METAPHYSICS

1   Here I am focusing on the brand of leftism that is atheistic, agnostic, or otherwise doesn't subscribe to a spiritual or religious worldview. That seems to align best with the Great Reset's metaphysical vision (or lack thereof). However, it is possible for someone to hold spiritual or religious beliefs while subscribing to other leftist values. There are many potential combinations of beliefs within Left-leaning philosophies.

2   Stauffer, "Pfizer CEO Intros Horrifying Wireless 'Compliance' Device," https://www.westernjournal.com/pfizer-ceo-intros-horrifying-wireless-compliance-device/. Also see, "'The idea of a Soul, Free Will -- these are Over!' - Technocracy explained by Prof Yuval Harari," https://www.youtube.com/watch?v=NV0CtZga7qM and "Yuval Noah Harari | Why Does Yuval Noah Harari Say 'We Are Upgrading Humans Into Gods?,'" https://rumble.com/v1cpnzj-yuval-noah-harari-non-human-world-new-gods-what-does-the-world-look-like.html.

3   McWhorter, *Woke Racism*, 23–60.

4   I know scientists personally who have told me that this happens.

5   Radin, *Real Magic*, 97. Tressoldi, *Extraordinary claims require extraordinary evidence: The case of non-local perception, a classical and Bayesian review of evidences*; Williams, *Revisiting the ganzfeld ESP debate: A basic review and assessment*; Mossbridge, Tressoldi, & Utts, *Predictive physiological anticipation preceding seemingly unpredictable stimuli: A meta-analysis*; Bem, Tressoldi, Raberyon, & Duggan, *Feeling the future: A meta-analysis of 90 experiments on the anomalous anticipation of random future events*; Bosch, Steinkamp, & Boller, *Examining psychokinesis: The interaction of human intention with random number generators—a meta-analysis*; Radin, Nelson, Dobyns, & Houtkooper, *Re-examining psychokinesis: Commentary on the Bösch, Steinkamp and Boller meta-analysis*; Nelson, Radin, Shoup, and Bancel, *Correlations of continuous random data with major world events*; global mind.org/results.html. Additionally, for a summary of Dr. Radin's studies, see https://www.

deanradin.com/publications.

6   See Gober, *An End to Upside Down Thinking*, chapter 4.

7   Utts, "An Assessment of the Evidence for Psychic Functioning," https://www.ics.uci.edu/~jutts/air.pdf.

8   Cardeña, "The Experimental Evidence for Parapsychological Phenomena: A Review," https://psycnet.apa.org/record/2018-24699-001.

9   Wahbeh et al., "What if consciousness is not an emergent property of the brain? Observational and empirical challenges to materialistic models," https://www.frontiersin.org/articles/10.3389/fpsyg.2022.955594/full#B64.

10 I've had discussions with scientists who state that this happens.

11 Rupert Sheldrake" Wikipedia page, accessed on November 12, 2022, https://en.wikipedia.org/wiki/Rupert_Sheldrake.

12 *Skeptiko*, "Dr. Mario Beauregard, Frontier Science Wake Up Call |538|," https://www.youtube.com/watch?v=8i-Q0MTJFls&t=2114s.

13 See *An End to Upside Down Thinking*, chapters 10 and 11. Also see the peer-reviewed research from the Windbridge Research Center, https://www.windbridge.org/research/.

14 See Gober, *An End to Upside Down Thinking*, chapter 9. Also see Gober, *An End to Upside Down Contact*, chapters 1 and 2.

15 van Lommel, Pim, et al. "Near-Death Experience in Survivors of Cardiac Arrest: A Prospective Study in the Netherlands." *The Lancet* 9298 (2001): 2039–45. http://www.thelancet.com/journals/lancet/article/PIIS0140673601071008/fulltext.

16 See Gober, *An End to Upside Down Thinking*, 140-43. Also see *Where Is My Mind?* Podcast, Ep. 5 "Near-Death Experiences."

17 See *Where Is My Mind?* Podcast, Ep. 2: "Blindfolded."

18 See Moody, *Glimpses of Eternity*.

19 Shared Crossing Research Initiative, "Shared Death Experiences: A Little-Known Type of End-of-Life Phenomena Reported by Caregivers and Loved Ones," https://pubmed.ncbi.nlm.nih.gov/33813876/.

20 See Gober, *An End to Upside Down Thinking*, 149–50 for a discussion of the shared life review.

21 See *Where Is My Mind?* Podcast, Ep. 6: "The Life Review." Also see *An End to Upside Down Liberty*, chapter 7.

22 Greyson, "Near-Death Experiences," in Kelly and Marshall (Ed.), *Consciousness Unbound*, 24 (Kindle edition).

23 Long, *God and the Afterlife*, 40.

24 Greyson, *After*, 182.

25 McKie, *Royal Mail's Nobel guru in telepathy row*, https://www.theguardian.com/uk/2001/sep/30/robinmckie.theobserver.

26 See Gober, *An End to Upside Down Living*, 64-68.

27 For example, see Schwab and Malleret, *COVID-19: The Great Reset*, 17.

28 Chen, "Community of people who believe they are animals," https://www.fox26houston.com/news/community-of-people-who-believe-

they-are-animals; Cain, "FOOL OF THE WILD This Morning viewers left stunned as woman reveals she identifies as a wolf and can even howl," https://www.thesun.co.uk/tv/17495428/this-morning-viewers-stunned-woman-identifies-wolf/.

29   Others have speculated about the link between transgender-related movements and transhumanism. For example, see Dreher, "Transgenderism As Transhumanism," https://www.theamerican conservative.com/transgenderism-as-transhumanism/.

30   For example, see descriptions in Gober, *An End to Upside Down Contact*, 57–66.

31   Sean Stone, *Best Kept Secret*, https://www.seanstone.info/bestkeptsecret. Also see SATAN'S CHILDREN — SATANIC RITUAL ABUSE (60 MINUTES AUSTRALIA), https://www.bitchute.com/video/ I1bHD2JyfmEg/; *Illinois Statutes Chapter 720. Criminal Offenses §-33. Ritualized abuse of a child*, https://codes.findlaw.com/il/chapter-720-criminal-offenses/il-st-sect-720-5-12-33.html; *Idaho Statutes*, https://legislature.idaho.gov/statutesrules/idstat/Title18/T18CH15/ SECT18-1506A/; "RAW: Sean Stone with Jay Parker," https://robert-davidsteele.com/sean-stone-with-jay-parker/; Noblitt and Noblitt (Ed.), *Ritual Abuse in the Twenty-First Century*, http://casra.org.uk/ prosecuted-cases/; and Gober, *An End to Upside Down Contact*, 57-66.

32   Murdock, "'Minor-Attracted Person': Inside The Growing Effort To Destigmatize Pedophilia," https://www.dailywire.com/news/minor-attracted-person-inside-the-growing-effort-to-destigmatize-pedophilia.

33   Gays Against Groomers, https://www.gaysagainstgroomers.com/about.

34   Bokhari, "'Gays Against Groomers' Activist Group Blacklisted by Google, PayPal, Venmo," https://www.breitbart.com/tech/2022/09/21/ gays-against-groomers-activist-group-blacklisted-by-google-paypal-venmo/. Also see Buttons, "BREAKING: Gays Against Groomers suspended from Twitter," https://thepostmillennial.com/breaking-gays-against-groomers-suspended-from-twitter.

35   Lungariello, "Video of drag queen gyrating in front of child has Texas pols pushing for legislative action," https://nypost.com/2022/10/18/ video-of-drag-queen-gyrating-next-to-child-sparks-backlash/; Chuldy, "Hate-fuelled 'Gays Against Groomers' invited on Fox News about being suspended from Twitter," https://www.pinknews.co.uk/2022/08/ 22/gays-against-groomers-founder-fox-news-twitter-ban/.

36   Langton, "Ban pornographic books in school libraries," https://www. washingtonexaminer.com/restoring-america/community-family/ban-pornographic-books-in-school-libraries. Binion, "Graphic novel pulled from Olympic High shelves, but parent wants school prosecuted over book," https://www.kitsapsun.com/story/news/2021/11/01/graphic-novel-gender-new-front-battle-school-library-books-criminal-charges/ 6201721001/. Springmagazine, "'Lawn Boy' IS pedophilic. Here's why. (Explicit)," https://thespringmagazine.com/2022/01/28/lawn-boy-is-pedophilic-heres-why-explicit/.

37   Hauf, "Biden administration funds studies on danger of transgender hormonal treatments even as it pushes them on kids," https://www.foxnews.com/politics/biden-funds-studies-dangers-transgender-hormone-treatments.

38   Golden, "Doctors Give Kids Drugs That Can Chemically Castrate Them – Just Like Pedophiles," https://www.westernjournal.com/doctors-give-kids-drugs-can-chemically-castrate-just-like-pedophiles/. Martyn, "New report describes dangers of giving Lupron to kids," https://www.consumeraffairs.com/news/new-report-describes-dangers-of-giving-lupron-to-kids-020317.html.

39   Liang, "Gender Affirmation Surgeries," https://www.hopkinsmedicine.org/health/wellness-and-prevention/gender-affirmation-surgeries.

40   Schwab, *The Fourth Industrial Revolution*, 82.

41   Downey, "Biden Claims School Children Don't Belong to Parents 'When They're in the Classroom,'" https://www.nationalreview.com/news/biden-claims-school-children-dont-belong-to-parents-when-theyre-in-the-classroom/.

CONCLUSION: SOCIETAL EVOLUTION

1   Future Thinkers, Who Are The 2nd Tier Thinkers? – Ken Wilber, https://www.youtube.com/watch?v=8o2_dbLq070.

2   Related to Dennis Prager's notion that good intentions aren't enough ("The road to Hell is paved with good intentions").

3   Mentioned as one of ten approaches to living in Gober, *An End to Upside Down Living*, 98-100.

4   Heldt, "American Psychological Association Labels 'Traditional Masculinity' as 'Harmful,'" https://townhall.com/tipsheet/briannaheldt/2019/01/07/american-psychological-association-labels-traditional-masculinity-as-harmful-n2538637.

5   Lukianoff and Haidt, *The Coddling of the American Mind*, 30.

6   Future Thinkers, "Clean Up, Wake Up, Grow Up," https://www.youtube.com/watch?v=2mROP49BeJc. Also see BuddhaAtTheGasPump, "Ken Wilber – Buddha at the Gas Pump Interview," https://www.youtube.com/watch?v=T1eOUIt4zUE&t=4278s.

7   Future Thinkers, "Showing Up For Life – Ken Wilber," https://www.youtube.com/watch?v=2-K-k0YrR1w.

8   Seth Dillon, Twitter, August 30, 2022, https://twitter.com/sethdillon/status/1564607389785100295?s=21&t=UIDRbWruXmp3rpi68EBYuA.

BIBLIOGRAPHY

Airaksinen, Toni. "Prof: Algebra, geometry perpetuate white privilege." Campus Reform website, October 23, 2017. https://www.campusreform.org/article?id=10005.

Aitken, Peter. "Swedish COVID vaccine pass microchip maker addresses privacy concerns." Fox Business, December 23, 2021. https://www.foxbusiness.com/technology/swedish-covid-vaccine-pass-microchip-privacy-concerns.

Alexander, Harriet. "Google's right-wing blacklist: Ex-engineer at tech giant says glitch which blocked some conservative websites from appearing in their search may have exposed a secret internal list which suppresses certain outlets." *Daily Mail*, July 21, 2020. https://www.dailymail.co.uk/news/article-8547049/Ex-engineer-Google-says-glitch-blocked-conservative-websites-exposed-secret-internal-list.html.

Alinsky, Saul. *Rules for Radicals*. New York: Vintage Books, 1989.

Al Jazeera. "Africa being 'punished' by fossil fuel investment ban – Niger." Al Jazeera, June 15, 2022. https://www.aljazeera.com/news/2022/6/15/africa-punished-by-investment-clamp-on-fossils-says-niger.

The American Report. "KLAUS SCHWAB TRUDEAU AND OTHER YOUNG GLOBAL LEADERS PENETRATED

CABINETS." YouTube video, January 29, 2022. https://www.
youtube.com/watch?v=RxtiD8Z6gBI&t=10s.

Andrews, Evan. "Where Did the Terms 'Left Wing' and 'Right Wing'
Come From?" History website, December 5, 2019. https://www.
history.com/news/how-did-the-political-labels-left-wing-and-
right-wing-originate.

Athas, Iqbal et al. "Sri Lanka Prime Minister says he's willing to resign
as protesters storm President's residence." CNN, July 9, 2022.
https://www.cnn.com/2022/07/09/asia/sri-lanka-protest-
president-saturday-intl-hnk/index.html.

Auken, Ida. "Welcome To 2030: I Own Nothing, Have No Privacy
And Life Has Never Been Better." *Forbes*, November 16, 2016.
https://www.forbes.com/sites/worldeconomicforum/2016/11/10/
shopping-i-cant-really-remember-what-that-is-or-how-
differently-well-live-in-2030/?sh=7d71814d1735.

Baldwin, Richard. "An Ethnography of Breastaurant Masculinity:
Themes of Objectification, Sexual Conquest, Male Control, and
Masculine Toughness in a Sexually Objectifying Restaurant."
Sex Roles, 79, 762 (2018) https://ia802809.us.archive.org/22/
items/20181002-Mike_Nayna-Academics_expose_corruption_
in_Grievance_Studies-kVk9a5Jcd1k/Papers/HootersPublished.
pdf.

Baldwin, Richard. "When the Joke Is on You: A Feminist Perspective
on How Positionality Influences Satire." *Hypatia: A Journal of
Feminist Philosophy*. https://ia802809.us.archive.org/22/items/
20181002-Mike_Nayna-Academics_expose_corruption_in_
Grievance_Studies-kVk9a5Jcd1k/Papers/HoH2%20TYPESET.
pdf.

Baldwin, Richard. "Who are they to judge? Overcoming anthropometry through fat bodybuilding." *Fat Studies*, Vol. 7, Issue 3 (2018).
https://www.tandfonline.com/doi/abs/10.1080/21604851.2018.
1453622

Barbier, Edward. "Transitioning to green energy is key to both tackling climate change and creating sustainable economies. Here's
why." July 11, 2022. https://www.weforum.org/agenda/2022/07/
green-energy-transition-democracy-economy/.

Bastasch, Michael. "Al Gore Was Wrong, Polar Bears Survived When
The Arctic Was Ice-Free." The *Libertarian Republic*, n.d. https://

thelibertarianrepublic.com/al-gore-was-wrong-polar-bears-survived-when-the-arctic-was-ice-free/.

Beck, Glenn, with Justin Haskins. *The Great Reset: Joe Biden and the Rise of 21st Century Fascism*. Mercury Radio Arts, Inc.: 2022.

Bem, Daryl et al. "Feeling the Future: A Meta-Analysis of 90 Experiments on the Anomalous Anticipation of Random Future Events." *F1000 Research* 4 (2015): 1188. https://f1000research.com/articles/4-1188/v1.

The Best Schools. "What is a Safe Space in College?" Best Schools website, October 11, 2022. https://thebestschools.org/resources/safe-space-college/.

Big Think. "Jordan Peterson: The fatal flaw in leftist American politics | Big Think." YouTube video, April 12, 2018. https://www.youtube.com/watch?v=8UVUnUnWfHI.

Binion, Andrew. "Graphic novel pulled from Olympic High shelves, but parent wants school prosecuted over book." *Kitsap Sun* website, November 1, 2021. https://www.kitsapsun.com/story/news/2021/11/01/graphic-novel-gender-new-front-battle-school-library-books-criminal-charges/6201721001/.

BizNews Radio. "'There's no emergency' – dissident climatologist Dr Judith Curry on the 'manufactured scientific consensus' on climate change." *Apple Podcast*, 2022. https://podcasts.apple.com/us/podcast/theres-no-emergency-dissident-climatologist-dr-judith/id1441394221?i=1000581672289.

Boghossian, Peter, and James Lindsay. *How to Have Impossible Conversations: A Very Practical Guide*. New York: Hachette, 2019.

Bokhari, Allum. "'Gays Against Groomers' Activist Group Blacklisted by Google, PayPal, Venmo." *Breitbart* website, September 21, 2022. https://www.breitbart.com/tech/2022/09/21/gays-against-groomers-activist-group-blacklisted-by-google-paypal-venmo/.

Bokhari, Allum. "Google Is Still Erasing Breitbart Stories About Joe Biden from Search." Breitbart, November 3, 2020. https://www.breitbart.com/tech/2020/11/03/google-is-still-erasing-breitbart-stories-about-joe-biden-from-search/.

Borysenko, Karlyn. *Actively Unwoke: The Ultimate Guide for Fighting Back Against the Woke Insanity in Your Life*. New York: Bombardier Books, 2022.

Bosch, Holger, Fiona Steinkamp, and Emil Boller. "Examining Psychokinesis: The Interaction of Human Intention with Random Number Generators; A Meta-Analysis." *Psychological Bulletin* 132, no. 4 (2006): 497–523.

Breggin, Peter, and Ginger Ross. *COVID-19 and the Global Predators: We Are the Prey*. Ithaca, NY: Lake Edge Press, 2021.

Brimelow, Hannah Claire. "Prime Minister Justin Trudeau Says Unvaccinated Are Usually 'Racist' and 'Misogynist.'" Timcast website, December 31, 2021. https://timcast.com/news/prime-minister-justin-trudeau-says-unvaccinated-are-usually-racist-and-misogynist/.

Britannica. "Edward Lorenz." Britannica website, n.d. https://www.britannica.com/biography/Edward-Lorenz.

Britannica ProCon.org. "FDA-Approved Prescription Drugs Later Pulled from the Market by the FDA." Britannica ProCon.org website, December 1, 2021. https://prescriptiondrugs.procon.org/fda-approved-prescription-drugs-later-pulled-from-the-market/.

Bruce-Lockhart, Anna, and Ross Chainey. "'Normal wasn't working' – John Kerry, Phillip Atiba Goff, and others on the new social contract post-COVID." World Economic Forum website, June 24, 2020. https://www.weforum.org/agenda/2020/06/great-reset-social-contract-john-kerry-phillip-goff/.

BuddhaAtTheGasPump. "Ken Wilber – Buddha at the Gas Pump Interview." YouTube video, April 30, 2018. https://www.youtube.com/watch?v=T1eOUIt4zUE&t=4278s.

Buttons, Christina. "BREAKING: Gays Against Groomers suspended from Twitter." The Post Millennial, July 29, 2022. https://thepostmillennial.com/breaking-gays-against-groomers-suspended-from-twitter.

Cain, Dan. "FOOL OF THE WILD This Morning viewers left stunned as woman reveals she identifies as a wolf and can even howl." *The Sun*, January 31, 2022. https://www.thesun.co.uk/tv/17495428/this-morning-viewers-stunned-woman-identifies-wolf/.

Cardeña, Etzel. "The experimental evidence for parapsychological phenomena: A review." *American Psychologist*, 73(5) (2018), 663–77. https://doi.org/10.1037/amp0000236.

Cecco, Leyland. "Polar bear numbers in Canadian Arctic pose threat to Inuit, controversial report says." *The Guardian*, November 13, 2018. https://www.theguardian.com/world/2018/nov/13/polar-bear-numbers-canadian-arctic-inuit-controversial-report

Chen, Angela. "Community of people who believe they are animals." Fox26, May 24, 2016. https://www.fox26houston.com/news/community-of-people-who-believe-they-are-animals.

Chua, Amy. *Political Tribes*. New York: Penguin Press, 2018.Chuldy, Emily. "Hate-fuelled 'Gays Against Groomers' invited on Fox News about being suspended from Twitter." *Pink News*, August 22, 2022. https://www.pinknews.co.uk/2022/08/22/gays-against-groomers-founder-fox-news-twitter-ban/.

CISION PRWeb. "Starving Polar Bear Images Inspired Climate Activist Greta Thunberg but Dr. Crockford Says Polar Bears are Thriving in a New Video from Friends of Science," CISION PRWeb, November 15, 2022. https://www.prweb.com/releases/starving_polar_bear_images_inspired_climate_activist_greta_thunberg_but_dr_crockford_says_polar_bears_are_thriving_in_a_new_video_from_friends_of_science/prweb16267141.htm.

Clifford, Catherine. "White House is pushing ahead research to cool Earth by reflecting back sunlight." CNBC, October 13, 2022. https://www.cnbc.com/2022/10/13/what-is-solar-geoengineering-sunlight-reflection-risks-and-benefits.html.

Clown World *Honk Honk.* "'Covid is critical because this is what convinces people to accept, to legitimize, total biometric surveillance.'" YouTube video, May 21, 2022. https://www.youtube.com/watch?v=hm7lTEoTe_Q.

The Committee to Unleash Prosperity. "The Tragedy of Sri Lanka: A Cautionary Tale On 'Going Green.'" The Committee to Unleash Prosperity website, July 11, 2022. https://committeetounleashprosperity.com/hotlines/the-tragedy-of-sri-lanka-a-cautionary-tale-on-going-green/.

Concha, Joe. "Jane Fonda calls coronavirus 'God's gift to the left.'" *The Hill*, October 7, 2020. https://thehill.com/homenews/media/520039-jane-fonda-calls-covid-19-gods-gift-to-the-left/.

Congress.gov. "H.Res.109 – Recognizing the duty of the Federal Government to create a Green New Deal." Congress.gov, February 7, 2019. https://www..gov/bill/116th-congress/house-resolution/109/text.

Corsi, Jerome. *The Truth About Energy, Global Warming, and Climate Change.* New York: Post Hill Press, 2022.

Courtois, Stephane et al. *The Black Book of Communism: Crimes, Terror, Repression.* Cambridge, MA: Harvard University Press, 1999.

Crockford, Susan. *The Polar Bear Catastrophe That Never Happened.* The Global Warming Policy Foundation, 2019.

Crowe, Jack. "Ocasio Cortez: 'The World is Going to End In Twelve Years If We Don't Address Climate Change.'" Yahoo! News, January 22, 2019. https://news.yahoo.com/ocasio-cortez-world-going-end-150517060.html.

Curl, Joseph. "Experts Finally Declare Imperial College Coronavirus Model That Predicted 2.2M Dead In U.S. 'Totally Unreliable.'" *The Daily Wire*, May 17, 2020. https://www.dailywire.com/news/experts-finally-declare-imperial-college-coronavirus-model-that-predicted-2-2m-dead-in-u-s-totally-unreliable.

Curry, Judith. "The paradox of the climate change consensus." Judith Curry website, April 17, 2016. https://judithcurry.com/2016/04/17/the-paradox-of-the-climate-change-consensus/.

DailyTruthReport. "World Economic Forum: 'By 2030, you'll own NOTHING and you'll be happy about it.'" Rumble video, January 31, 2021. https://rumble.com/vdgi1h-world-economic-forum-by-2030-youll-own-nothing-and-youll-be-happy-about-it.html.

D'Angelo, Chris. "93 Percent Of The Great Barrier Reef Is Practically Dead." *HuffPost*, April 21, 2016. https://www.huffpost.com/entry/climate-change-destroying-great-barrier-reef_n_571918e6e4b0d912d5fde8d4.

Deenan, Patrick. *Why Liberalism Failed.* New York: Yale University Press, 2018.

Desmet, Mattias. *The Psychology of Totalitarianism.* London: Chelsea Green Publishing, 2022.

DiAngelo, Robin. *White Fragility.* Boston: Beacon Press Books, 2018.

Dillon, Seth. Twitter post, August 30, 2022. https://twitter.com/sethdillon/status/1564607389785100295?s=21&t=UIDRbWruXmp3rpi68EBYuA.

DiLorenzo, Thomas. *The Politically Correct Guide to Economics*. Washington, DC: Regnery, 2022.

DiLorenzo, Thomas. *The Problem with Socialism*. Washington, DC: Regnery, 2026.

DiLorenzo, "The Rise of Economic Fascism in America." *LewRockwell.com*, September 7, 2021. https://www.lewrockwell.com/2021/09/thomas-dilorenzo/the-rise-of-economic-fascism-in-america/.

Disclose.tv. Twitter post, October 2, 2022. https://twitter.com/disclosetv/status/1576522107051446273?s=21&t=WnTR7d4uoO5gid-Defbu9AA.

Donner, Tim. "The Sports Media: Just as Biased as Their 'News' Brethren." *Liberty Nation News*, February 26, 2017. https://www.libertynation.com/sports-media-bias/.

Downey, Caroline. "Biden Claims School Children Don't Belong to Parents 'When They're in the Classroom.'" *National Review*, April 27, 2022. https://www.nationalreview.com/news/biden-claims-school-children-dont-belong-to-parents-when-theyre-in-the-classroom/.

Dreher, Rod. "Transgenderism As Transhumanism." *The American Conservative*, July 12, 2018. https://www.theamericanconservative.com/transgenderism-as-transhumanism/.

Duncan, Clifton. Twitter post, October 20, 2022. https://twitter.com/cliftonaduncan/status/1583207340936830976?s=21&t=0AmkdAJNruC4IAXOXEYcfQ.

Durden, Tyler. "Doug Casey On The WEF's Plan For Mankind And What Comes Next." *Zero Hedge*, November 9, 2022. https://www.zerohedge.com/geopolitical/doug-casey-wefs-plan-mankind-and-what-comes-next.

Ehrlich, Paul. *The Population Bomb*. New York: Ballantine Books, Inc., 1971.

Eisenstein, Charles. *Climate: A New Story*. Berkeley, CA: Creative Commons, 2018.

Elder, Larry. *Double Standards: The Selective Outrage of the Left*. Hermosa Beach, CA: Creators Publishing, 2017.

Elder, Larry. Twitter post, October 20, 2022. https://twitter.com/larryelder/status/1583310284143267841?s=21&t=BMo2tvw3vPfARQUmZVgnIA.

Elder, Larry, with Epoch Times. "Larry Elder SCHOOLS Woke Liberals | Larry Elder." YouTube video, November 13, 2020. https://www.youtube.com/watch?v=1xoDvfJK5yE.

Environmental Progress. *Environmental Progress* website, n.d. https://environmentalprogress.org/the-case-against-environmental-alarmism.

Epstein, Alex. *Fossil Future: Why Global Human Flourishing Requires More Oil, Coal, and Natural Gas—Not Less.* New York: Portfolio/Penguin, 2022.Epstein, Alex. Twitter post, August 31, 2022. https://twitter.com/AlexEpstein/status/1565009174194446336.

Epstein, Robert. "Why Google Poses a Serious Threat to Democracy, and How to End That Threat." American Institute for Behavioral Research and Technology, June 16, 2019. https://www.judiciary.senate.gov/imo/media/doc/Epstein%20Testimony.pdf.

Espaillat et al. "An exploratory study on microaggressions in medical school: What are they and why should we care?" *Perspectives on Medical Education.* 2019, 8(3): 143–51. https://www.ncbi.nlm.nih.gov/pmc/articles/PMC6565651/.

The European Union Times. "University of California says you are a racist if you say 'the human race.'" *The European Union Times,* August 13, 2015. https://www.eutimes.net/2015/08/university-of-california-says-you-are-a-racist-if-you-say-the-human-race/.

Fernandez, Henry. "Facebook CEO Mark Zuckerberg acknowledges Silicon Valley left-wing bias." FOXBusiness, April 10, 2018. https://www.foxbusiness.com/politics/facebook-ceo-mark-zuckerberg-acknowledges-silicon-valley-left-wing-bias.

Feshbach, Murray, and Alfred Friendly, Jr. *Ecocide in the USSR: Health and Nature Under Siege.* New York: Basic Books, 1992.

Firing Line with Margaret Hoover | PBS. "Ai Weiwei | Full Episode 11.12.21 | Firing Line with Margaret Hoover | PBS." YouTube video, November 12, 2021. https://www.youtube.com/watch?v=OjYjhxGJ-sI.

Fleischer, Ari. *Suppression, Deception, Snobbery, and Bias: Why the Press Gets So Much Wrong—And Just Doesn't Care.* New York: Broadside Books, 2022.

Fleming, Sean. "Good grub: why we might be eating insects soon." World Economic Forum website. July 16, 2018. https://www.weforum.org/agenda/2018/07/good-grub-why-we-might-be-eating-insects-soon/.

Fleming, Sean. "This 3D-printed steak could help us reduce meat consumption." World Economic Forum website, July 8, 2020. https://www.weforum.org/agenda/2020/07/3d-printed-steak-cut-meat-consumption/.

Forgas, et al. (Ed.). *Social Psychology and Politics*. New York: Routledge, 2015.

The Fort with Chris Powers. "Alex Epstein – The Future is Fossil Fuels." YouTube video, May 11, 2022. https://www.youtube.com/watch?v=TQUh9lsfRYc.

The Forum of Young Global Leaders Shaping the Future. Search page, November 4, 2022. https://www.younggloballeaders.org/community?utf8=%E2%9C%93&q=&x=0&y=0&status=&class_year=&sector=&region=#results.

Fox News. "Martin Luther King Jr.'s famous 'I Have a Dream' speech: Full text." Fox News website, January 27, 2022. https://www.foxnews.com/us/transcript-of-martin-luther-king-jr-s-i-have-a-dream-speech.

The Freedom Records. "Growing Up In The Cultural Revolution, Xi Van Fleet The Freedom Records." YouTube video, June 12, 2022. https://www.youtube.com/watch?v=4wl0fS0aIDw.

Funnell, Dominica. "Northern Territory placed into lockout until noon on Monday, unvaccinated residents to enter lockdown." Sky News Australia, January 6, 2022. https://www.skynews.com.au/australia-news/coronavirus/northern-territory-placed-into-lockout-until-noon-on-monday-unvaccinated-residents-to-enter-lockdown/news-story/85112b44c171b0196694c65807d1ed63.

Future Thinkers, "Clean Up, Wake Up, Grow Up," YouTube video, December 30, 2019. https://www.youtube.com/watch?v=2mROP49BeJc.

Future Thinkers. "Showing Up For Life – Ken Wilber." YouTube video, January 2, 2020. https://www.youtube.com/watch?v=2-K-k0YrR1w.

Future Thinkers. "Who Are The 2nd Tier Thinkers? – Ken Wilber." YouTube video, December 22, 2019. https://www.youtube.com/watch?v=8o2_dbLq070.

Gays Against Groomers. "About" page. Gays Against Groomers website, n.d. https://www.gaysagainstgroomers.com/about.

Gleick, James. *Chaos*. New York: Open Road Media, 1987.

Gober, Mark. *An End to Upside Down Contact: UFOs, Aliens, and Spirits—and Why Their Ongoing Interaction with Human Civilization Matters*. Cardiff-by-the-Sea, CA: Waterside Press, 2022.

Gober, Mark. *An End to Upside Down Liberty: Turning Traditional Political Thinking on Its Head to Break Free from Enslavement*. Cardiff-by-the-Sea, CA: Waterside Press, 2021.

Gober, Mark. *An End to Upside Down Living: Reorienting Our Consciousness to Live Better and Save the Human Species*. Cardiff-by-the-Sea, CA: Waterside Press, 2020.

Gober, Mark. *An End to Upside Down Thinking: Dispelling the Myth That the Brain Produces Consciousness, and the Implications for Everyday Life*. Cardiff-by-the-Sea, CA: Waterside Press, 2018.

Gober, Mark, and Blue Duck Media. *Where Is My Mind?* Podcast (Eps. 1 through 8). June–September 2019.

Golden, C. Douglas. "Doctors Give Kids Drugs That Can Chemically Castrate Them—Just Like Pedophiles." *Western Journal*, June 6, 2022. https://www.westernjournal.com/doctors-give-kids-drugs-can-chemically-castrate-just-like-pedophiles/.

Golding, Bruce. "79% say 'truthful' coverage of Hunter Biden's laptop would have changed 2020 election." *New York Post*, August 26, 2022. https://nypost.com/2022/08/26/2020-election-outcome-would-differ-with-hunter-biden-laptop-coverage-poll/.

Greyson, Bruce. *After: A Doctor Explores What Near-Death Experiences Reveal about Life and Beyond*. New York: St. Martin's Essentials, 2021.

Groseclose, Tim. *Left Turn: How Liberal Media Bias Distorts the American Mind*. New York: St. Martin's Griffin: 2011.

Gross, Neil. "Why Is Hollywood So Liberal?" *New York Times*, January 27, 2018. https://www.nytimes.com/2018/01/27/opinion/sunday/hollywood-liberal.html.

Haidt, Jonathan. *The Righteous Mind: Why Good People are Divided by Politics and Religion*. New York: Vintage Books, 2012.

Hansas, John. "The Myth of the Rule of Law," 1995. In *The Anarchist Handbook*, organized by Michael Malice. Michael Malice, 2021.

Hare, Robert. *Without Conscience: The Disturbing World of the Psychopaths Among Us*. New York: The Guilford Press, 1999.

Harrington, Mary. "Climate change is not making children obese." Unherd, August 15, 2022. https://unherd.com/thepost/climate-change-is-not-making-children-obese/.

Harris, Nicholas. "Greta Thunberg throws in her lot with the anti-capitalist Left." Unherd, October 31, 2022. https://unherd.com/thepost/greta-thunberg-throws-her-lot-in-with-the-anti-capitalist-left/.

Hart, Robert. "France's Macron Vows To 'Piss Off' Unvaccinated With New Restrictions." *Forbes*, January 5, 2022. https://www.forbes.com/sites/roberthart/2022/01/05/frances-macron-stokes-outrage-after-vowing-to-anger-unvaccinated-with-tough-new-restrictions/?sh=117430ff2c0f.

Harvey, Fiona. "Equivalent of Covid emissions drop needed every two years – study," *The Guardian*, March 3, 2021. https://www.theguardian.com/environment/2021/mar/03/global-lockdown-every-two-years-needed-to-meet-paris-co2-goals-study.

Hathaway, Candace. "CEO announces 11% cut to staff, promises 'anti-racist' layoffs." Blaze Media, September 15, 2022. https://www.theblaze.com/news/twilio-anti-racist-firings.

Hauf, Patrick. "Biden administration funds studies on danger of transgender hormonal treatments even as it pushes them on kids." Fox News, October 20, 2022. https://www.foxnews.com/politics/biden-funds-studies-dangers-transgender-hormone-treatments.

Hayek, Friedrich. *The Fatal Conceit*. London: Routledge, 1988. https://mises.at/static/literatur/Buch/hayek-the-fatal-conceit.pdf.

Hayek, Friedrich. *The Road to Serfdom*. London and New York: Routledge Classics, 2001.

Heldt, Brianna. "American Psychological Association Labels 'Traditional Masculinity' as 'Harmful.'" Townhall website, January 7, 2019. https://townhall.com/tipsheet/briannaheldt/2019/01/07/

american-psychological-association-labels-traditional-masculinity-as-harmful-n2538637.

Hewer, Christopher, and Evanthia Lyons (Ed.). *Political Psychology: A Sociological Approach*. Hoboken, New Jersey: Wiley Blackwell, 2018.

Hoffer, Eric. *The True Believer: Thoughts on the Nature of Mass Movements*. New York: HarperCollins, 2002.

Holthaus, Eric. Twitter post, October 7, 2018. https://twitter.com/EricHolthaus/status/1049339997827084295.

Hoppe, Hans-Hermann. *Democracy: The God that Failed: The Economics and Politics of Monarchy, Democracy, and Natural Order*. New York: Routledge, 2001.

Housman, Dylan. "Euthanasia Is Now A Leading Cause Of Death In Canada, And Ethicists Are Freaking Out." *Daily Wire*, August 12, 2022. https://dailycaller.com/2022/08/12/canada-euthanasia-disability-human-rights-mental-health/.

Huber et al., "UN Sustainable Development Goals—The Leading ESG Framework for Large Companies." Harvard Law School-Forum on Corporate Governance, October 4, 2018. https://corpgov.law.harvard.edu/2018/10/04/un-sustainable-development-goals-the-leading-esg-framework-for-large-companies/.

Icax. *Absolute Zero* Report. Icax website, n.d., https://www.icax.co.uk/Absolute_Zero_Report.html.

Ice Age Farmer Resources. "'The idea of a Soul, Free Will -- these are Over!' - Technocracy explained by Prof Yuval Harari." YouTube video, September 23, 2021. https://www.youtube.com/watch?v=NV0CtZga7qM.

Imanuelson, Peter. "The credit card that tracks your CO2 emissions." *The Freedom Corner with PeterSweden*, July 27, 2022. https://petersweden.substack.com/p/card-co2-tracking.

Impact Team Report. *The Weather Conspiracy: The Coming of the New Ice Age*. New York: Ballantine Books, 1977.

Investor's Business Daily. "Media Bias: Pretty Much All Of Journalism Now Leans Left, Study Shows," November 16, 2018. https://www.investors.com/politics/editorials/media-bias-left-study/.

James, Alexander. "More than 75 colleges host blacks-only graduation ceremonies." *The Washington Examiner*, May 21, 2019. https://www.washingtonexaminer.com/red-alert-politics/more-than-75-colleges-host-blacks-only-graduation-ceremonies.

The Joe Rogan Experience. "#1877-Jann Wenner." Spotify, October 2022. https://open.spotify.com/episode/4yb794L4eMgchIFx1d JtaW.

The Joe Rogan Experience. "#1776-Steven E. Koonin." Spotify, February 2022. https://open.spotify.com/episode/76RdMG5T-ne7H9jaP7mhkdk?si=VrAXD3pxTfeY4p-ygxVdbA&context=spotify%3Ashow%3A4rOoJ6Egrf8K2IrywzwOMk&nd=1.

Jezard, Adam. "Even as birth rates decline overpopulation remains a global challenge." World Economic Forum website, April 5, 2018. https://www.weforum.org/agenda/2018/04/almost-everywhere-people-are-having-fewer-children-so-do-we-still-need-to-worry-about-overpopulation.

Jones, Alex. *The Great Reset and the War for the World*. New York: Skyhorse Publishing, 2022.

Kahneman, Daniel. *Thinking, Fast and Slow*. New York: Farrar, Straus and Giroux, 2011.

Kasprak, Alex. "Did UN Official Say Nations Would Vanish If Global Warming Not Reversed by 2000?" Snopes, September 20, 2019. https://www.snopes.com/fact-check/nations-vanish-global-warming/.

Keene, Houston. "Republicans baffled that Ketanji Brown Jackson can't say what a woman is: 'It is a simple question.'" Fox News, March 23, 2022. https://www.foxnews.com/politics/republicans-baffled-ketanji-brown-jackson-define-woman.

Kelly, Edward et al. (Ed.) *Beyond Physicalism: Toward Reconciliation of Science and Spirituality*. Lanham, MD: Rowman & Littlefield,2015.

Kelly, Edward, and Paul Marshall et al. (Ed.) *Consciousness Unbound: Liberating Mind from the Tyranny of Materialism*, Lanham, MD: Rowman & Littlefield, 2021.

Kelly, Edward et al. (Ed.). *Irreducible Mind: Toward a Psychology For the 21st Century*. Lanham, MD: Rowman & Littlefield, 2010.

Kendi, Ibram X. *Antiracist Baby*. New York: KOKILA, 2020.

Kendi, Ibram X. *How to Be an Antiracist*. New York: Penguin Random House, 2019.

Kennedy Jr., Robert F. *A Letter to Liberals: Censorship and COVID: An Attack on Science and American Ideals*. New York: Skyhorse Publishing, 2022.

Kiderlin, Sophie. "Oil protesters arrested after throwing tomato soup at Van Gogh painting." CNBC, October 14, 2022. https://www.cnbc.com/2022/10/14/oil-protesters-arrested-after-throwing-tomato-soup-at-van-gogh-painting.html.

Kline, Jennifer. "Alyssa Milano on why Hollywood is so politically left-leaning." AOL, August 28, 2017. https://www.aol.com/article/entertainment/2017/08/30/alyssa-milano-on-why-hollywood-is-so-politically-left-leaning/23188416/.

Kling, Arnold. *The Three Languages of Politics: Talking Across the Political Divides*. Washington, DC: Cato Institute, 2017.

Knaus, Christopher and Nick Evershed. "Great Barrier Reef at 'terminal stage': scientists despair at latest coral bleaching data." *The Guardian*, April 9, 2017. https://www.theguardian.com/environment/2017/apr/10/great-barrier-reef-terminal-stage-australia-scientists-despair-latest-coral-bleaching-data.

Koonin, Steven. *Unsettled: What Climate Science Tells Us, What It Doesn't, and Why It Matters*. Dallas: BenBella Books, 2021.

Kraychick, Robert. "WEF Adviser Yuval Harari: 'We Just Don't Need the Vast Majority of the Population' in Today's World." Breitbart, August 10, 2022. https://www.breitbart.com/economy/2022/08/10/wef-adviser-yuval-harari-we-just-dont-need-the-vast-majority-of-the-population-in-todays-world/.

Kruger, Justin and David Dunning. "Unskilled and unaware of it: how difficulties in recognizing one's own incompetencelead to inflated self-assessments." *Journal of Personality and Social Psychology*, November 30, 1999. https://www.semanticscholar.org/paper/Unskilled-and-unaware-of-it%3A-how-difficulties-in-to-Kruger-Dunning/f2c80eef3585e0569e93ace0b9770cf76c8eb abc?p2df.

Lakoff, George. *Moral Politics: How Liberals and Conservatives Think*. Chicago: The University of Chicago Press, 2016.

Langton, Stacy. "Ban pornographic books in school libraries." *Washington Examiner*, November 16, 2021. https://www.washington examiner.com/restoring-america/community-family/ban-pornographic-books-in-school-libraries.

Lawton, Andrew. Twitter post, May 24, 2022. https://twitter.com/andrewlawton/status/1529045188764921856?s=21&t=_Oxr CqlGTguU2to_46w-2g.

Ledsom, Alex. "France Travel: Many Short-Haul Flights Outlawed From April." *Forbes*, April 3, 2022. https://www.forbes.com/sites/alexledsom/2022/04/03/france-travel-many-short-haul-flights-outlawed-from-april/?sh=71a0d2e27618.

Lee, Alexander. "What is programmable money?" *FEDS Notes*, June 23, 2021. https://www.federalreserve.gov/econres/notes/feds-notes/what-is-programmable-money-20210623.htm.

Lee, Michael. "'Strongly biased in favor of liberals': Psychologist says Google manipulated content ahead of election that swayed votes." *Washington Examiner*, November 25, 2020. https://www.washingtonexaminer.com/news/strongly-biased-in-favor-of-liberals-psychologist-says-google-manipulated-content-ahead-of-election-that-swayed-votes.

Levin, Mark. *American Marxism*. New York: Simon & Schuster, 2021.

Liang, Fan. "Gender Affirmation Surgeries." *Johns Hopkins Medicine*, n.d. https://www.hopkinsmedicine.org/health/wellness-and-prevention/gender-affirmation-surgeries.

LibertyInOurTime. "Society Without State: Private Law Society | Hans-Hermann Hoppe." YouTube video, May 17, 2012. https://www.youtube.com/watch?v=TlWGA9H5An4.

Lindsay, James. *Race Marxism: The Truth About Critical Race Theory and Praxis*. Orlando, FL: New Discourses, 2022.

Lindsay et al. "Academic Grievance Studies and the Corruption of Scholarship." Areo website, n.d. https://areomagazine.com/2018/10/02/academic-grievance-studies-and-the-corruption-of-scholarship/.

Lomborg, Bjorn. *False Alarm: How Climate Change Panic Costs Us Trillions, Hurts the Poor, and Fails to Fix the Planet*. New York: Hachette, 2021.

Lomborg, Bjorn. "More people die of cold: Media's heat-death climate obsession leads to lousy fixes." *New York Post*, July 14, 2021. https://nypost.com/2021/07/14/more-die-of-cold-medias-heat-death-climate-obsession-leads-to-lousy-fixes/.

Long, Jeffrey, with Paul Perry. *God and the Afterlife: The Groundbreaking New Evidence for God and Near-Death Experience*. New York: HarperCollins, 2016.

Love, Charles. *Race Crazy: BLM, 1619, and the Progressive Racism Movement*. New York: Emancipation Books, 2021.

Lukianoff, Greg and Jonathan Haidt. *The Coddling of the American Mind: How Good Intentions and Bad Ideas Are Setting up a Generation for Failure*. New York: Penguin Random House, 2019.

Lundgren, David. "Hide the Decline." *U.S. Senate Committee on Environment & Public Works*, December 14, 2019. https://www.epw.senate.gov/public/index.cfm/press-releases-all?ID=8F16552A-802A-23AD-465F-8858BEB85AC2.

Lungariello, Mark. "Video of drag queen gyrating in front of child has Texas pols pushing for legislative action." *New York Post*, October 18, 2022. https://nypost.com/2022/10/18/video-of-drag-queen-gyrating-next-to-child-sparks-backlash/.

Mackey, John, and Raj Sisodia. *Conscious Capitalism: Liberating the Heroic Spirit of Business*. Boston: Harvard Business School Publishing Corporation, 2013.

Magness, Phillip. "Imperial College Predicted Catastrophe in Every Country on Earth. Then the Models Failed." American Institute for Economic Research, May 5, 2021. https://www.aier.org/article/imperial-college-predicted-catastrophe-in-every-country-on-earth-then-the-models-failed/.

Mancini, Maggie. "Dr. Rachel Levine named as one of USA Today's Women of the Year." Philly Voice, March 12, 2022. https://www.phillyvoice.com/rachel-levine-health-secretary-women-of-the-year-usa-today/.

Marshall, Winston. Twitter post. November 14, 2022, https://twitter.com/mrwinmarshall/status/1592236611898834944?s=21&t=ti6PMV0ysGvpjPPELiHp6A.

Mastercard, "DO Black – the world's first credit card with a carbon limit." Mastercard website, April 30, 2019. https://www.master

card.com/news/europe/sv-se/nyhetsrum/pressmeddelanden/
sv-se/2019/april/do-black-the-world-s-first-credit-card-with-
a-carbon-limit/.

Martyn, Amy. "New report describes dangers of giving Lupron to
kids." *Consumer Affairs*, February 3, 2017. https://www.consumer
affairs.com/news/new-report-describes-dangers-of-giving-
lupron-to-kids-020317.html.

McCarthy, Michael. "ESPN's own study indicates big chunk of
viewers perceive network has liberal bias." *Sporting News*, June
6, 2017. https://www.sportingnews.com/us/other-sports/news/
espn-political-bias-liberal-conservative-langer-research-
associates-hank-williams-jr-colin-kaepernick-curt-schilling/
5goo5xpn3hhd1eiwiqm9vmahl.

McFarlane, Sarah and Karen Abnett. "'African nations tell COP27
fossil fuels will tackle poverty.'" Reuters, November 10, 2022.
https://www.reuters.com/business/cop/african-hosted-climate-
talks-give-fossil-fuel-voice-2022-11-10/.

McKenna, John. "Fancy a bug burger? A Swiss supermarket is selling
food made from insects." World Economic Forum website,
August 22, 2017. https://www.weforum.org/agenda/2017/08/
fancy-a-bug-burger-a-swiss-supermarket-is-selling-food-
made-from-insects.

McKie, Robin. "President 'has four years to save Earth.'" *The Guardian*,
January 17, 2009. https://www.theguardian.com/environment/
2009/jan/18/jim-hansen-obama.

McKie, Robin. "Royal Mail's Nobel Guru In Telepathy Row." *The
Observer*, September 29, 2001. https://www.theguardian.com/
uk/2001/sep/30/robinmckie.theobserver.

McMaken, Ryan. "The Alex Jones Verdict Shows the Danger of Defamation Laws." Mises Institute website, October 13, 2022. https://
mises.org/power-market/alex-jones-verdict-shows-danger-
defamation-laws.

McMaken, Ryan. *Breaking Away: The Case for Secession, RadicalDe-
centralization, and Smaller Polities.* Auburn, AL: Mises Institute,
2022.

McTaggart, India. "Greta Thunberg: It's time to transform the West's
oppressive and racist capitalist system." *The Telegraph*, November
2, 2022. https://www.msn.com/en-gb/entertainment/music/

greta-thunberg-its-time-to-overthrow-the-wests-oppressive-and-racist-capitalist-system/ar-AA13Ebby.

McWhorter, John. *Woke Racism: How a New Religion Has Betrayed Black America*. New York: Portfolio/Penguin, 2021.

Migdon, Brooke. "Canadian woman becomes first person diagnosed as suffering from 'climate change.'" *The Hill*, November 8, 2021. https://thehill.com/changing-america/sustainability/climate-change/580527-canadian-woman-becomes-first-person-diagnosed/.

Miller, Jennifer Jean. "Twitter CEO Admits Censoring Hunter Biden Story Was 'Wrong,'" *Western Journal*, November 17, 2020. https://www.westernjournal.com/twitter-ceo-admits-censoring-hunter-biden-story-wrong/.

Miller, Joshua Rhett. "Transgender swimmer Lia Thomas sets pool record in 500-yard freestyle win at Ivy League Championship." *New York Post*, February 18, 2022. https://nypost.com/2022/02/18/trans-swimmer-lia-thomas-wins-500-yard-freestyle-at-ivy-league-championship/.

Miltimore, Jon. "Hayek: Social Justice Demands the Unequal Treatment of Individuals." *FEE Stories*, November 13, 2018. https://fee.org/articles/hayek-social-justice-demands-the-unequal-treatment-of-individuals/.

misesmedia. "The Attractiveness of Austrian Economics | Thomas E. Woods, Jr." YouTube video, July 21, 2013. https://www.youtube.com/watch?v=DStLhWMRERM.

misesmedia. "An Austrian Critique of Mainstream Economics | Walter Block." YouTube video, August 2, 2016. https://www.youtube.com/watch?v=ua_tJbdmNmo.

misesmedia. "The Birth of the Austrian School | Joseph T. Salerno." YouTube video, July 16, 2019. https://www.youtube.com/watch?v=xdepDj8C4D0.

misesmedia. "The Curse of Economic Nationalism | Thomas J. Dilorenzo." YouTube video, July 22, 2021. https://www.youtube.com/watch?v=GNW5cMJOsPw.

misesmedia. "The Mises View: "Income Inequality" | Joseph T. Salerno." YouTube video, February 6, 2014. https://www.youtube.com/watch?v=HBIkj6UdlQg.

misesmedia. "Property and the Social Order | Hans-Hermann Hoppe." YouTube video, August 19, 2011. https://www.youtube.com/watch?v=AQmMe2IeGPU.

misesmedia. "Rothbard's Case Against the Fed." YouTube video, February 5, 2021. https://www.youtube.com/watch?v=Pv4CwF-579s.

misesmedia. "Taking Rights Seriously | Judge Andrew P. Napolitano." YouTube video, July 13, 2020. https://www.youtube.com/watch?v=3QMSDJn2wSU.

misesmedia. "Tate Fegley: Crime and Punishment in a Libertarian Society." YouTube video, July 9, 2015. https://www.youtube.com/watch?v=8Tonyri5Xys.

misesmedia. "Ten Things You Should Know About Socialism | Thomas J. DiLorenzo," YouTube video, July 22, 2019.

misesmedia. "What Is Cronyism?" YouTube video, February 4, 2021. https://www.youtube.com/watch?v=4b5cyrVmafU&t=4s.

Moody, Raymond. *Glimpses of Eternity: An Investigation into Shared Death Experiences.* London: Rider, 2011.

Moore, Mark. "Sen. Hawley called transphobic in heated exchange with woke prof over pregnancy." *New York Post,* July 12, 2022. https://nypost.com/2022/07/12/sen-hawley-called-transphobic-in-heated-exchange-with-woke-prof-over-pregnancy/.

Moore, Patrick. *Fake Invisible Catastrophes and Threats of Doom.* Comox, B.C.: Ecosense Environmental Inc., 2021.

Morano, Marc. *The Great Reset: Global Elites and the Permanent Lockdown.* Washington, DC: Regnery Publishing, 2022.

Morano, Marc. *Green Fraud: Why the Green New Deal Is Even Worse Than You Think.* Washington, DC: Regnery Publishing, 2021.

Morrison, Chris. "Satellite Temperature Data Show Almost All Climate Model Forecasts Over the Last 40 Years Were Wrong." *Daily Skeptic,* October 8, 2022. https://dailysceptic.org/2022/10/08/satellite-temperature-data-show-almost-all-climate-model-forecasts-over-the-last-40-years-were-wrong/.

Mossbridge J., P. Tressoldi, and J. Utts. "Predictive Physiological Anticipation Preceding Seemingly Unpredictable Stimuli: A Meta-Analysis." *Frontiers in Psychology* 3 (2012): 390. https://www.frontiersin.org/articles/10.3389/fpsyg.2012.00390/full.

Murdock, Corinne. "'Minor-Attracted Person': Inside The Growing Effort To Destigmatize Pedophilia." *Daily Wire*, n.d. https://www.dailywire.com/news/minor-attracted-person-inside-the-growing-effort-to-destigmatize-pedophilia.

Murray, Douglas. *The War on the West*. New York: HarperCollins, 2022.

Nelson, Roger et al. "Correlations of Continuous Random Data with Major World Events." *Foundations of Physics Letters*, 15 (2002): 537–50.

Nisbett, Richard. "Fundamental Attribution Error." *Edge*, 2017. https://www.edge.org/response-detail/27014.

Notheis, Asher. "'Don Lemon says unvaccinated people should be 'shunned' or 'left behind.'" Yahoo! News, September 16, 2001. https://news.yahoo.com/don-lemon-says-unvaccinated-people-175300636.html.

O'Neill, Natalie. "Fauci says attacks on him are 'attacks on science.'" *New York Post*, June 9, 2021. https://nypost.com/2021/06/09/fauci-says-attacks-on-him-are-attacks-on-science/.

Onians, Charles. "Snowfalls are now just a thing of the past." *The Independent*, March 20, 2000. https://web.archive.org/web/20130422045937/http://www.independent.co.uk/environment/snowfalls-are-now-just-a-thing-of-the-past-724017.html.

Orwell, George. *Animal Farm*. New York: Signet Classics, 2020.

Palumbo, Matt. "Why Larry Summers Doesn't Understand Economic Inequality." Mises Institute website, May 5, 2015. https://mises.org/library/why-larry-summers-doesnt-understand-economic-inequality.

Parsa, Cyrus. *The Great Reset*. La Jolla, CA: The AI Organization, 2021.

Paul, Rand, with Kelly Ashby Paul. *The Case Against Socialism*. New York: Broadside Books, 2019.

Paul, Ron. *End the Fed*. New York, NY: Grand Central Publishing, 2009.

Paul, Ron. "The 'Great Reset' is about Expanding Government Power and Suppressing Liberty."

Ron Paul Institute for Peace and Prosperity website, January 4, 2021. http://www.ronpaulinstitute.org/archives/featured-articles/2021/

january/04/the-great-reset-is-about-expanding-government-power-and-suppressing-liberty/.

Paul, Ron. *Liberty Defined: 50 Essential Issues That Affect Our Freedom.* New York: Grand Central Publishing, 2011.

Perlroth, Nicole. "One Man's Fight With Google Over a Security Warning." *New York Times,* January 5, 2012. https://archive.nytimes.com/bits.blogs.nytimes.com/2012/01/05/one-mans-fight-with-google-over-a-security-warning/.

Peters, William. *At Heaven's Door: What Shared Journeys to the Afterlife Teach About Dying Well and Living Better.* New York: Simon & Schuster, 2022.

PhilosophyInsights. "Roger Scruton: Why Intellectuals are Mostly Left." YouTube video, March 26, 2019. https://www.youtube.com/watch?v=FYo4KMhUx9c.

Pierre, Dion. "Demands for Segregated Housing at Williams College Are Not News." *The National Review,* May 8, 2019. https://www.nationalreview.com/2019/05/american-colleges-segregated-housing-graduation-ceremonies/.

Piro, Graham. "Yang: Climate Change May Require Elimination of Car Ownership." *Washington Free Beacon,* September 19, 2019. https://freebeacon.com/politics/yang-well-eliminate-car-ownership-to-fight-climate-change/.

Pluckrose et al. "Understanding the 'Grievance Studies Affair' Papers and Why They Should Be Reinstated: A Response to Geoff Cole," *Sociological Methods & Research.* Vol. 50, Issue 4 (2021). https://journals.sagepub.com/doi/full/10.1177/00491241211009946.

Pluckrose, Helen, and James Lindsay. *Cynical Theories: How Activist Scholarship Made Everything about Race, Gender, and Identity—and Why This Harms Everyone.* Durham, NC: Pitchstone Publishing, 2020.

Plume, Karl. "Could insect farms meet our food demands of the future?" World Economic Forum website, https://www.weforum.org/agenda/2018/04/insect-farms-gear-up-to-feed-soaring-global-protein-demand.

Plumer, Bradford. "Rebranding Global Warming." *New Republic,* September 19, 2010. https://newrepublic.com/article/77820/rebranding-global-warming.

Pollak, Joel. "Don't Charge that Electric Vehicle: California Braces for Energy Shortage Thru Labor Day." Breitbart, August 31, 2022. https://www.breitbart.com/economy/2022/08/31/dont-charge-that-electric-vehicle-california-braces-for-energy-shortage-thru-labor-day/.

Prager, Dennis. "If the Road to Hell Is Paved With Good Intentions, With What Do We Pave the Road to Heaven?" *The Dennis Prager Show*, June 7, 2022. https://dennisprager.com/column/if-the-road-to-hell-is-paved-with-good-intentions-with-what-do-we-pave-the-road-to-heaven/.

Prager, Dennis. "Leftism Is Not Liberalism." *The Dennis Prager Show* website, September 12, 2017. https://dennisprager.com/column/leftism-is-not-liberalism/.

PragerU. "Does it Feel Good or Does it Do Good? Left vs. Right #2." PragerU website, December 14, 2015. https://www.prageru.com/video/does-it-feel-good-or-does-it-do-good-left-vs-right-2.

PragerU. "Religion of Green." YouTube video, September 25, 2020. https://www.youtube.com/watch?v=UTgNtvTuYRU.

PragerU, "Students vs. Chinese: Cultural Appropriation." YouTube video, October 23, 2019. https://www.youtube.com/watch?v=GNXm7juuM-8.

PragerU. "Students vs. Mexicans: Cultural Appropriation." YouTube video, October 24, 2018. https://www.youtube.com/watch?v=IT2UH74ksJ4.

Prior, Ian. "The definitive proof critical race theory is being taught in our schools." Fox News, June 20, 2022. https://www.foxnews.com/opinion/proof-critical-race-theory-taught-schools.

Project Veritas. "PART 1: CNN Director ADMITS Network Engaged in 'Propaganda' to Remove Trump from Presidency... 'Our Focus Was to Get Trump Out of Office'...'I Came to CNN Because I Wanted to Be a Part of That.'" *Project Veritas*, April 13, 2021. https://www.projectveritas.com/news/part-1-cnn-director-admits-network-engaged-in-propaganda-to-remove-trump/.

Psychology Today Staff, "Dunning-Kruger Effect." Psychology Today website, n.d. https://www.psychologytoday.com/us/basics/dunning-kruger-effect.

Radin, Dean. "Publications." Dean Radin website, n.d. https://www.deanradin.com/publications.

Radin, Dean. *Real Magic: Ancient Wisdom, Modern Science, and a Guide to the Secret Power of the Universe*. New York: Harmony, 2018.

Radin, Dean. *Supernormal: Science, Yoga, and the Evidence for Extraordinary Psychic Abilities*. New York: Random House, 2013.

Radin, Dean, Nelson Roger, Dobyns York, Houtkooper Joop. "Reexamining psychokinesis: comment on Bösch, Steinkamp, and Boller." *Psychological Bulletin*. 2006;132(4):529–32; discussion 533–7.

Ramaswamy, Vivek. *Nation of Victims*. New York: Hachette Book Group, 2022.

Ramaswamy, Vivek. *Woke, Inc.: Inside Corporate America's Social Justice Scam*. New York: Center Street, 2021.

Rasheed, Zaheena, and Rathindra Kuruwita. "Sri Lanka faces 'man-made' food crisis as farmers stop planting." Al Jazeera, May 18, 2022. https://www.aljazeera.com/news/2022/5/18/a-food-crisis-looms-in-sri-lanka-as-farmers-give-up-on-planting.

Rathnakumar S. "Andrew Dessler vs. Steven Koonin: Climate Change Debate." YouTube video, September 6, 2022. https://www.youtube.com/watch?v=IGNSGyhK_z0.

ReasonTV. "Russia and the Global Green Energy Crisis: Live With Michael Shellenberger." YouTube video, October 6, 2022. https://www.youtube.com/watch?v=H9qdQ1u_BDQ.

Rectenwald, Michael. *Beyond Woke*. London: New English Review Press, 2020.

Reilly, Patrick. "Teammates say they are uncomfortable changing in locker room with trans UPenn swimmer Lia Thomas." *New York Post*, January 27, 2022. https://nypost.com/2022/01/27/teammates-are-uneasy-changing-in-locker-room-with-trans-upenn-swimmer-lia-thomas/.

Reilly, Patrick. "Transgender Rikers inmate sentenced to 7 years for raping female prisoner." *New York Post*, April 25, 2022. https://nypost.com/2022/04/25/transgender-rikers-inmate-gets-7-years-for-raping-female-prisoner/.

Revkin, Andrew. "A Climate Scientist Who EngagesSkeptics." *New York Times*, November 27, 2009. https://archive.nytimes.com/dotearth.blogs.nytimes.com/2009/11/27/a-climate-scientist-on-climate-skeptics/.

Richardson, Valerie. "No racial bias in police shootings, study by Harvard professor shows." *Washington Times*, July 11, 2016. https://www.washingtontimes.com/news/2016/jul/11/no-racial-bias-police-shootings-study-harvard-prof/.

Richardson, Valerie. "Republican recall frontrunner Larry Elder called 'Black face of white supremacy.'" *Washington Times*, August 20, 2021. https://www.washingtontimes.com/news/2021/aug/20/los-angeles-times-column-larry-elder-black-face-wh/.

Richardson, Valerie. "Susan Crockford fired after finding polar bears thriving despite climate change." *Washington Times*, October 20, 2019. https://www.washingtontimes.com/news/2019/oct/20/susan-crockford-fired-after-finding-polar-bears-th/.

Rindsberg, Ashley. *The Gray Lady Winked: How the New York Times's Misreporting, Distortions, & Fabrications Radically Altered History.* New York: Midnight Oil Publishers LLC, 2021.

Robinson, Charlie. *Hypocrazy: Surviving in a World of Cultural Double Standards.* Charlie Robinson, 2021.

Robinson, Nathan. *Why You Should Be a Socialist.* New York: All Point Books, 2019.

Rogers, Zachary. "Nearly half of Dems say fines, prison time appropriate for questioning vaccines, poll says." ABC7, January 17, 2022. https://katv.com/amp/news/nation-world/half-of-dems-believe-fines-prison-time-appropriate-for-questioning-vaccine-poll-says.

Romeo, John. "Disinformation is a growing crisis. Governments, business and individuals can help stem the tide." World Economic Forum website, October 11, 2022. https://www.weforum.org/agenda/2022/10/how-to-address-disinformation/.

Rose, Larken. *The Most Dangerous Superstition.* Larken Rose, 2012.

Rossini, Chris. Twitter post, September 26, 2022. https://twitter.com/ChrisRossini/status/1574431709701062657.

Rothbard, Murray N. *America's Great Depression.* Auburn, AL: The Ludwig von Mises Institute, 2000.

Rothbard, Murray N. *Anatomy of the State.* Auburn, AL: The Ludwig von Mises Institute, 2009.

Rothbard, Murray N. *The Case Against the Fed.* Auburn, AL: The Ludwig von Mises Institute, 2007.

Rothbard, Murray N. "Egalitarianism as a Revolt Against Nature and Other Essays." Auburn, AL: Ludwig von Mises Institute, 2000. https://cdn.mises.org/Egalitarianism%20as%20a%20Revolt%20Against%20Nature,%20and%20Other%20Essays_2.pdf.

Rothbard, Murray N. *The Ethics of Liberty.* New York: New York University Press, 2002.

Rothbard, Murray N. *For a New Liberty: The Libertarian Manifesto.* Auburn, AL: The Ludwig von Mises Institute, 2006.

Rothbard, Murray N. "A Future of Peace and Capitalism," Lew Rockwell website, August 3, 2020. https://www.lewrockwell.com/2020/08/murray-n-rothbard/a-future-of-peace-and-capitalism/.

Rothbard, Murray N. *Man, Economy, and State: A Treatise on Economic Principles with Power and Market: Government and the Economy.* Auburn, AL: The Ludwig von Mises Institute, 2009.

Rothbard, Murray N. "Myth and Truth About Libertarianism." The Mises Institute website, July 20, 2019. https://mises.org/library/myth-and-truth-about-libertarianism.

Rothbard, Murray N. *Society Without a State.* December 28, 1974. https://www.lewrockwell.com/1970/01/murray-n-rothbard/how-anarchism-can-work/.

Rubin, Dave. *Don't Burn This Book: Thinking for Yourself in an Age of Unreason.* New York: Sentinel: 2020.

The Rubin Report. "Conservatives, Black Lives Matter, Racism | Larry Elder | POLITICS | Rubin Report." January 15, 2016. https://www.youtube.com/watch?v=IFqVNPwsLNo.

Saad, Gad. *The Parasitic Mind: How Infectious Ideas Are Killing Common Sense.* Washington, DC: Regnery, 2020.

Salerno, Joseph. "Mises on Nationalism, the Right of Self-Determination, and the Problem of Immigration." Mises Institute web-site, March 28, 2017. https://mises.org/wire/mises-nationalism-right-self-determination-and-problem-immigration.

Samuels, Robert. *The Psychopathology of Political Ideologies*. New York: Routledge, 2022.

Sanandaji, Nima. *Debunking Utopia: Exposing the Myth of Nordic Socialism*. New York: Post Hill Press, 2021.

Scafetta, Nicola. "CMIP6 GCM ensemble members versus global surface temperatures." *Climate Dynamics*, August 31, 2022. https://link.springer.com/content/pdf/10.1007/s00382-022-06493-w.pdf.

Schwab, Klaus. *The Fourth Industrial Revolution*. New York: Penguin Random House, 2017.

Schwab, Klaus. "Now is the time for a 'great reset.'" World Economic Forum website, June 3, 2020. https://www.weforum.org/agenda/2020/06/now-is-the-time-for-a-great-reset/.

Schwab, Klaus. *Stakeholder Capitalism: A Global Economy that Works for Progress, People and Planet*. Hoboken, NJ: John Wiley & Sons, 2021.

Schwab, Klaus, and Thierry Malleret. *COVID-19: The Great Reset*. Geneva: World Economic Forum, 2020.

Schwab, Klaus, and Thierry Malleret. *The Great Narrative: For a Better Future*. Geneva: World Economic Forum, 2020.

Science Direct. "Availability Heuristic." Science Direct website, n.d. https://www.sciencedirect.com/topics/computer-science/availability-heuristic.

Shabecoff, Philip. "U.N. ECOLOGY PARLEY OPENS AMID GLOOM." *New York Times*, May 11, 1982. https://www.nytimes.com/1982/05/11/world/un-ecology-parley-opens-amid-gloom.html.

Shared Crossing Research Initiative. "Shared Death Experiences: A Little-Known Type of End-of-Life Phenomena Reported by Caregivers and Loved Ones." *American Journal of Hospice and Palliative Medicine*, Volume 38, Issue 12, 1479–1487 (2021).

Sheldrake, Rupert." Wikipedia, accessed November 12, 2022. https://en.wikipedia.org/wiki/Rupert_Sheldrake.

Shellenberger, Michael. *Apocalypse Never: Why Environmental Alarmism Hurts Us All*. New York: Harper, 2020.

Shellenberger, Michael. "The Woke Grift." Michael Shellenberger Substack website, November 10, 2022. https://michaelshellenberger.substack.com/p/the-woke-grift.

Shir-Raz et al., "Censorship and Suppression of Covid-19 Heterodoxy: Tactics and Counter-Tactics." Minerva, 2022. https://link.springer.com/article/10.1007/s11024-022-09479-4.

Shrier, Abigail. *Irreversible Damage: The Transgender Craze Seducing Our Daughters.* Washington, DC: Regnery Publishing, 2021.

Simpson, Craig. "Woke dance school drops ballet from auditions as it is 'white' and 'elitist.'" *The Telegraph,* July 16, 2022. https://www.telegraph.co.uk/news/2022/07/16/woke-dance-school-drops-ballet-auditions-white-elitist/.

Skeptiko. "Dr. Mario Beauregard, Frontier Science Wake Up Call |538|." YouTube video, February 1, 2022. https://www.youtube.com/watch?v=8i-Q0MTJFls&t=2114s.

Sky News Australia, "Dave Rubin on his 'wake-up call' to 'twisted, evil, woke cult.'" YouTube video, October 16, 2022. https://www.youtube.com/watch?v=sAte3bVhcnY.

Smith, M. "Going in Through the Back Door: Challenging Straight Male Homohysteria, Transhysteria, and Transphobia Through Receptive Penetrative Sex Toy Use." *Sexuality & Culture,* 22, 1542 (2018). https://link.springer.com/article/10.1007/s12119-018-9536-0.

Something is Not Right Series. "Klaus Schwab of World Economic Forum boasting of his infiltration into governments." Rumble video, January 27, 2022. https://rumble.com/vtfrxk-klaus-schwab-of-world-economic-forum-boasting-of-his-infiltration-into-gove.html.

Sowell, Thomas. *Black Rednecks and White Liberals.* New York: Encounter Books, 2005.

Sowell, Thomas. *Discrimination and Disparities.* New York: Hachette Book Group, Inc., 2019.

Sowell, Thomas. *Dismantling America.* New York: Basic Books, 2010.

Sowell, Thomas. *Economic Facts and Fallacies.* New York: Basic Books, 2011.

Sowell, Thomas. *Intellectuals and Society.* New York: Basic Books, 2011.

Sowell, Thomas. *The Vision of The Anointed: Self-Congratulations as a Basis for Social Policy*. New York: Basic Books, 1995.

springmagazine. "'Lawn Boy' IS pedophilic. Here's why. (Explicit)." *The Spring Magazine* website, January 28, 2022. https://thespring magazine.com/2022/01/28/lawn-boy-is-pedophilic-heres-why-explicit/.

Starnes, Todd. "First grader sent to office for 'misgendering' fellow student." Fox News, September 25, 2017. https://www.foxnews.com/opinion/first-grader-sent-to-office-for-misgendering-fellow-student.

Stauffer, Elizabeth. "Pfizer CEO Intros Horrifying Wireless 'Compliance' Device." *Western Journal*, May 23, 2022. https://www.westernjournal.com/pfizer-ceo-intros-horrifying-wireless-compliance-device/.

Steamboat Institute. "Should America Rapidly Eliminate Fossil Fuel Use to Prevent Climate Catastrophe?" YouTube channel, March 14, 2022. https://www.youtube.com/watch?v=4AIVpK4oACs.

Stone, Sean. *Best Kept Secret*. Sean Stone website, 2021. https://www.seanstone.info/bestkeptsecret.

Stone, Sean. "G Edward Griffin on 'Collectivism.'" YouTube video, April 8, 2021. https://www.youtube.com/watch?v=-nH2Igq1gh8.

Stone, Sean. *New World Order: A Strategy of Imperialism*. Chicago, IL: Independent Publishers Group, 2012.

Street, Zoyander. "Yes, Men Can Have Periods and We Need to Talk About Them." *Daily Beast*, July 12, 2017. https://www.thedailybeast.com/yes-men-can-have-periods-and-we-need-to-talk-about-them.

Subramanian, Tara. "Parts of Great Barrier Reef record highest amount of coral in 36 years." CNN, August 4, 2022. https://www.cnn.com/2022/08/04/australia/great-barrier-reef-high-coral-report-australia-climate-intl-hnk/index.html.

Swan, Bishop Talbert. Twitter post, October 14, 2022. https://twitter.com/talbertswan/status/1581103527585120257?s=21&t=Ylu Sewgwo9hHMr8Yk5LnFQ.

Thrivetime Show: The ReAwakening versus The Great Reset. "Yuval Noah Harari | Why Does Yuval Noah Harari Say 'We Are

Upgrading Humans Into Gods?'" Rumble video, July 18, 2022. https://rumble.com/v1cpnzj-yuval-noah-harari-non-human-world-new-gods-what-does-the-world-look-like.html.

TODAY. "Al Gore Talks Climate Crisis: 'This Is The Time For a Great Reset' | TODAY." YouTube video, June 19, 2020. https://www.youtube.com/watch?v=1iv6WkIZ2pI.

Townsend, Mark and Paul Harris. "Now the Pentagon tells Bush: climate change will destroy us." *The Guardian*, February 21, 2004. https://www.theguardian.com/environment/2004/feb/22/usnews.theobserver.

Tressoldi, P. E. "Extraordinary Claims Require Extraordinary Evidence: The Case of Non-Local Perception, a Classical and Bayesian Review of Evidences." *Frontiers in Psychology* 2, no. 117 (2011).

Twenge, Jean and Keith Campbell. *The Narcissism Epidemic: Living in the Age of Entitlement.* New York: Atria Paperback, 2009.

United Nations. "Google teams up with UN for verified climate information." *United Nations* website, April 22, 2022. https://www.un.org/en/climatechange/google-search-information.

Utts, Jessica. "Appreciating Statistics." *Journal of the American Statistical Association* 111 (2016): 1373–80. https://www.tandfonline.com/doi/full/ 10.1080/01621459.2016.1250592.

Utts, Jessica. "An Assessment of the Evidence for Psychic Functioning." *Journal of Parapsychology* 59, no. 4 (1995): 289–320.

Utts, Jessica. "An Assessment of the Evidence for Psychic Functioning." Division of Statistics, University of California, Davis, 1995. http://www.ics.uci.edu/~jutts/air.pdf.

Utts, Jessica. "From Psychic Claims to Science: Testing Psychic Phenomena with Statistics." Department of Statistics, University of California, Davis, August 3, 2006. http://www.ics.uci.edu/~jutts/Sweden.pdf.

van Lommel, Pim, et al. "Near-Death Experience in Survivors of Cardiac Arrest: A Prospective Study in the Netherlands." *The Lancet* 9298 (2001): 2039–45. http://www.thelancet.com/journals/lancet/article/ PIIS0140673601071008/fulltext.

Volokh, Eugene. "UC teaching faculty members not to criticize race-based affirmative action, call America 'melting pot,' and more."

The Washington Post, June 16, 2015. https://www.washingtonpost.com/news/volokh-conspiracy/wp/2015/06/16/uc-teaching-faculty-members-not-to-criticize-race-based-affirmative-action-call-america-melting-pot-and-more/.

von Mises, Ludwig. *Human Action: A Treatise on Economics*. Auburn, AL: The Ludwig von Mises Institute, 1998.

von Mises, Ludwig. *Liberty & Property*. Auburn, AL: The Ludwig von Mises Institute, 2009. https://cdn.mises.org/Liberty%20and%20Property_3.pdf

Wahbeh et al. "What if consciousness is not an emergent property of the brain? Observational and empirical challenges to materialistic models." *Frontiers in Psychology*, September 7, 2022. https://www.frontiersin.org/articles/10.3389/fpsyg.2022.955594/full#B64.

Wallace, Tim. "Bank of England tells ministers to intervene on digital currency 'programming.'" *The Telegraph*, June 21, 2021. https://www.telegraph.co.uk/business/2021/06/21/bank-england-tells-ministers-intervene-digital-currency-programming/.

Walsh, Matt. "Environmentalism Gets Even More Genocidal | Ep. 993." YouTube video, July 26, 2022. https://www.youtube.com/watch?v=HwxnWIgQEvM.

Walsh, Matt. *What Is a Woman? Daily Wire*, 2022. https://get.dailywire.com/wiaw/subscribe?cid=wiaw&mid=b&xid=0&hsa_acc=6411461344&hsa_cam=429594023&hsa_grp=1326012504412860&hsa_ad=&hsa_src=s&hsa_tgt=kwd-82876595724471%3Aloc-190&hsa_kw=mat+walsh+what+is+a+woman&hsa_mt=p&hsa_net=adwords&hsa_ver=3&msclkid=14a0abb8944d1fcba372c8cc8e799cd8.

Walsh, Michael (Ed.). *Against the Great Reset: Eighteen Theses Contra the New World Order*. New York, Post Hill Press: 2022.

Watson, Paul Joseph. "Environmental Activist Says Cheese is Racist, Dairy Shouldn't Be Served in Schools." *Summit News*, April 14, 2021. https://summit.news/2021/04/14/environmental-activist-says-cheese-is-racist-dairy-shouldnt-be-served-in-schools/.

Weiss, Bari. "'The Psychopathic Problem of the White Mind.'" Common Sense by Bari Weiss website, June 4, 2021. https://www.commonsense.news/p/the-psychopathic-problem-of-the-white#comments.

Weller, Chris. "Gun control in four countries around the world," World Economic Forum website, February 21, 2018. https://www.weforum.org/agenda/2018/02/these-4-countries-have-nearly-eliminated-gun-deaths-heres-what-the-us-can-learn/.

Wiggershaus, Rolf. *The Frankfurt School*. Cambridge: The MIT Press, 1995.

Wignaraja, Kanni and Balazs Horvath. "Universal basic income is the answer to the inequalities exposed by COVID-19." World Economic Forum website, April 17, 2020. https://www.weforum.org/agenda/2020/04/covid-19-universal-basic-income-social-inequality/.

"Wikipedia co-founder: I no longer trust the website I created." Unherd website, July 14, 2021. https://unherd.com/thepost/wikipedia-co-founder-i-no-longer-trust-the-website-i-created/. Wilber, Ken. *The Integral Vision: A Very Short Introduction*. Boulder, CO: Shambhala, 2018.

Williams, B. J. "Revisiting the Ganzfeld ESP Debate: A Basic Review and Assessment." *Journal of Scientific Exploration* 25, no. 4 (2011): 639–61.

Wilson, Greg. "Evidence Of FBI Meddling In 2020 Election Mounts After Zuckerberg's Hunter Biden Laptop Revelation." *Daily Wire*, August 26, 2022. https://www.dailywire.com/news/evidence-of-fbi-meddling-in-2020-election-mounts-after-zuckerbergs-hunter-biden-laptop-revelation.

Wolf, Naomi. *The Bodies of Others: The New Authoritarians, COVID-19 and the War Against the Human*. Fort Lauderdale, FL: All Seasons Press, 2022.

World Economic Forum. "History." World Economic Forum website, n.d. https://www.weforum.org/about/history.

World Economic Forum. "Klaus Schwab and Prince Charles on why we need a Great Reset – listen to the podcast." World Economic Forum website, June 4, 2020. https://www.weforum.org/agenda/2020/06/the-great-reset-this-weeks-world-vs-virus-podcast/.

World Economic Forum. "Leadership and Governance." World Economic Forum website, n.d. https://www.weforum.org/about/leadership-and-governance.

World Economic Forum. "Our Mission." World Economic Forum website, n.d. https://www.weforum.org/about/world-economic-forum.

World Economic Forum. "Our Partners." World Economic Forum website, n.d. https://www.weforum.org/partners#J.

World Economic Forum. "Will the Future Be Human? – Yuval Noah Harari." YouTube video, January 25, 2018. https://www.youtube.com/watch?v=hL9uk4hKyg4.

Yglesias, Matthew. "Denmark's prime minister says Bernie Sanders is wrong to call his country socialist." Vox, October 31, 2015. https://www.vox.com/2015/10/31/9650030/denmark-prime-minister-bernie-sanders.

Zilber, Ariel. "Twitter suspends Babylon Bee for naming RachelLevine 'Man of the Year.'" *New York Post*, March 21, 2022. https://nypost.com/2022/03/21/twitter-suspends-babylon-bee-over-rachel-levine-man-of-the-year-title/.

INDEX

ABOUT THE AUTHOR

Mark Gober is the author of *An End to Upside Down Thinking* (2018), which won the Independent Publisher (IPPY) award for best science book of the year. He is also the author of *An End to Upside Down Living* (2020), *An End to Upside Down Liberty* (2021), and *An End to Upside Down Contact* (2022); and is the host of the podcast *Where Is My Mind?* (2019). Additionally, he serves on the board of the Institute of Noetic Sciences and the School of Wholeness and Enlightenment. Previously, Gober was a partner at Sherpa Technology Group in Silicon Valley and worked as an investment banking analyst in New York. He has been named one of *IAM's Strategy 300: The World's Leading Intellectual Property Strategists*.

Gober graduated magna cum laude from Princeton University, where he wrote an award-winning thesis on Daniel Kahneman's Nobel Prize–winning "Prospect Theory" and was elected a captain of Princeton's Division I tennis team.

Made in the USA
Middletown, DE
13 February 2023

24784812R00136